THE BATTLE OF MAIDA
1806

THE BATTLE OF MAIDA 1806

FIFTEEN MINUTES OF GLORY

by

RICHARD HOPTON

LEO COOPER

First published in Great Britain in 2002 by
LEO COOPER
an imprint of
Pen & Sword Books Ltd
47 Church Street
Barnsley
South Yorkshire
S70 2AS

Copyright © 2002 Richard Hopton

ISBN 0 85052 845 3

A catalogue record for this book is available
from the British Library.

Typeset in 10.5/12.5pt Plantin by
Phoenix Typesetting, Ilkley, West Yorkshire

Printed in England by
CPI UK

TO THE MEMORY OF
MY MOTHER
1936–2001

CONTENTS

MAPS

ACKNOWLEDGEMENTS

I have been helped by numerous people in the process of writing this book, in particular the staffs of the British Library and the National Army Museum, whose prompt and courteous service made my researches so much less stressful than they might otherwise have been. Patrick Mercer kindly read an early version of the book and made many thoughtful and helpful suggestions for improvements. Leo Cooper encouraged me from the start, while my father brought his great fund of historical knowledge to bear on many aspects of the book. Tom Hartman, who edited the book, has put me right on numerous occasions as well as providing amusing anecdotes over the lunch table.

I have quoted from the correspondence between Sir John Stuart and Sir Sidney Smith with the gracious permission of Her Majesty the Queen.

Many friends have listened to me droning on about Maida over the last few years and to all of them I extend my heartfelt thanks for their forbearance. Finally, I should like to thank Caroline, who, luckily for her, missed the writing of the book, but whose wit and love has brightened the last stages of its genesis.

London
January 2002

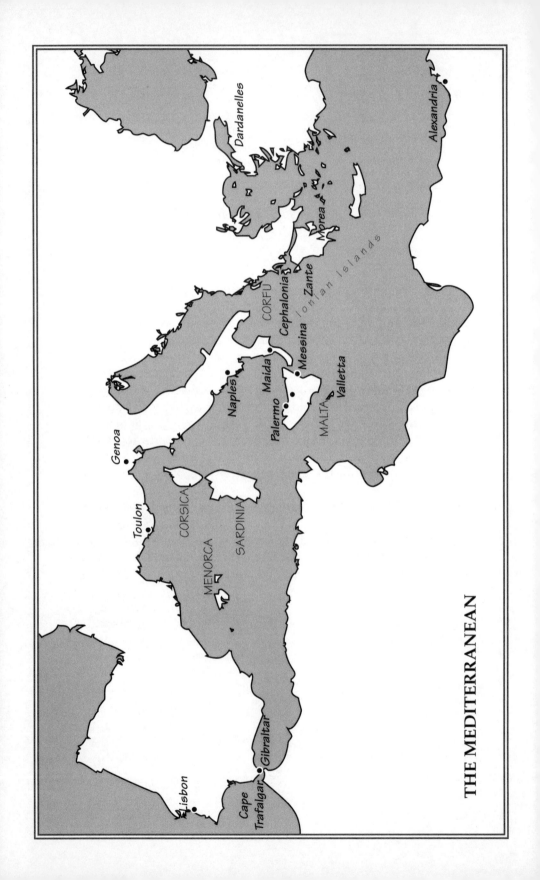

THE MEDITERRANEAN

INTRODUCTION

On Sunday 13 March 1803, Lord Whitworth, the British Ambassador in Paris, attended a court *levée* at the Tuileries. He was taking some English visitors to the ceremony in order to present them to Madame Bonaparte. It was a formal occasion, with some two hundred people present, held in the magnificent state rooms of the palace whose elaborate decoration, gilded ceilings and imposing portraits reflected the power and glory of France's greatest monarch Louis XIV, *le roi soleil*. When Whitworth arrived at the *levée* Napoleon, in a state of "very considerable agitation", confronted him and in a voice loud enough for everyone thronging the room to hear said: "So you are determined to go to war?"

Five days earlier, on 8 March, Parliament had unanimously voted an increase of 10,000 men to the strength of the Royal Navy, in reply to a Royal Message calling for defensive precautions in the face of warlike preparations in the ports along the French and Dutch coasts. By the time of Whitworth's visit to the Tuileries this news had reached Paris, throwing the First Consul into a towering rage.

"We have already fought for fifteen years," he said, brushing aside Whitworth's attempts at conciliation. "You want to carry on fighting for another fifteen years and you will force me into it." Napoleon moved off towards the Russian and Spanish Ambassadors who were standing nearby and, in the same vein, continued, "The English want war but if they are the first to draw the sword I shall be the last to put it away".

Napoleon stalked off, doing his rounds of the room, evidently still very angry. Shortly afterwards he confronted Whitworth once more: "Why these armaments? Against whom are you taking these precautions? I have not got a single ship of the line in any port in France, but if you want arms, I too will arm. If you want to fight, I too will fight. You may perhaps be able to destroy France but you will never intimidate her. It is vital to abide by treaties, a curse on those who do not abide by treaties; they shall answer for it to all Europe." With this Napoleon stormed out of the room, repeating the final sentence as he went.

This celebrated scene is a milestone on the descent of England and France back into war in 1803. The violence of Whitworth's description of the incident stands out from the usual polished, courtly diplomatic phrases; he remarks on "the extreme impropriety of [Napoleon's] conduct". Indeed, Napoleon's tirade displayed a "total want of dignity as well as of decency" that was quite shocking to contemporaries.[1] Negotiations continued throughout March and April between Whitworth and the French Foreign Minister, Talleyrand. The principal sticking-point was the fate of Malta: by the terms of the Peace of Amiens the British government had agreed to relinquish the island, but the arrangements for its future security were deemed inadequate. Article Ten of the Peace nominated the Tsar of Russia as the guarantor of Malta's independence, but he was reluctant to become embroiled in a cause so far from home and declined to accept the responsibility. Faced with increasing evidence of Napoleon's belligerence after the Peace of Amiens, the British refused to evacuate the island until a satisfactory solution could be found to protect it from French aggression.

Various compromises were mooted, but the two sides failed to reach a settlement. On 23 April Whitworth was sent his final instructions by the Cabinet in which he was ordered to insist, as a minimum, on a ten-year lease of Malta and, if the French government would not agree to this, he was to leave Paris. On 4 May Whitworth had a further and inconclusive interview with Talleyrand, at which he was persuaded to refer another French officer to his government. This he did; it was refused. When the news of the Cabinet's refusal reached Paris Whitworth requested his passports and, on 12 May, left for home. Britain declared war on France on 18 May.

So Britain and France were once more at war. The respite provided by the Peace of Amiens had lasted a mere fourteen months and the war which now resumed would continue for a further eleven years.

This long period of visceral struggle against the Napoleonic Empire falls, from the British perspective, into three phases: The War of the Third Coalition, the Peninsular War and the final, triumphant act of 1814 and 1815.

The Third Coalition, as is well known, achieved mixed results. Nelson's victory at Trafalgar ended any pretensions the French had to challenge the British mastery of the seas. Austerlitz, on the other hand, scotched all hope that the Coalition's armies might have had of defeating Napoleon's ambitions on Continental Europe. Ulm and Austerlitz allowed Napoleon to dictate terms to Austria and sent the Russian army scuttling home, but, despite these crushing victories, there was for the allies one small chink of light in the surrounding gloom: the Battle of Maida. The campaign on the Danube in the autumn and winter of 1805, which ended in disaster, was only a part (albeit the major part) of the strategy adopted by the leaders of the Third Coalition. They had hoped to mount an effective campaign in North Germany but were frustrated by Prussia's refusal to join the alliance. The Mediterranean theatre was important, too; here they did manage to put a combined force of British and Russian troops into the field even if, in the event, it achieved very little.

The Anglo-Russian expedition which landed near Naples in November 1805 retreated, ingloriously, without firing a shot in anger in January 1806, the Russians to Corfu and the British to Sicily. There the British troops remained to guard the island against the expected French attack. It was this small army that, striking into the French-occupied mainland, won the Battle of Maida on 4 July 1806. It was the only conclusive victory achieved by the armies of the Third Coalition.

Maida was fought in Calabria, on the western side of the Italian peninsula, about fifty miles north of the Straits of Messina. It was a small battle – there were only 11,000 combatants in total – fought on a distant shore far from the hub of affairs. Neither, strictly, can it be said to form part of the story of the Third Coalition, which had been pronounced dead at the Peace of Pressburg six months earlier. But Maida was a child of this alliance, albeit a posthumous one. The history of the combination against Napoleon between 1804 and 1806 and its strategy explains why the British troops were at Maida in this distant part of Italy at all.

William Windham, the Secretary of War at the time of Maida, proclaimed on receiving news of the victory that it ranked along with Poitiers, Crecy and Agincourt in the annals of British military history.[2] Undoubtedly Windham was guilty of over-exaggeration; perhaps *The Times* was nearer the mark when it reported the news under the headline "Glorious Victory".[3] Neither can one claim that Maida, the youngest offspring of the alliance, in any way makes up for the failings of the parent at Ulm and Austerlitz. Nevertheless, Maida was a signal victory and has sunk into an historical obscurity it does not deserve.

The *grognards* of the Army of Naples disparagingly referred to "*l'affaire de Sainte Euphemie*" (their term for Maida) as "*la bataille d'un quart d'heure*" – the fifteen minutes of my subtitle – and it is almost as if the Napoleonic establishment decided to erase any recollection of that brief yet painful battle from the collective memory, such is the lack of contemporary French reference to it.

Perhaps not surprisingly the British, by contrast, were greatly heartened by the battle. It showed how to defeat the mighty French and, as such, presaged the triumphs of the Peninsular War. Sir Charles Oman, writing in the early twentieth century, observed:

> "But for all of those who were present, or who received the report of an intelligent eye-witness, the little-remembered Calabrian battle of Maida was an epoch-making day in British military history. On the sandy plain of the Amato 5,000 infantry in line received the shock of 6,000 in column, and inflicted on them one of the most crushing defeats on a small scale that took place during the whole war."

The moral, Oman wrote, was unmistakable; neither did it escape the attention of some of those who fought in the battle.

> "It is worthwhile remembering that some of the officers who were afterwards to be Wellington's most trusted lieutenants were present at Maida, and understood its meaning, among them Cole, who later commanded the Peninsular 4th Division, the brigadiers Kempt and Oswald, and Colborne the famous colonel of the 52nd Light Infantry."

This book tells the story of the battle, of the men who fought in it, of the generals and the tactics they employed. It sets Maida in the wider, European, diplomatic and political context in order to explain how a British army came to fight a battle on the shores of the Mediterranean so far down the boot of Italy.

Chapter One

WAR AND PITT (*BIS*)

Napoleon's astonishing public tirade against Lord Whitworth was neither the beginning nor the end of the road towards the resumption of war between Britain and France but a marker along the way. Relations between the two countries were soured by deep mutual suspicions long before Whitworth received his dressing-down at the Tuileries and war was not declared for nearly another two months.

The administration headed by Henry Addington which took up the reins of government following the resignation of Pitt in March 1801 was determined to seek an end to the war with France. Negotiations began almost at once and on 1 October 1801 the Preliminaries were signed. The terms of the Preliminaries were widely regarded as unsatisfactory, but such was the general desire for peace after so many years of war that these shortcomings were overlooked. Men hoped that the final form of the treaty would clear up the difficulties and ambiguities that were all too apparent in the Preliminaries. The two most unsatisfactory aspects of the draft agreement were the lack of any provision for the future of the Low Countries – the original *casus belli* – and the fate of Malta.

Addington's government has had a bad press down the years, perhaps being seen as an administration that tried to appease a dictator. Contemporaries were frequently scathing about Addington himself; he was widely referred to as "The Doctor", a snobbish jibe at his relatively humble origins. Neither was his Cabinet greatly distinguished by administrative talent or, importantly, by oratical prowess in Parliament. "The most important offices in the state were bestowed on decorous and laborious mediocrity," as Lord Macaulay succinctly put it.[4]

Those who had been prepared to accept the shortcomings of the Preliminaries in the hope that they would thereby "give peace a chance" were soon to be disillusioned. In the six months between the Preliminaries and the signing of the final treaty in March 1802 it became evident that Napoleon's aggressively expansionist policy had not been in any way curtailed by the outbreak of peace. During that short period the French acquired the vast territory of Louisiana and sent troops to San Domingo. Both of these were direct threats to the important British commercial and strategic interests in the West Indies. Nearer to home Napoleon severed the canton of Valais from Switzerland, bringing it under French control. This gave France at a stroke sole use of the Alpine passes of Simplon and St Bernard, thereby improving the access for his armies to Italy.

In the summer and autumn of 1802 Napoleon continued on his course of expansion and aggression in Europe. Displaying a blithe disregard for the terms of the treaties that had so recently been signed, he annexed both Piedmont and Parma in northern Italy and refused to evacuate French troops from around Flushing or Utrecht. These were serious breaches of the European settlement that the Powers had enunciated at Amiens and at the earlier Peace of Luneville (1801) but raised little by way of protest from Addington's government. The nation and its rulers were enjoying the fruits of peace too much, it seemed – and after so many years at war who could blame them? – to pay any great heed to events across the Channel.

In October 1802 Napoleon invaded the remainder of Switzerland – whose integrity was supposedly guaranteed by Luneville – on the most feeble of pretexts. Addington, taking up the cudgels on behalf of a small country under threat, formally protested to Paris. The Cabinet dispatched an agent to offer arms and money, an empty gesture given the respective geographic positions of the two countries and the fact that Switzerland, being landlocked, was beyond the reach of the Royal Navy.

Addington's ill-considered action had put the government in an awkward position: unable, materially or militarily, to help the Swiss, it had nevertheless succeeded in angering Napoleon. The Swiss, seeing that help would not be forthcoming, gave in to the inevitable and capitulated to the French. Napoleon, delighting in another example of Britain's powerlessness to intervene in continental affairs, issued a reminder in the *Moniteur*, the official newspaper of the regime in Paris, that Britain, not being a signatory to Luneville, was not entitled to appeal to its terms.

But for all the toothlessness of Addington's response to the Swiss crisis it did represent a turning point. No longer would the British government look supinely on at European events, nor would it continue to regard the encroachments of the French with indifference. The stiffening of British resolve was exemplified by the instructions issued in November 1802 to Lord Whitworth on his appointment as Ambassador in Paris. Whitworth was ordered to insist to the French government on Britain's right to intervene in the affairs of the Continent, a right that Napoleon had specifically denied.

In January 1803, hard upon the Swiss débâcle, the *Moniteur* published a highly provocative report by Colonel Sebastiani, a French agent, of his activities in the eastern Mediterranean and the Near East. It reinforced British suspicions that French ambitions in the area were still very much alive. The Sebastiani report also acted as a reminder to the government of the importance of Malta as a base from which to defend British interests in the Mediterranean.

The fate of Malta had not been settled satisfactorily by the Peace of Amiens. The island's importance lay in its commanding position in the Mediterranean and in its powerful and easily defensible harbour. Napoleon captured the island from the Knights of St John, who had ruled it since the sixteenth century, on his way to Egypt in June 1798. Shortly afterwards, following Nelson's victory at the Battle of the Nile (1 August 1798), a British fleet commanded by Sir Alexander Ball blockaded Valetta and, after a two-year siege, the French garrison surrendered to the British in September 1800.

The treaty required the British to evacuate the island and Article Ten formally invited Alexander, the new Tsar of Russia, to act as guarantor of its security. Russia was the only power acceptable to Britain as a safeguard for Malta's independence, but the Tsar refused, offering instead only mediation between Britain and France in the matter. As the evidence of French aggression accumulated during the summer and autumn of 1802 it became increasingly clear that the French had no intention of abiding by the terms of the Peace of Amiens. The Sebastiani report confirmed this impression as well as pointedly reminding the Cabinet of the importance of the Mediterranean theatre. In such circumstances it would have been little short of grossly negligent to give up Malta.

The refusal of the British government to surrender Malta may have been *prima facie* the cause of the resumption of war in 1803, but Napoleon deserves an equal measure of the blame. The First Consul had never regarded peace as anything more than a temporary respite and an opportunity to build up his strength, *reculer pour mieux sauter*. His conduct during 1802, before and after the signing of the Peace of Amiens, demonstrates that he had no intention of forgoing his territorial ambitions, whatever any treaty might say.

By the end of 1802 Napoleon's popularity and prestige in France were at their height; his reputation as a dashing general, forged in Italy, Germany and Egypt was now further enhanced by his achievement in reaching a reconciliation with the Catholic Church – the Concordat of 1801. The Concordat, in establishing a *modus vivendi* between the Church and the Consulate, did much to heal the schism caused by the Revolution. The two peace treaties, Amiens and Luneville, added further lustre to the First Consul's name; the victor of Marengo was now cast as the wise ruler of his people and the people approved of what they saw. In 1802 a plebiscite voted, according to the official returns, by three and a half million to eight thousand in favour of bestowing the Consulate for life. Where Napoleon led, it seemed, the French would follow.

Napoleon's undisputed preeminence in France and his restless ambitions made the resumption of war inevitable. As the First Consul himself remarked, "Between old monarchies and a young republic the spirit of hostility must always exist. In the existing situation every treaty of peace means to me no more than a brief armistice: and I believe that, while I fill my present office, my destiny is to be fighting almost continually."[5]

*   *   *

With the resumption of hostilities on 18 May 1803, the war settled quickly back into the pattern it had assumed before 1801: the French enjoying an unquestioned hegemony over the Continent, the British commanding the seas. Neither side could take the fight to the other; it was a stalemate.

On 19 May, the day after the war began again, Admiral Cornwallis and five ships of the line took up their station off Brest, thereby renewing the blockade of that port. The following day Nelson left Portsmouth in his flagship *Victory* for the Mediterranean, where he had been appointed Commander-in-Chief. It was not long before the Navy was once again, as it had been throughout the 1790s, blockading all the important ports of France and the Low Countries, from Toulon in the Meditteranean to Texel in the North Sea.

Napoleon, for his part, although able to do little to combat the British at sea, had unlimited freedom of action on the Continent and immediately moved on to the offensive. On 18 May two French ships had been captured at sea by the Royal Navy. Enraged by this act, as he saw it, of aggression, Napoleon ordered that, in retaliation, all British subjects of military age in France should be arrested and incarcerated. Imprisoning civilians in this way – they were locked up in the fortress at Verdun – was contrary to all contemporary notions of the conduct of war.

As well as venting his spleen on those British subjects who were unfortunate enough to be in France when war was declared Napoleon attacked British interests in other, more material ways. He closed the Continental ports, including the supposedly free ports of Bremen and Hamburg, to British merchantmen and began preparations for the occupation of Hanover. He also started to prepare for the invasion of Britain. He instituted an ambitious programme of barge building and, in the summer, toured the Channel ports – accompanied by the Bayeux Tapestry, a powerful source of inspiration no doubt – to inspect progress. The threat of a French invasion was to become the dominant theme of Britain's politics and her war strategy for the next two and a half years until it was permanently removed by Trafalgar.

Faced with this threat of imminent invasion, Addington's government set about raising men to defend the country. There were several and overlapping ways in which soldiers could be recruited: Militias, Volunteer regiments and the Army of Reserve. Martial spirit was abroad in England that summer and the response to the government's recruitment drive was excellent; by the autumn of 1803 340,000 men had joined the Volunteer Associations.[6] William Pitt, absent from the main political stage, spent the summer of 1803 at Walmer Castle in

Kent organizing the defence of Kent in his capacity as a Warden of the Cinque Ports. Here too men flocked to the colours; by the end of the year more than 10,000 Kentishmen had enlisted as Volunteers and a further 1,040 in the Army of Reserve.[7] The government was overwhelmed by the tidal wave of recruits. There was a shortage of modern weapons; there are reports of formations drilling with pikes. Nor was the Cabinet able to decide on the most efficient way in which men should be recruited and embodied. Indeed, disagreements on proposals for the Army of Reserve would ultimately open the way for Pitt's return to office in 1804.

On 23 May 1803, five days after the declaration of war, Pitt spoke in the Debate in the House of Commons on the resumption of war. The former Prime Minister had retreated into the background since resigning office in 1801, content to support Addington from afar, but on 20 May resumed his seat in the House. He spoke with all the fire and vigour of old, supporting the Cabinet and denouncing Napoleon's aggression. His precise words were not recorded by Hansard's reporters but Sheridan described the speech as "one of the most magnificent pieces of declamation that ever fell from that rascal Pitt's lips".[8]

Rousing as this speech was, it did not mark the return of Pitt to the centre stage. The summer he spent soldiering at Walmer Castle was one of several lengthy absences from the political scene, absences that are in part explained by the fact that Pitt was in a dilemma. At the time of his resignation in 1801 Pitt had pledged his support to Addington's administration and continued to consider himself bound to honour it. On the other hand there had been several attempts to persuade Pitt to join the government, all of which had foundered on his insistence that he would only take office as head of the administration. This, of course, flew in the face of his pledge to support Addington. His fullest modern biographer has characterized this as being the conflict between 'Character' and 'Duty'.[9] In other words Pitt's need to maintain his 1801 pledge appeared to be at odds with the needs of the country and his public duty.

This dilemma grew more acute once the war was resumed. It became clear during the latter half of 1803 that the government was unable to cope with the pressures of wartime administration and by the beginning of 1804 Addington was in difficulties. He lacked effective performers in Parliament and Lord St Vincent, the First Lord of the Admiralty, was coming under increasing criticism for his management of the Navy. With the nation back at war, a steady and experienced hand was needed at the helm and who better to provide it than Pitt, who had steered the country through the troubled waters of the 1790s?

In March 1804 Pitt moved into the attack against the government's administration of the Navy, with a speech delivered on the 15th in the House of Commons. On 23 April he attacked the government's policy for the army. Ministers were, he said, "incapable of acting upon anything like system, of adopting or executing any well-digested or energetic plan for . . . defence". The spirit of the nation must be "separated from the tardiness, langour, and imbecility of ministers".[10]

The government won the vote on the motion on 23 April by a majority of only 37 but, thanks to Pitt's intervention, it lost the argument. Addington's administration was failing and on 29 April the Prime Minister told colleagues that he was prepared to step aside in favour of Pitt. The next day, 30 April, the Lord Chancellor, Lord Eldon, called on Pitt to inform him that the King would like to see his ideas for the formation of a new ministry.

Pitt hoped that he would be able to form the widely-based government which was so clearly desirable in time of war; one of the principal weaknesses of Addington's ministry had been its narrow base. Pitt was hopeful of persuading Lord Grenville, who had been his Foreign Secretary in the 1790s, and his political allies to join the government. Grenville, however, refused to be a member of a Cabinet that did not include Fox, and Pitt was wholly unable to induce George III to accept Fox as a member of the Cabinet.

On 10 May 1804 Addington delivered the seals of office and Pitt was once more Prime Minister. His failure to construct a broadly-based Cabinet meant that he was forced to rely on a combination of his own supporters and some of those who had been in the previous Cabinet. Of the former category, Pitt's old friend Henry Dundas (now Lord Melville) was sent to the Admiralty, Lord Camden to the War Office and Lord Harrowby to the Foreign Office. Of those who had served in Addington's Cabinet, Lord Eldon continued as

Lord Chancellor and Lord Hawkesbury was appointed to the Home Office. Pitt was back in the saddle but with a government weaker that he would have liked, he himself in far from perfect health and with the threat of invasion looming large on the south side of the Channel.

Chapter Two

THE THIRD COALITION IN PROSPECT

Once Pitt had returned to office he immediately started to examine the prospects of rekindling the European coalitions of the 1790s. Such coalitions, subsidized by British guineas, were the only way by which the Cabinet could engage the French armies on the Continent on anything like equal terms. The massing of French troops in the Pas de Calais and the threat of invasion added an urgency to the need for Pitt to find Continental allies, a spur to "set Europe at Napoleon's back".

Pitt had been the architect of the two coalitions of the 1790s and was now, in 1804, pinning his hopes on those same countries who had fought against France in the previous decade. A *tour d'horizon* of Britain's former allies will show how the years of war had affected them, undermined or fortified their will to fight, and given an indication of the support, or lack of it, that Pitt might expect in reviving the anti-French coalition.

Russia

It was to St Petersburg that Pitt first looked for support against the French; he regarded the Russians as the lynchpin of any European alliance against Napoleon. Indeed, once the negotiations for a European coalition were under way, Pitt was content to allow the Russians to bargain with the other Powers – and offer them British subsidies. This illustrates the importance that Pitt attached to an alliance with Russia and the high regard he had for her influence in the councils of Europe.

Russia had taken part in both of the coalitions of the 1790s, with varying degrees of enthusiasm. Catherine the Great had lent Russia's

14

weight to the First Coalition (1793–6), but had in fact provided little assistance against France as she was more concerned with the conquest and partition of Poland. Her successor, Tsar Paul, was one of the moving spirits of the Second Coalition (1799–1801) and his armies took an active part in the war against the French. The Russian contribution to the war was supported by a British subsidy which, in 1798–9, amounted to £35 a man.[11] The veteran Marshal Suvorov achieved sweeping successes in the Italian campaign of 1799 in which he reconquered Lombardy and Piedmont from the French, leading his troops to the very borders of France. Suvorov's successes were undermined by bickering between the allies and, in 1800, Napoleon regained the ground lost the previous summer. The defeat of Suvorov in Switzerland in 1799 and dissent within the alliance caused the Tsar to become increasingly disenchanted with his Coalition partners.

Tsar Paul suffered from mental instability that made him an unreliable ally and it was not long before the Russian alliance turned sour for Britain. The Tsar, disillusioned with his Coalition partners and blaming them for Suvorov's defeats, was assiduously courted by Napoleon, a courtship that reaped its reward when, at the end of 1800, Paul revived the Armed Neutrality. The Baltic countries – Denmark, Prussia and Sweden joined the Russians – were contesting the long-maintained British claim to the search and confiscation of illegal cargo in neutral shipping. Britain's Maritime Code had for years been a bone of contention, but the revival of the Armed Neutrality now threatened her all-important trade with the Baltic, the source of timber, naval supplies and grain. Any interruption to Britain's trade in the Baltic was a serious matter, nor, in time of war, was the Cabinet prepared to countenance any challenge to the Navy's right to search neutral shipping, an essential weapon in the fight against the French.

The British government acted immediately to counter the threat posed by the Armed Neutrality and dispatched a fleet to the Baltic. The expedition was commanded by Admiral Sir Hyde Parker; Nelson was the second-in-command. The fleet's first target was Denmark as the British could not risk entering the Baltic to attack the Russians with the Danes undefeated in their rear. After an unsuccessful attempt to resolve the matter by diplomacy, Nelson defeated the Danish fleet at the Battle of Copenhagen (2 April 1801). This victory, a brilliant feat of navigation in the sandbanks, shoals and fast channels of the waters around Copenhagen, knocked out an enemy fleet which was moored under the cover of its own heavy shore batteries.

On the night of the 25 March, while Parker and Nelson were preparing to strike at the Danish navy, Tsar Paul was murdered in St Petersburg by some of his own drunken officers. The head of the northern alliance against Britain had, with a single stroke, been lopped off. The Tsar's murder and the victory at Copenhagen signalled the collapse of the Armed Neutrality and the rift was formally healed by a Convention signed in May 1801. By the terms of this agreement the Russians affirmed the legality of the right to search neutral vessels and seize hostile goods. Settled for the time being, the question returned to bedevil Anglo-Russian relations in the summer of 1805, at a vital moment in the formation of the Third Coalition.

The signing of the Convention marked an end to the Armed Neutrality and the hostility between Britain and Russia, but it did not herald an immediate return to the active cooperation that had existed between the two countries in the days of the Second Coalition. The new Tsar, Alexander, was not as anxious as his father to play a leading role on the European stage. Indeed, he made his intentions clear when, within days of acceding to the throne, he announced that he would not succeed his father as Grand Master of the Order of the Knights of St John. The Tsar's reluctance to guarantee Malta's future integrity was the first evidence of Alexander's desire to withdraw Russia from European affairs.

If Alexander's policy in the wake of his accession in 1801 was to steer his country away from the wider stage, by the time Pitt returned to office in 1804 the Tsar was manifesting a much greater enthusiasm for adopting a European role. Napoleon's continued territorial aggression after the Peace of Amiens and his disregard for the niceties of international convention did much to stir the Russians from their introspective torpor.

Alexander's appointment of Prince Adam Czartoryski as head of the Foreign Ministry in late 1803 was another step towards a more positive role in European affairs. Under his predecessor, Vorontsov, Russia's "leading principle . . . was to be on good terms with all the world, and not to interfere in European affairs".[12] Czartoryski, a Pole by birth, (he said of himself that "I was merely there [in Russia] by accident, like an exotic flower in a foreign land") brought a more actively anti-French, pro-British line to Russian foreign affairs.[13]

If the central direction of Russian foreign affairs was, by 1804, turning more towards Britain and against France then the appointment, at the end of 1802, of Markov as the Russian Ambassador to Paris had contributed to the change. Markov was not the most conciliatory of envoys and his presence in Paris did much to disturb the equilibrium of Franco-Russian relations. Apparently he "spoke excellent French, but what he said was generally harsh, trenchant, disagreeable and totally devoid of feeling".[14] As Czartoryski, in effect his boss, said, with heavy irony, of him, "Such was the pearl of Russian diplomatists sent to Napoleon by Russia in evidence of her desire to be on good terms with him".[15]

Markov's presence in Paris was not calculated to foster good relations between the two countries. By contrast, the Russian representative in London, Simon Vorontsov, brother of Czartoryski's predecessor at the Foreign Ministry, was widely respected and liked in British political circles. Vorontsov fully reciprocated these sentiments, to the extent that Czartoryski said of him that "he loved [England] more than the most bigoted of Tories".[16] While the Russian's anglophilia did much to improve relations between the two countries after the rupture of the Armed Neutrality his government worried that it impaired the objectivity of his reports. Czartoryski was concerned that Vorontsov had "gone native". This explains, in part, why, when the negotiations for an alliance began in earnest in late 1804, the Russians sent a second envoy, Novosiltsov, to London.

Ambassadors are important figures, both as conduits of their governments' policy and as the immediate representatives of a nation. They can, and do, influence relations between two countries but the impetus for alliances most often derives from a deeper calculation of common interests. So it was with Britain and Russia. By the time of Pitt's return to office the threat that Napoleon's expansionist policy posed to both nations could no longer be ignored. His depredations in Switzerland, Italy and Germany, in particular the invasion of Hanover, are well known and were a matter of great concern to both governments. So too was the First Consul's cavalier disregard for the conventions which governed international relations. The kidnapping of the Duc d'Enghien in March 1804 was only the most blatant example of this.

Alarming as events in central Europe were to both Russia and Britain, it was in the eastern Mediterranean that the interests of the two countries most closely overlapped. The situation in the eastern and central Mediterranean was complex, but, in essence, the interests of Britain and Russia converged in their desire to maintain the integrity of the Ottoman Empire. They may have had different reasons for wishing to protect the Porte but both were convinced of the necessity to shield it from French aggression.

The Russians had, since their conquest of the northern littoral of the Black Sea in the late eighteenth century, taken an increasing interest in the affairs of the Balkans. By a treaty between Russia and the Ottoman Empire signed in 1774 the Russians acquired the right to free commercial navigation in Turkish waters; this included, most importantly, the right of passage through the Dardanelles to the Mediterranean. The same treaty gave the Tsar a role as spiritual protector of the Sultan's Orthodox subjects.

By 1804 the Russians had established a Mediterranean base in the Ionian Isles. The seven islands, of which Corfu, Cephalonia and Zante were the largest and most important, had become a self-governing republic ("The Republic of the Seven United Isles") set up under Russian tutelage in 1800. The islands, which the Russians had taken from the French in 1798–99, were both economically and strategically valuable. Economically, the islands were capable of providing any conqueror with an immediate financial return, provided of course, that trade could be kept open. Corfu was rich in olive groves while Zante's huge crops of currants were greatly in demand in Britain, where they were a staple ingredient of puddings.

Strategically, the islands provided a base from which a fleet could control the Adriatic and range more widely over the Mediterranean. They also, given their proximity to the mainland mass of the western Balkans, afforded a position from which to exert a powerful political influence in the region. Napoleon had realized the political potential of the archipelago in the 1790s and continued to be alive to the possibilities that it offered even after the French had lost control of the islands.

Colonel Sebastiani's report in the *Moniteur* (January 1803), was a sharp reminder to Britain and Russia of French ambitions in the eastern Mediterranean. By the time the report was published, the west

18

coast of the Balkan peninsula was in turmoil: Russian, Austrian and French agents were swarming everywhere, fomenting trouble; French privateers were cruising the coast distributing arms. The principal target of this activity was Ali Pasha, the ruler of Albania. Nominally a subject of the Ottoman Empire, he was constantly trying both to enlarge his territory and to loosen his ties with Constantinople. As an overmighty and troublesome subject of the Porte, he was an important ally for those who wished to destabilize the Turkish regime in the western Balkans.

The Russians were worried that the French would attack some part of the Turkish dominions, possibly as the first stepping stone in a campaign in the East. They thought that the most likely target was the Morea, the modern Peloponnese. Nelson, who left England for the Mediterranean at the outbreak of war, confirmed the threat to the Morea from the build-up of French forces in the region. Writing to Addington on 28 June 1803 he reported that "It is perfectly clear that the French are at work in that country, either to prepare for their own reception, or to induce the Greeks to revolt against the Porte, and either way, it is a chain for their getting to Egypt".[17]

The French menace in the region had become more pronounced in the summer of 1803. At the resumption of war French forces commanded by General Saint-Cyr reoccupied Apulia, part of the Kingdom of the Two Sicilies. Saint-Cyr moved so quickly that Nelson, in his report to the Prime Minister barely five weeks after the declaration of war, estimated that the French had 13,000 men in the Kingdom of the Two Sicilies. Apulia being on the eastern side of Italy it was these troops who posed the most immediate threat to the Ionian Islands, to the Ottoman dominions in the Balkans and to the Morea. Only the narrow seas between the heel of Italy and Corfu separated the French and Russians.

The government in St Petersburg was alarmed by the build-up of French forces in southern Italy. Ministers worried not only because of the threat to the Ionian Islands but also because the French forces under Saint-Cyr had violated the territory of the King of the Two Sicilies. The integrity of the Two Sicilies was one of the principal aims of Russian policy in the Mediterranean and, as we will see, under the auspices of the Third Coalition, Russian troops landed at Naples to assist in its defence.

The Russian government reacted to the increasing French threat in the Adriatic by, in November 1803, deciding to reinforce the garrison of Corfu. This decision coincided with the arrival of Czartoryski as Foreign Minister and was symptomatic of the new, more outward-looking attitude in St Petersburg. The first reinforcements reached Corfu by the end of March 1804 and by August the Russians had 11,000 men in the Ionian Islands, together with two ships of the line, three frigates and twelve gunboats.[18]

By May 1804 the Russians were aware of the threat that the French posed to European stability in general and to their interests in the eastern Mediterranean in particular. Importantly, the government in St Petersburg had shown that it was willing and able to act in defence of the Ionian Islands; the might of Russia was now ready once more to engage in the European theatre. One historian of the period, writing about the Mediterranean put it thus: "The massing of French and Russian troops on opposite sides of the Adriatic was to be a chief reason for Russia's participation in the War of the Third Coalition".[19]

This, then, was the position that confronted Pitt when he returned to office. The Russians had, thus far, refused to ally themselves with Britain but the diplomatic channels between London and St Petersburg had remained open. Now, with a more positive attitude abroad in the Tsar's councils and an obvious and ever-increasing French threat to the Ionian Islands and the Balkans (not to mention elsewhere in Europe), the Russians had every reason to seek an alliance with Britain. Indeed, in March 1804 the two countries had agreed that they would oppose the partition of the Ottoman Empire. Furthermore, the British government was asked if it would be willing to strengthen the Russian forces then arriving in Corfu with men drawn from the garrison of Malta. The road to a full treaty was to prove circuitous and fraught with difficulty, but at least there was now common ground, a basis for negotiation. This was radically different from the state of affairs that had prevailed during the crisis of the Armed Neutrality only three years previously.

Austria

Pitt may have regarded Russia as the keystone of any new European coalition against the French but no such alliance would be complete

20

without the Austrians. The Hapsburg Empire occupied a position of immense strength in central Europe, dominating the Danube, Austria herself, Hungary and vast tracts of the former Poland. To the south, the Austrians were the only power capable of resisting French ambitions in Italy. In Germany, by virtue of the fact that the Emperor was the Holy Roman Emperor, the Hapsburgs still wielded great, if somewhat diminished, influence. Voltaire's jibe that the Holy Roman Empire was "neither holy, nor Roman, nor an empire" may have contained more than a germ of truth but ignores the fact that in 1804 it covered a huge swathe of Germanic Europe from the Adriatic in the south to the Baltic in the north and from the Rhine in the west to the Oder and beyond in the east. Its Emperor was, inevitably, an important figure.

The Austrians had been the first to take up arms against the Jacobin menace of Revolutionary France. Marie Antoinette, Louis XVI's Queen, was sister to the Emperor Leopold (who died in March 1792, to be succeeded by Francis II) and the French Royal family looked principally to their Austrian relations for salvation. Family ties apart, the Austrians were the most immediately at risk of all European states from the crusading armies of the Revolution. In addition to their homelands and their interests in Germany, they had extensive possessions in the Netherlands, a few short days' march from Paris.

The War of the First Coalition began badly for the Austrians with defeat at the hands of the French general Dumouriez at the battle of Jemappes (6 November 1792). By the time the Prussians made a separate peace with the French at Basle in April 1795 the Austrians had lost their possessions in the Netherlands to the Revolutionary army. Thereafter, the spotlight shifted to Italy when the Austrians took the offensive in the Po Valley in the summer of 1795. But it was the Italian campaign of 1796 that destroyed Austria's armies and, with them, the First Coalition.

This campaign marked the start of Napoleon's career as the most feared, most brilliant general in Europe. Having struck through the Alpine passes in April, he terrified the King of Savoy into submission and launched himself against the Austrians. His victory at the Bridge of Lodi (10 May) was only the first in a series of defeats for the Austrian army that culminated in the humiliations of the Treaty of Campo Formio, formally signed in October 1797. By the terms of this treaty the Austrians acknowledged the loss of their possessions in the Netherlands and were deprived of much of their territory in northern Italy. They were partly compensated for these losses by the grant of the mainland provinces of the now-defunct Venetian republic. They had retained a foothold in Italy, but, with the French in possession of Lombardy, it was an unstable settlement which was unlikely to result in lasting peace.

The War of the Second Coalition began when the French launched an attack eastwards across the Rhine on 1 March 1799. The allies had the better of the exchanges in 1799: Marshal Suvorov rolled the French out of Italy, capturing Turin and Milan in the process. The Archduke Charles, commanding the Austrian armies to the north, forced the French to abandon Zurich in June. By the end of the campaigning season Massena had defeated Suvorov and, although the seeds of discord were starting to germinate, the alliance was nevertheless in a very strong position.

The allies' successes in 1799 were achieved in the absence of the man who had destroyed their armies in Italy in 1796. It was as if the leading actor had been cut from the play. Napoleon had been campaigning in Egypt and the Middle East, beating the Mamalukes and exploring the Pyramids, for a year when, in August 1799, having received news from France, he abandoned his troops and returned home. He arrived at Saint-Raphael in early October and made quickly for Paris. Fretting that he would miss his opportunity, he in fact had arrived in the nick of time and, by the *coup d'état* of 18 Brumaire, seized power. Napoleon had now *de facto* achieved supreme power and henceforward France danced to the tune called by the First Consul.

1799 was the zenith of the fortunes of the Second Coalition, 1800 its nadir. Over the winter Napoleon built up the strength of his armies, massing a reserve at Dijon, from where he was able to keep his enemies guessing as to his intentions. Moreau was to advance across the Rhine while Napoleon attacked the Austrians in Italy. In early May the Army of Italy slipped over the Great St Bernard and debouched into the plains of Lombardy.

The Italian campaign of 1800 was short and, for Melas, the Austrian commander, disastrous. On 2 June Napoleon entered Milan and, within a week was marching his troops south-west to bring the Austrian army to battle. The decisive engagement was fought at

Marengo on 14 June. The battle itself was a close-run thing, the French victory being secured only by Desaix's desperate counter-attack and Kellerman's cavalry charge when the Austrians appeared to hold the upper hand.

Marengo was not the end of the war in Italy but it had re-established the French hegemony achieved at Campo Formio. The fighting continued in the north along the Danube until the Austrians were decisively defeated by Moreau at Hohenlinden (December 1800). This defeat forced the Austrians to sue for peace and a treaty was signed between the two countries at Luneville in February 1801. This peace was a new humiliation for Austria: not only were the arrangements put in place by Campo Formio reinstated but she was forced to make further concessions. The treaty recognized the Rhine and, in Italy, the River Adige (in the Veneto) as the French frontier and acknowledged French possession of the former Austrian Netherlands.

By 1804 the accepted view in Whitehall was that the Austrians were likely to be most reluctant to commit themselves to another war against the French. The Cabinet was encouraged in this belief by the reports of its Ambassador to Vienna, Sir Arthur Paget. It is indicative of Paget's opinion of the direction of Austrian policy at this time that he reported in June 1803 "that not even a remonstrance has been made by the Court of Vienna to the French Government against the invasion of Hanover".[20] It appeared that the Emperor and his advisors were most anxious not to give offence to the French.

They did, indeed, have every reason to wish to avoid another conflict. By 1804 the Austrians had been forced to sue twice for peace within seven years. Defeats at the hands of the French during the wars of the First and Second Coalitions in Italy and Germany had left them militarily weakened and virtually bankrupt. The wars had been ruinously expensive and in 1804 the Hapsburg system was tottering for lack of money. The exchequer owed Britain £6.2 million, a loan outstanding from 1795.[21] The government had been compelled to print paper money to finance the cost of the war, which had, in its turn, fuelled inflation and undermined confidence. Furthermore, the loss of the Netherlands and the possessions in Italy reduced the government's income at a time when it was struggling to meet its outgoings.

War against France had crippled the Hapsburgs financially and militarily; the peace was to sap at their political influence in Germany. As we have seen, Luneville confirmed France in her "natural boundaries", which in the East meant the Rhine. France's gains in the Rhineland were at the expense of a number of German states which were, however, compensated for their territorial losses under a redistribution of territory known as Secularizations. Enacted in 1802–3, the Secularizations suppressed ecclesiastical lands and 112 Imperial cities within the Holy Roman Empire and annexed them to those states which had lost out to France west of the Rhine. The principal beneficiaries of this redistribution of land were Prussia, Bavaria, Baden and Wurtemburg.

The Secularizations were a deathly blow to the prestige of Francis II as Holy Roman Emperor, but more serious still was the impact of the redistribution on Austria's political standing in Germany. Those states which were beneficiaries of the new secular order now looked to France rather than Austria as the arbiter of German affairs. It was a highly effective way of extending French influence in Germany at the expense of Austria. The fact that Bavaria sided with the French in the War of the Third Coalition illustrates the effectiveness of the Secularizations as an act of political patronage.

The reduced political status, military power and financial stability of the Austrian Empire by 1803–4 was reflected by events in diplomatic circles. In July 1803 the British government approached St Petersburg with the suggestion that the Russians might conclude an offensive alliance against France with Austria. The proposal was rebuffed, despite the offer of a subsidy, not least because the Russians were not confident of the willingness of the Austrians to go to war once more. Czartoryski later described Austrian foreign policy in the years after Luneville as "lachrymose and sentimental".[22]

By the spring of 1804 it did not appear in London or St Petersburg that there had been any significant stiffening of Austrian sinews. In April Czartoryski told Vorontsov, the Russian Ambassador in London, that he could not envisage Austria committing herself to a tripartite alliance with Britain and Prussia for war against France.[23] At the same time Sir John Warren reported from St Petersburg that Austria was "cowed" by her defeats in the previous war, worried about a French attack in Italy and would not entertain any overtures that might lead to war. Warren told the Foreign Secretary that, in Czartoryski's opinion, a defensive alliance of European powers based on the Luneville settlement was the most that could be hoped for.[24]

Sir Arthur Paget had a low opinion of the willingness of the Austrian government to resist the ambitions of the French and was pessimistic about the prospects of concerting action between the European powers to maintain the *status quo*. The Court of Vienna, Paget complained in April 1804, was guilty of "acts of unexampled weakness and humiliation towards the French government". In the same gloomy tone he continued:

> "In the three weeks I have been returned to Vienna I have seen treaties broken, territory violated, the rights of nations trampled upon, murder even committed, without having as yet discovered the slightest indication of any disposition [by the Emperor's ministers] to check the progress of this monstrous hostility, much less to avenge the insults which have been daily and directly levelled at the Imperial Crown."[25]

Paget could hardly have expressed his opinion of the tenor of Austria's policy towards France more clearly, but he was not as well-informed as he thought. Paget was convinced of the utter docility of the Emperor's government towards France and his despatches give no indication that he knew of the conflict being fought out in the councils of Vienna between the "war" party headed by the Archduke John and the "peace" party led, paradoxically enough, by the Empire's most renowned general, the Archduke Charles. As early as 1803 Cobenzl, the Emperor's chief minister, was convinced that only an alliance with the Russians could save Austria from Napoleon. He and his supporters could see that the First Consul had not abandoned the expansionist policies of the Revolution. But the Emperor was reluctant to commit his country to another damaging war and Charles, who knew better than anyone the state of the army, was utterly opposed to any war. For him peace was the only policy that offered any salvation to Austria.[26]

The "war" party operated in the deepest secrecy; there was no sense in offending the French and risk provoking an attack before the Austrians were ready. The diplomats had to secure the support of allies and the army be brought on to a war footing before Vienna could declare its hand: until these preparations were complete Austria would maintain a facade of neutrality. It was this facade that made Paget

25

despair for the future of Europe; little did he know that he was, quite deliberately, being kept in the dark by Cobenzl. The fewer people who were in on the secret, Cobenzl reasoned, the less the likelihood of it leaking out to the French.

For Pitt, surveying the courts of Europe on his return to office in May 1804, the prospects of an alliance with Austria must have seemed distant. Paget's pessimistic dispatches from Vienna held out no hope of any assistance from that quarter; the Austrian Court seemed bent on appeasing Napoleon, desperate to avoid the trauma of another war. But, for those perceptive enough to see it, there was a chink of light. In the same month in which Pitt returned to office Czartoryski in St Petersburg told Sir John Warren that, in his opinion, continued acts of aggression on the part of the French would, eventually, drive the other European powers into a coalition against France. It was to prove an uncannily accurate prophesy.

Prussia

Prussia was the third of the great European powers that had, in the 1790s, ranged itself against the regicidal revolutionaries of France. The King of Prussia had been one of the leading lights in the effort to preserve the French monarchy, in concert with the Emperor of Austria. Frederick William III was as horrified by the Revolution as the other crowned heads of Europe and in July 1792 Prussia declared war on France, entering the conflict in support of the Austrians, who had been at war since April.

To begin with, the Prussian forces, commanded by the Duke of Brunswick, advanced easily into France, encountering little opposition; by 1 September the Duke's troops had taken the fortress of Verdun. The Prussians advanced slowly, but seemingly inexorably, on Paris; the very existence of the Revolution seemed to hang in the balance. It was saved only by an unexpected victory at the Battle of Valmy (20 September 1792) in the Champagne country.

The defeat of Brunswick's troops at Valmy was as dispiriting for the Prussians as it was timely for the French. It was a far cry from the days of the Prussian military supremacy under Frederick the Great forty years earlier. Thereafter they played only a half-hearted role in the war against the French; this was despite receiving a heavy subsidy from the

26

British to the tune of, in 1794, £29 a man. The war against France was of secondary importance; in Berlin thoughts were concentrated on developments to the east, where, together with the two Emperors of Austria and Russia, Frederick William was picking over the corpse of Poland.

The Second and Third Partitions of Poland (1793 & 1795) offered Prussia an opportunity to expand her territory eastward; as a result of the First Partition in 1773 she had acquired a huge tranche of West Prussia, an acquisition which no doubt whetted her appetite for further substantial gains. In April 1795, after two and a half years of desultory fighting in the west, Prussia made peace with the French and withdrew from the war. As one British historian succinctly and damningly put it: "Prussia was the first to abandon the defence of Germany against the French".[27]

The Treaty of Basle allowed the Prussians to concentrate all their resources on the despoiling of Poland; the price they paid for this was to allow France to retain all the territory she had taken to the west of the Rhine until a general peace. If, by a future settlement, France held on to these lands, then Prussia would be compensated elsewhere. Here were the first straws in the wind of the mutual self-interest that would keep France and Prussia in a state of friendly neutrality for nearly a decade.

To Pitt, beginning his search for allies in the spring of 1804, Prussia would have seemed the least promising of all Britain's former partners. The craven attitude of the Prussians to the French was, it appeared, likely to be a serious obstacle in forming an effective alliance against Napoleon. The Prussians were the key to resisting French aggression in northern Germany – once they had made peace in 1795 the French were virtually unchallenged in the region – and, most importantly from a British point-of-view, their assistance was a prerequisite for retaking the Dutch Netherlands. It was the threat of a French invasion of Holland that had forced Britain into the war in 1793; no responsible government in London could allow the Dutch ports to fall into the hands of a hostile power. Ensuring that the Dutch ports remained in friendly hands was as much a priority in 1804 as it had been in 1793; Napoleon's refusal to evacuate his troops from Flushing in 1802, as demanded by the Peace of Amiens, was the cause of tension between the two countries during the period of peace.

27

Nor did it seem that the Prussians were likely suddenly to reverse their policy of the last ten years. They had, after all, benefited greatly from both their neutrality and their cooperation with France. Nine years of neutrality had given Prussia the opportunity for uninterrupted trade, without the restrictions that war placed on the trade of combatant nations. This led in turn to a healthy flow of revenue to the exchequer in Berlin at a time when other European countries were suffering from disruption of their trade and the consequent loss of income.

The Prussians had also, by 1804, made considerable territorial gains in the west to complement the acquisitions from Poland to the east in the 1790s. The territorial compensation for Prussia promised in the Treaty of Basle became reality under the settlement imposed on Europe by the Peace of Luneville. The Secularizations of 1802–3 were the first step in Napoleon's reorganization of Germany, a process which led to the abolition of the Holy Roman Empire and the establishment of the Confederation of the Rhine. The Secularizations entailed the redistribution of German ecclesiastical land and Imperial Cities to those states which had lost territory to France to the west of the Rhine. Prussia benefited greatly from the reorganization, as in 1803 she was able to annex large swathes of central Germany. Weimar, Gotha, Eichsfeld, Hildesheim, Paderborn, Essen and Munster all became part of Prussia as a result of the Secularizations. Territorial aggrandisement on this scale was a rare reward for mere neutrality. Frederick William was unlikely to wish to bite the hand that fed him.

There was one other major stumbling block to any possible alliance between Britain and Prussia: Hanover. The kingdom of Hanover covered a large belt of central Germany to the west of Prussia and for many reasons, not least its trade and the fact that it would furnish a deeper frontier against the French, its acquisition had long been the cherished ambition of the Kings of Prussia. The difficulty was that Hanover was ruled by the King of England. George III was devoted to his German subjects; the waspish Sir Philip Francis expressed it thus: "His [George III's] ruling passions were avarice and Hanover – for money not to be spent, and for a country he was determined never to see".[29] It was inconceivable that the British government would allow Hanover to be used as a bargaining chip in negotiations for an alliance with Prussia: the King simply would not countenance it. This being the case, it was all too evident to the Prussians that they would never secure the prize of Hanover by aligning themselves with England. It was much more likely to fall into their lap as a result of cooperation with the French, particularly once the French had occupied Hanover on the resumption of war in May 1803.

Perhaps not surprisingly, in view of their apparently pro-French stance, the Prussians did not enjoy the easiest of relations with either Austria or Russia, their potential partners in any coalition against France. Relations with Austria had been soured by events of the previous ten years. The Prussian withdrawal from the war in 1795 had left Austria exposed to French aggression in Germany and to devastating attacks in Italy. The redistributions of territory in Germany under the Secularizations which built up Prussia at Austria's expense were bitterly resented in Vienna and the Partitions of Poland had left a residue of jealousy and suspicion between the two countries.

Relations between the Russians and Prussians operated on two levels. The King and the Tsar had from the first enjoyed a good friendship. Shortly after Alexander's accession the monarchs had met at Memel and established a healthy rapport. Here, too, Czartoryski reports, the Tsar began a "Platonic coquetry" with the Queen.[29] The cordial relations of the two monarchs was not, if Czartoryski is to be believed, matched by similar feelings between their respective countries. "The relations of Russia with Prussia were purely personal between the two sovereigns, as there was no sympathy between the Cabinets, the armies, or the people of the two states.[30] Just as with Austria, here too the Partitions of Poland had left a residue of suspicion between the countries.

In the early summer of 1804 the prospects of inveigling Prussia into an alliance against France were not bright: Berlin was determinedly neutral, although to more impartial observers it was a neutrality with a distinctly pro-French flavour. George Jackson, the British *chargé d'affaires* in Berlin in 1804 bemoaned what he saw as the utter submission of Prussia to France.[31] Sir John Warren reported from St Petersburg in the summer that the Prussians had told Czartoryski they wished to remain strictly neutral.[32]

The government was dominated by Frederick William and his Francophile ministers whose policy of neutrality and cooperation with the French had paid huge dividends in the recent past and might, in

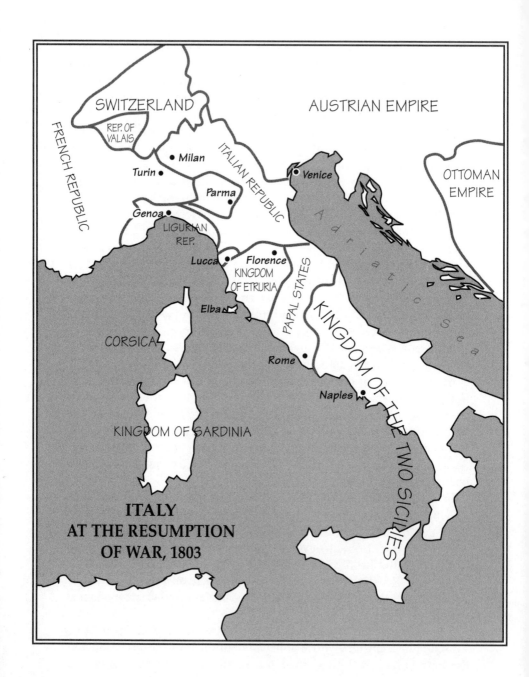

SWITZERLAND

REP. OF VALAIS

AUSTRIAN EMPIRE

FRENCH REPUBLIC

OTTOMAN EMPIRE

• Milan

Turin •

ITALIAN REPUBLIC

• Venice

Parma •

Genoa •

LIGURIAN REP.

Lucca •

Florence •

KINGDOM OF ETRURIA

PAPAL STATES

Adriatic Sea

Elba

CORSICA

Rome •

KINGDOM OF THE TWO SICILIES

Naples •

KINGDOM OF SARDINIA

**ITALY
AT THE RESUMPTION
OF WAR, 1803**

the future, deliver the ultimate prize, Hanover. This imperative of national self-interest was reinforced by fear, fear of the all-conquering Napoleonic armies. The Prussian army had performed poorly against the French in the 1790s and since then Napoleon and his young, dynamic marshals had swept all before them. There seemed little to gain and much to lose by taking up arms.

The Kingdom of the Two Sicilies

The Bourbon King Ferdinand who ruled the Kingdom of the Two Sicilies which consisted of the southern half of the Italian peninsula and the island of Sicily, had joined the First Coalition against Revolutionary France in 1793. He was a natural enemy of the Revolution, not least for dynastic reasons: the two branches of the Bourbon family, Neapolitan and French, were related and his Queen, Maria Carolina, and the Queen of France, Marie Antoinette, were sisters. And, if the Revolution had a particular *bête noire*, it was the House of Bourbon.

In the early years of the wars Naples was on the periphery of the military action, which took place far away in northern Europe. However, the defection of Prussia in 1795 allowed the French to turn their attention to Italy from 1796. Once Austria had been defeated and knocked out of the war in 1797 the Kingdom of the Two Sicilies had lost its principal bulwark against French aggression in Italy – only the flimsy defences of the Papal States stood between Naples and the armies of the Directory. In the autumn of 1798 the French overran the mainland portion of Ferdinand's kingdom and established a republic in Naples, organized along approved revolutionary lines. This was just one example of the many exported revolutions with which the French attempted to mould Europe in their own image.

Known as the Parthenopean Republic, it was a chaotic and short-lived experiment. King Ferdinand, having fled on HMS *Vanguard* to Sicily as the French advanced, reconquered his mainland possessions with the help of a subsidy of £100,000 from the British (December 1798). The reconquest was led by the splendid figure of Cardinal Ruffo, a war-mongering prelate of the type who figure so prominently in the history of Renaissance Italy. By June 1799 Ruffo had reached Naples, and on 11 July St Elmo's Castle, the rebels' stronghold,

31

surrendered, its resistance cut short by the threatening firepower of the Navy. By the end of the month the important fortresses of Gaeta and Capua had fallen and the Parthenopean Republic had been defeated. The reassertion of his authority over his mainland dominions did not, however, encourage Ferdinand to return to his people. He did accompany the doughty Cardinal Ruffo to Naples but refused to land in his capital, preferring to conduct state business from the safety of HMS *Foudroyant*, anchored in the Bay. Indeed, the King did not formally return to Naples until June 1802.[33]

The collapse of the Second Coalition after the battles of Marengo and Hohenlinden left the Two Sicilies exposed once more to French aggression. Faced with an overwhelming French presence in the north of Italy and a general European truce Ferdinand had little option but to sign the Treaty of Florence with Napoleon (March 1801). The terms of the treaty allowed Ferdinand to recover much of his kingdom, but only on condition that he remained strictly neutral and agreed to accept, pay and feed a French army of occupation until a general peace was signed.[34] For the perenially impoverished Neapolitan government this was a particularly onerous imposition, estimated to cost more than four million ducats a year.[35]

At the resumption of war in May 1803 the French armies reoccupied Apulia and Abruzzi. It was, among other things, the presence of Saint-Cyr's troops on the eastern side of Italy that caused, as we have seen, both the Russians and the British to become deeply suspicious of France's ambitions in the Balkans and the Middle East. It was here that the interests of Britain and Russia were most closely identified – both governments were anxious to preserve the integrity of the Ottoman Empire – and here that the first shoots of the Anglo-Russian cooperation which would result in the Third Coalition pushed above ground.

That the British had enjoyed a harmonious relationship with the Court of Naples during the 1790s was due in no small measure to the part played by Sir William Hamilton. Sir William was, until his recall in 1800, the British Minister at Naples for thirty-six years; he and, latterly, his wife Emma had become close to the Royal Family, particularly the Queen. It is a measure of the intimacy that existed between the Hamiltons and the Court that Arthur Paget, who succeeded Sir William as the British Minister, felt justified in complaining of his reception on taking up his appointment. "It is not," he wrote, "to be told the pains that were taken by Lady Hamilton to set the King and Queen & the whole Court against me, even before I had arrived. I was represented as a Jacobin and coxcomb, a person sent to bully and to carry them *bon gré, mal gré* back to Naples."[36] The Queen, for her part referred to "the accursed Paget".[37] It was also, of course, in Naples that the *vicace* Emma cast her spell over Nelson after his triumph at the Battle of Nile, thus ensuring her place in the pantheon of *femmes fatales*.

For the British the significance of the Two Sicilies as an ally lay not in her military and naval strength but in her geographic and strategic position. No one was more keenly aware than Pitt of the importance to the Navy of the ports of both Sicily and the mainland portion of Ferdinand's dominions. It was imperative that they should not be allowed to fall to the French, whether as a result of military action or diplomatic sleight of hand. The loss to the Royal Navy of these ports would severely curtail and perhaps end altogether Britain's dominance in the Mediterranean. Without the use of Messina and Naples it would be much more difficult for Nelson to command the central and eastern Mediterranean as he had done since the Battle of the Nile.

In the years before 1804 the British had several times given Ferdinand a helping hand in the defence of his kingdom. Nelson's role in the reconquest of the mainland possessions has already been noted; in the same year the British provided a garrison for the Sicilian port of Messina. Two regiments, commanded by General Sir Charles Stuart, were ordered to Sicily from the British base at Minorca to forestall any attempt by the French to launch a *coup de main* against the island. Moreover, the British continued to provide financial as well as practical assistance to their ally. In November 1803 Hugh Elliot, Paget's successor as Minister in Naples, was authorized by Addington to draw £170,000 from government funds in Malta, to help put the King's forces on to a war footing. Indeed Elliot, who arrived in Naples in June 1803, busied himself from the start with measures to safeguard Sicily against a French attack.

By the time of Pitt's return to office the ports of Sicily and southern Italy had assumed a greater significance owing to the fact that the majority of Britain's other naval bases in the Mediterranean, bar Malta, had been surrendered at the Peace of Amiens. The valuable bases on Corsica, Elba and Minorca had been lost in this way. The difficulty confronting Pitt was that the Two Sicilies was an unreliable ally in so far as it was unlikely to be able (or perhaps willing) to resist a full French invasion. This was compounded by the fact that to provide military assistance on a scale large enough to prove effective was likely to present almost insurmountable practical problems.

The capacity of the Two Sicilies to resist a French invasion was impaired by a lack of money which prevented the maintenance of an adequate army. In 1805 Ferdinand's army amounted to 9–10,000 men; when the French eventually invaded in 1806 they did so with around 30,000 men. She was not a rich nation and her public finances had suffered badly at the hands of the Parthenopean Republic. Paget reported, in 1800, "the total discredit into which the paper Money has fallen . . . It now sells at Naples at 68% discount."[38] Public credit was further undermined by the extortionate demands of the French for payment of her troops following the treaty of 1801. Financially, the kingdom paid a high price for her continued independence.

The parlous state of the public finances was reflected in the condition of the body politic and the country as a whole. Paget, who may not have been the most impartial observer, reported that "Every department in the State, ecclesiasticall [sic], civil, and military, has assumed the most untoward appearance. Instead of Religion, there is an excess of bigotry, corruption has succeeded to Justice, and the fact of calling the assistance of Foreign Troops in itself proves what the state of the Army must be".[39]

Neither did the country as a whole seem to Paget to be in good order. "The Provinces are, in general, in a very unpleasant state of Insubordination, particularly in Calabria and the Abruzzi, where people live in a state of licentiousness and anarchy . . .". Another English traveller, writing ten years later, seemed to confirm Paget's opinions. "The Sicilians appear to me a sorry set of people – the nobles are illiterate, and little to be respected; in the middle orders I see no character at all; the lower orders are knavish and more horribly filthy than anything you can imagine."[40]

This country was ruled over by King Ferdinand and his Queen, Maria Carolina, a couple whose sometimes eccentric spirit infuses the story of events leading to the Battle of Maida. They are always in the wings giving prompts and, occasionally, emerging on to the stage itself. Ferdinand had acceded to the throne of the Kingdom of the Two Sicilies in 1759 but had never taken any interest in the affairs of state. His great passion was shooting and he devoted himself to the sport with an almost religious intensity as an English officer described after a visit to one of Ferdinand's hunting lodges, La Favorita, near Palermo. "The Gardens . . . are full of game, too full indeed to afford sport to an Englishman. Hares and rabbits start up on every side and hardly think it worth their while to run from you. The partridges & pheasants . . . are not less numerous . . . When his majesty comes there to shoot . . . he takes seat in an open spot made on purpose his Gamekeepers & Rangers beat up the game & drive it towards him. His Majesty fires away as fast as his servants can put guns into his hands, & when he is tired, which may be after having killed 200 head of different sorts, the sport ceases. Noble Diversion!!"[41]

A large, coarse-mannered man, nicknamed "Il Nasone", Ferdinand was, for all his lack of attention to the business of government and his passion for shooting, very popular with the mass of his subjects, particularly with the *lazzaroni*, the mendicant underclass of Naples. When on 27 June 1802 he rode back into Naples after an absence of three years he received a rapturous welcome.

Others, seeing him in a different light, were more critical. Paget held no brief for him at all: "The King . . . is timid and bigoted and, as is often the case in the same disposition, cruel and revengeful".[42] Another, more balanced view from a British diplomat who knew the King well, described his "great gawky body, his plebian manners, his superstitious, diffident mind and his burst of Neapolitan bonhomie – here was . . . a man who might be trusted to act sensibly and loyally if only he was not bedevilled by intrigue."[43]

His Queen, Maria Carolina, was the polar opposite of her husband. Clever, energetic and hard-working, she, with the royal ministers, ruled the kingdom. She was an indefatigable letter writer: over a twenty-year period, for example, she wrote Count Gallo, the Ambassador in Paris and one of the Queen's confidants, 1400 letters. The French Ambassador to the Court of Naples described her, most unflatteringly, as "this famous wreck of bygone graces and gallantries". But he did continue his pen portrait by saying that "The Queen is neither good nor bad . . . Born with a great deal of intelligence and natural grace and . . . endowed with more knowledge than women

35

usually possess, she had a fair claim to govern, when she came to Naples and found a man on the throne incapable of governing".[44] Another, this time British, observer agreed, saying "that with exceeding good abilities, she probably never had any common sense and that her mind enfeebled by age, by vast quantities of opium and by the operation of violent passions had reached a state little short of insanity."[45]

The Queen's principal aim was to preserve the integrity and independence of her husband's kingdom by staving off the menace of French invasion. In the periods when the mainland had been overrun and the Court forced to take refuge in Sicily – the Queen hated Palermo – this entailed leaving no stone unturned in an effort to reconquer the lost territory. The Queen would write letters by the hundred, imploring support, scheming, cajoling, pleading. Her hopes of salvation habitually rested with her family in Vienna and were, equally habitually, disappointed.

Maria Carolina also looked to London for support. British naval power had been the saviour of the Royal Family in 1799, spiriting them away from the revolutionaries to Sicily, and was to be so again in 1806. After the first flight from Naples, the Queen wrote, "The English have shown themselves most faithful, zealous and loyal". "Without them," she continued, "we would already be pensioners or beheaded or imprisoned . . . They have saved us personally, preserved Sicily, and will recover Naples."[46]

The Queen was grateful to Britain for her help in times of need and was an admirer of Nelson, the Hamiltons and later Elliot, although she loathed Paget, but Britain's best hope of securing the cooperation of the Two Sicilies lay in the person of the First Minister, Sir John Acton. Sir John, an English baronet, had commanded the Neapolitan land and sea forces and came in time to wield almost absolute power in the councils of the King.

His presence at the head of the government in Naples was particularly galling to the French, who considered, with some justice, that he inclined the Two Sicilies to favour a conjunction with Britain. Napoleon wrote to the Queen telling her that "I have therefore decided as a wise precaution to consider Naples as a country ruled by an English minister".[47] His Ambassador in Naples was even more forthright: "What can we expect from the Court of Naples when it is directed by a British subject? Everything about Chevalier Acton is English: titles, hopes, speeches and material fortune". He hammered the point home: "When [Acton] speaks of the British he says 'we'."[48] The French in the period between 1800 and 1803 were constantly scheming to secure Acton's dismissal, either by browbeating the King and Queen or by political machination. In May 1804 they eventually succeeded when Acton was goaded into resigning. The French victory was only partially complete, however, as, despite his age – he was 68 in 1804 – he continued to exert his influence from behind the scenes. Retiring with a pension to Sicily he kept abreast of affairs by reading all the important state papers.

The British government, under both Addington and Pitt, gave the highest priority to keeping the ports of southern Italy and, particularly, Sicily out of French hands. To this end it assiduously courted the Neapolitan government as well as paying it subsidies. This policy resulted in cooperation with the Russians, the dispatch of a British army to the Mediterranean and, ultimately, the maintenance of a British garrison in Sicily until the end of the war. It would also, and not that directly, lead to the Battle of Maida.

Chapter Three

RELUCTANT ALLIES & A PROVOCATIVE ENEMY: THE BIRTH OF THE THIRD COALITION

On the night of 14 March 1804 a small contingent of French soldiers commanded by Generals Caulaincourt and Ordener crossed the Rhine near Strasbourg into the principality of Baden. They made for the town of Ettenheim where the young Bourbon prince, the Duc d'Enghien, was living in exile. As ordered, the soldiers kidnapped Enghien and spirited him back to Paris, arriving at the castle of Vincennes on the afternoon of 20 March. Having got its man, the Privy Council met to decide his fate. It ordered that he should be tried by a court martial established by Murat in his capacity as Governor of Paris; the members of the Privy Council can have been under no illusion as to the verdict this body would return. Murat's court convened at 1 am on 21 March and Enghien was speedily condemned to death. He requested an interview with Napoleon, but this was refused and at 2.30 am on the same morning he was shot by firing squad in the castle's disused moat.

Enghien was a scion of one of the most distinguished families in France; his grandfather was the Prince de Condé and his father the Duc de Bourbon. Enghien was undeniably a prominent royalist and recently Paris had seethed with rumours of royalist plots against Napoleon's life. The most threatening of these supposedly involved Georges Cadoudal, who, along with his co-conspirators, had been arrested in February. The First Consul jumped to the wrong conclusion; there was no evidence among Enghien's papers that he was involved in any of these supposed Royalist plots. But Napoleon, obsessed about threats on his life, was determined to strike at his enemies, whatever the cost, wherever he could find them. Nor did the

Privy Council, in conclave on 20 March, do anything to restrain the First Consul. Only Cambacérès voted against Enghien's execution. Both Fouché and Talleyrand were present and both assented to the proposal; equally the two men both subsequently tried to deny responsibility for the murder.

Other rulers at other times have committed atrocities that have left a permanent blemish on their reputations; one thinks, for example, of Henry II and Thomas à Becket; the murder, for that was what it was, of the Duc d'Enghien is an indelible stain on Napoleon's character. It seemed to demonstrate that "vaulting ambition, which o'erleaps itself". This single act, more than any other, compromised Napoleon's reputation as a hero and a statesman. The brave victor of Marengo, the wise Consul who, by his negotiation of the Concordat, had reconciled France to the Pope, this Olympian figure, had stooped to common murder.

Europe was outraged. The Tsar, horrified by the episode, ordered the Court of St Petersburg into mourning for the murdered prince. His Ambassador in Paris, d'Oubril, was commanded to make an official protest to the French government. The Queen of the Two Sicilies described the affair as a "dark stain" on Napoleon's character: "He has," she wrote, "violated the law he had sworn to uphold . . . he has violated human rights."[49]

The ways in which the nations of Europe reacted to the news of Enghien's murder give the clearest possible indication of the stance taken by each individual country towards France and Napoleon. The Duke of Baden, whose territory had been violated by French soldiers in the kidnapping, was too terrified of retribution even to register the meekest of protests. Baden was a small principality adjoining France, so the Duke's fears were perhaps understandable; Austria and Prussia had no such excuse. Paget, in Vienna, bemoaned the lack of a proper response from the Austrian cabinet to the incident: Cobenzl, the Austrian Foreign Minister, had reacted, he said, with a "display of so much ignorance, weakness, and pusillanimity on the part of any individual calling himself a Statesman".[50] British and Russian diplomats alike looked on in disgust as the Prussians, in their turn, failed to register any form of official protest with the French government.

The murder of the Duc d'Enghien is the first and perhaps the best example of how Napoleon managed to provoke his enemies into combining against him. In March 1804 only Britain of all the European nations was at war with France; all the other countries, in varying degrees, were pursuing the path if not of peace with France, then certainly of least resistance to her. It is true that there was a burgeoning recognition of common interest between Britain and Russia in the eastern Mediterranean and the Balkans, but that was far from the flowering of a full military alliance. Such a wantonly provocative act on the part of Napoleon was the best possible catalyst for an anti-French alliance. For Pitt, back in office and casting round for potential allies, it was manna from heaven.

Enghien's murder immediately raised the diplomatic temperature. The Tsar ordered that a stiff protest be lodged with the French government. Talleyrand replied, expressing his surprise that the Russian government should concern itself with matters relating to the security of another state and pointedly reminding the Russians that France had not seen fit to interfere after the murder of Tsar Paul. This reply was calculatedly rude; Czartoryski described it as "harsh and insulting".[51]

The Russians were still considering Talleyrand's tactless reply when Napoleon stirred the hornet's nest once more by graciously allowing a *senatus-consultum* in Paris to declare him Emperor on 18 May. This new insult was again taken lying down by both Austria and Prussia, the latter meekly acknowledging Napoleon's new title. But for the Russians, coming as it did so soon after *l'affaire d'Enghien*, it merely served to stiffen their resolve. Czartoryski composed an ultimatum to the French government, which he described as a "band of brigands", demanding proof of its friendly intentions and moderation and setting out the terms on which a European settlement could be made.[52]

In the early autumn of 1804 d'Oubril presented this ultimatum to the French government, who failed to provide a satisfactory reply within the twenty-four hours demanded by the Russians. D'Oubril, obeying his instructions, accordingly asked for his passports and left Paris. Diplomatic relations between France and Russia had been broken off.

Hardly had the dust settled on the Enghien affair and Napoleon's assumption of an Imperial title than European sensibilites were again outraged by another example of French high-handedness and disregard for the niceties of international law. On 24 October 1804 Sir George Rumbold, the British *chargé d'affaires* in Hamburg, was kidnapped by French agents, allegedly because he was involved in a conspiracy against the Napoleonic government. Fortunately Sir George did not share the fate of the hapless Duc d'Enghien; he was allowed to return to his family in England, but it was another example of Napoleon's talent for galvanizing his enemies into action against him. It can be no accident that a fortnight after Sir George's abduction the previously supine Austrian government signed a treaty, albeit only defensive one, with the Russians.

Earlier in the summer the new Ministry in London had opened on a positive note. Less than a month after taking office the Foreign Secretary, Lord Harrowby, wrote to the Russian Ambassador in London, Simon Vorontsov, setting out the policy of Pitt's new government. The British, Harrowby wrote, hoped to unite the European Powers by entering into an alliance with Russia. Britain was prepared to pay lavish subsidies in return for commitments to active military opposition to France. Furthermore, the Russians, as trusted partners, were authorized to inform both Austria and Prussia of London's intentions so far as subsidies were concerned.[53]

The new, more constructive relationship between Britain and Russia was exemplified by two fresh diplomatic appointments, one on each side. Sir John Warren, the British Ambassador in St Petersburg, was recalled in July; he had been a competent if somewhat uninspiring envoy, although Czartoryski described him as being the "perfect representative of the nullity and incapacity of the Addington Ministry that had appointed him".[54] In fairness to Warren it should be noted that he had asked to be recalled in order to resume his naval career.

His replacement was Lord Granville Leveson Gower, a young but worldly *protégé* of Pitt's. He was appointed to the post in July but did not arrive in St Petersburg until November. Leveson Gower is a central figure in the formation of the Third Coalition; he was involved in lengthy and difficult negotiations with Czartoryski and, latterly, Count Stadion for the Austrians. He also left, in his private correspondence, a wonderfully spicy, indiscreet and amusing description of diplomatic life in St Petersburg.

The Russians, for their part, sent Count Novosiltsov to London to take charge of the negotiations. He too arrived in November. Novosiltsov was the ideal man to fill the role: he was an anglophile, had lived in England and spoke English. He came armed with the

41

Tsar's blueprint for the post-war settlement of Europe. This document, it turned out, was long on theory but somewhat short on practical detail. Pitt and Novosiltsov, however, established a strong working relationship and matters proceeded apace in London in the late autumn and winter of 1804.

Pitt's view of the shape of post-war Europe, that is, the terms on which the allies would be prepared to accept peace, was set out in a state paper of 19 January 1805. It is signed by Lord Mulgrave, the new Foreign Secretary, Harrowby's replacement, but is recognized as the work of Pitt and had been drawn up in response to a speculatively insincere offer of peace from Napoleon. The new Emperor had addressed the proposal directly to George III, monarch to monarch, a presumption the King found most offensive. The state paper also formed the basis of the draft treaty that was, two days later, sent to Leveson Gower in St Petersburg from which he was to negotiate with the Russian government.

The rapport that built up between Pitt and Novosiltsov masked the considerable differences that existed between the two governments on the question of the post-war settlement. The Tsar and Czartoryski favoured a European political map based on principles of national self-determination; Pitt, by contrast, was anxious only to establish a stable political system, a balance of power. For him nationalist aspirations were wholly subordinate to political realities. The other principal difference between the two governments lay in the question of territorial inducements to potential allies, that is, who should get what for joining in the fight against Napoleon. Pitt was in favour of the expulsion of the French from Italy, with the consequent aggrandisement of the Austrians; the Russians opposed this. Similarly, Pitt proposed to establish the Prussians as guarantors of the integrity of the Low Countries, an essential goal of British foreign policy; the Russians, likewise, were not anxious to allow Prussian influence in the west to grow.

Political arrangements for the future of Europe and territorial inducements for fighting were important matters for negotiation. So too was the question of subsidy. Britain's allies had become accustomed during the wars of the 1790s to receiving substantial subsidies to underpin their efforts against the French and Pitt was under no illusions as to their importance in putting together another coalition. The question was, how much? In the draft treaty sent to Leveson Gower the rate at which subsidy was to be offered was set at £1,250,000 per 100,000 men put into the field. This rate, Leveson Gower was told, was not open to negotiation. As the government calculated that an army of between 400–500,000 men would be needed to stand any realistic chance of success against Napoleon, this implied a total expenditure of between £5m and £6.25m. To put this sum into perspective while the government's total revenue in 1804 exceeded £46m, the following year its expenditure on the Navy amounted to just over £15m.[55] So, even allowing for taking figures from two years together, the government was applying approaching half of its annual revenue to the Navy and to subsidizing its foreign allies.

It seemed likely that the war would be won in central Europe, but Britain and Russia had other, shared interests in the eastern Mediterranean to which both attached great importance. These negotiations, less constrained by the dawdling Austrians, galloped ahead. Leveson Gower's initial instructions, given to him in October 1804, emphasize the importance of operations in southern Italy and by the beginning of November Warren, in his last despatch from St Petersburg, relayed Russian proposals for joint action in Naples. By the end of the month Leveson Gower was reporting that the question of a unified command of the Anglo-Russian forces had been discussed. A week later Leveson Gower told the government in London that General Lacy, a seventy-year-old Russian commander who had seen service in the Seven Years War, had been ordered to make a military survey of the Kingdom of Naples.[56]

On arrival in St Petersburg Leveson Gower at once established a rapport with Czartoryski. However, while negotiations continued in London between Pitt and Novosiltsov, he was left somewhat out on a limb. The text of the draft treaty did not reach him until the end of February and communications with London were always difficult during the hard northern winters. Matters were exacerbated by Harrowby's accident in December, who is said to have fallen downstairs during an epileptic fit, which left the Foreign Secretaryship vacant until Mulgrave took over on 11 January.

Diplomatic representation in the age before instant worldwide communications was a more leisurely, long-drawn-out activity than it is today; bursts of frantic, tiring negotiation were interspersed with

43

periods when there was little to do. In St Petersburg, the *longueurs* hung heavily on Leveson Gower. He describes a typical day.

"For the last three or four Days I have had no public Business whatever to do, and my Days have thus passed: I get up at eleven; dressing, breakfast, and Newspaper Reading last till about one; I then read some idle book till towards three; I ride or drive till five, dine, go to the Spectacle, and finish as usual my Evening with the Barbarian [Princess Galitzine], where I stay till 2 – the last two hours are tête-à-tête; we talk politics, Metaphysics, Literature, Beaux arts, Scandal, Love."[57]

Leveson Gower found the formalities of diplomatic convention and the trite, endlessly repetitive small talk extremely boring and complained vociferously about it in his letters home. Indeed, there seemed to be little about St Petersburg to recommend it to His Britannic Majesty's Ambassador-Extraordinary. He grumbled about the ruinous expense of living in the city and the ramshackle condition of his quarters: "It is the custom of the Russians when their houses are completely out of order, and the furniture all broken, to travel, and let their house to some Foreigner."[58] But this, one senses, was a mere triviality when compared to the ultimate humiliation for the self-respecting man-about-town: "Amongst my misfortunes here I must mention my not being able to procure a Box at the Theatre."[59]

However, once the draft treaty arrived from London at the end of February, Leveson Gower and Czartoryski got down to work. The two men had got on well from the start; Leveson Gower remarked shortly after arriving in Russia that "I like Czartoryski's manner very much; it is rather cold and distant, but he is quiet and very gentlemanlike"; and there was much to be done.[60] There was considerable pressure on the two diplomats from their respective governments to reach agreement on the terms of a treaty; the British were anxious to start constructing a coalition and to have a voice in its direction and the Russians for their part needed the financial support and diplomatic clout that a British alliance offered.

The negotiations, however, did not get off to a promising start. The British proposals on the all-important question of subsidy were received "in a cold manner". Czartoryski is said to have described them as "nugatory". These difficulties were overcome and, by the end of the first week of April, Leveson Gower was able to write to Mulgrave setting out the terms that had been agreed and on 11 April the Provisional Treaty was signed. It was, for the most part, substantially the same as the draft sent from London in January, with some minor amendments, notably in the arrangements for the territorial settlement of northern Italy. Leveson Gower had also been obliged to concede a further £1m "primer" subsidy to help the Austrians bring their army to a war footing. This extra money would not, it was agreed, be recoverable in the event that war did not break out.

There were, however, two clauses in the draft treaty which Leveson Gower knew would not endear him to his superiors in London. The first was a statement that the Russians would promise the French to use their influence with His Majesty's Government to bring about reform of the British Maritime Code. The Code, under which the Royal Navy claimed rights over neutral shipping, had long been a contentious issue and was at the root of the Armed Neutrality of 1800. Clearly it still rankled the Russians, but Leveson Gower knew that the Cabinet would never consent to any restrictions to the Navy's rights under the Code. By the time the Provisional Treaty was signed on 11 April he had brought Czartoryski round to the British view and the clause was simply expunged from the text.

The second sticking-point concerned the vexed question of Malta. Czartoryski insisted on the inclusion in the Treaty of a clause providing for the British evacuation of Malta. Once the British had left the Russians would undertake to garrison the island. Leveson Gower knew that this arrangement would be wholly unacceptable to the Cabinet, which regarded Malta as the key to British control of the Mediterranean. Czartoryski was equally insistent: the clause must form part of the Treaty between the two countries. The best that Leveson Gower could do to mitigate the position was to persuade the Russians to insert a rider to the effect that the government in London would have to consent to the clause. This, he knew, was most unlikely to happen. Indeed he was prepared to break off the negotiations rather than allow the inclusion of this provision, unmodified, into the Treaty. With these compromises incorporated into the text, the two diplomats were able to sign the Provisional Treaty but it still required ratification by their respective governments. The issue of Malta, in particular, had many miles yet to run and would bring the negotiations to the brink of collapse.

While Leveson Gower and Czartoryski were hammering out the Treaty, point by point, in St Petersburg, in London the government was putting the finishing touches to its plan to send an expeditionary force to the Mediterranean. The presence in southern Italy of a large number of French troops and the parlous state of the defences of the Kingdom of the Two Sicilies had persuaded the Cabinet that action was needed, and needed urgently, if Sicily was to be saved from the French. So the government began to assemble a force that would be large enough to defend the Sicilian ports from the French. It is a measure of the importance Pitt attached to Sicily that he was willing to detach a substantial force at such a crucial moment from home defence duties and send it to the Mediterranean. For in the spring of 1805 Napoleon's Grande Armée was massed at Boulogne; invasion was anticipated weekly; Britain's very existence was in peril.

The government appointed General Sir James Craig to lead the expedition, as commander of British Land Forces in the Mediterranean. His second in command was General Sir John Stuart; of both men we will hear much as the story unfolds. Craig received his orders in several parts, the first on 28 March 1805. It is tempting, given the continuing negotiations between the British and Russian governments and their common interest in the Mediterranean, to view Craig's expedition as part of a strategy of formal cooperation with the Russians. This would, however tempting, be wrong. As Craig's orders make abundantly clear, his main task was to secure Sicily from the French. In the first batch of orders, dated 28 March 1805, Lord Camden, the Secretary of War, wrote: "It being of the utmost importance that Sicily should not fall into the hands of the French, the protection of the Island is to be considered as the principal object to which the Force you are to command is destined".[61]

Lord Camden then addressed the various circumstances in which the British might find themselves; clearly Craig might have to act without Ferdinand's cooperation, as well as with it. If Ferdinand asked for his help in securing Sicily, then Craig was to "afford every Assistance in Your Power to secure the possession of that Island to the King of Naples".[62] If Ferdinand was prepared to cooperate with the British then the task, diplomatically at least, would be more straightforward.

The bulk of the orders of 28 March, however, addressed the

situation in which, for whatever reason, Ferdinand was unwilling or unable to cooperate with the British in securing Sicily. Craig was to take possession of the island if Ferdinand ordered the exclusion of British vessels from his ports and he was to prevent any attempt the French might make to invade. If, on arriving in the Mediterranean, the General found that the French had landed on the island, he should attempt to dislodge them. This part of Craig's instructions was composed with particular circumstances in mind, but Camden could not safely stop at that. One of the greatest problems that the British government and its commanders in the Mediterranean faced was the sheer distance separating them. The overland route was closed and a boat from Palermo could take up to ten weeks to reach London and the same to return to Sicily. An exchange of letters could therefore take up to five months. By the time a report arrived in London from the Mediterranean it was likely to have been overtaken by events. It was essential therefore that the local commander should be given a wide measure of discretion.

The most interesting part of Camden's orders of 28 March concerns the exercise of this discretion and reveals the British government's doubts about Ferdinand's reliability as an ally. Craig was to occupy Sicily at once if circumstances suggested that waiting for Ferdinand's consent to an occupation would jeopardize the security of the island. Camden assured the General that the government would place a liberal construction on any exercise of his discretion. The Cabinet was not willing to allow the whims of another monarch, however friendly and well-intentioned, to stand in the way of vital British interests. To this end it was prepared to order its commander to override the conventions of international diplomacy and occupy the territory of a friendly Power, regardless of whether that Power gave its consent to the occupation or not. This is yet another indication of the importance that the British government attached to Sicily.

The government was determined to prevent Sicily falling into the hands of the French – so much was crystal clear – and this was the principal object of the expedition. However, the Cabinet issued further instructions ordering Craig to act in concert with the Russians and even the Austrians on the mainland of Italy should the circumstances demand it. Cooperation with the Russians was, at this stage, a secondary consideration for the British; Camden's first set of orders

47

make no mention of it whatsoever. At the end of March, when Craig was given his orders, there was no formal treaty between the two countries, however cordial relations might have been and however much both governments hoped that the diplomats could agree terms.

Formal treaty or not, there is no doubt, however, that there was a connection between the military planning and the diplomatic activity. One historian of the period asserts that the willingness of the British government to send a force to the Mediterranean was "the touchstone of Russian confidence" in the future of the alliance. Given the shared interest of the two countries in containing the growing French threat in the area this is hardly surprising.[63] Certainly the news of the departure of Craig's expedition was well received when it arrived in St. Petersburg.[64]

There is a further twist to the tale. John Ehrman, Pitt's most authoritative biographer, asserts that the second part of Craig's orders, those instructing him to act in concert with the Russians on the Italian mainland, were only added as an afterthought to scotch a rumour that had reached London to the effect that the Russians were suspicious of British intentions *vis-à-vis* Sicily. St Petersburg, it was said, although anxious that Pitt send troops to the Mediterranean, was worried that his sole object was the occupation of Sicily. That this rumour, emanating as it did from an unreliable source, was both believed and acted upon, is an eloquent testimony to the importance the British government attached to the Russian alliance.[65]

Having kissed hands with the King, Craig set sail from Portsmouth with more than 4,000 men in thirty-six transport vessels on 19 April 1805. Whatever the uncertainties underlying his orders, his expedition had other, more immediate dangers to confront. It was widely expected that Villeneuve, the French admiral in Toulon, would try to evade the British blockade and escape into the Atlantic. This would make the army's passage to Malta extremely hazardous. In fact, unknown to the government in London, Villeneuve had already escaped by the time Craig's force left England.

As the Secret Expedition, as it was known, was ploughing down the Channel towards the Bay of Biscay, no doubt nervously scanning the horizon for any sign of Villeneuve's squadron, Leveson Gower and Czartoryski were running into troubled waters of their own in St Petersburg. The British Ambassador, when informing the Cabinet of the signing of the Provisional Treaty, had voiced the opinion that the Russians did not attach any great significance to the questions of the Maritime Code and the surrender of Malta. Thus far, he asserted, the Russians were merely using them as a procedural device to delay the ratification of the Treaty until it was clearer which way the Austrians were going to jump.

Leveson Gower had been able to put the question of the Maritime Code to one side, but his prognosis proved over-optimistic so far as Malta was concerned: it was to become a serious stumbling block in the negotiations. Once the text of the Provisional Treaty arrived in London the government got to work. The Foreign Secretary wrote to Vorontsov, the Russian Ambassador, explaining why Malta could never be considered as a negotiable interest. It provided, he wrote, a secure base for operations against the French in the Mediterranean and the interests of Europe were best served by the island remaining in British hands. "It is," he concluded, "as a British port and arsenal alone that it can contribute to check the progress (in that quarter) of the present common enemy of Europe."[66]

This cut no ice in St Petersburg. By the beginning of June the Foreign Secretary informed Leveson Gower that the Russians had made it plain that they regarded the evacuation of the British garrison from Malta as a *sine qua non* of any alliance. Britain had shown that she was amenable to compromise on most matters, but Malta was sacrosanct. Leveson Gower was to spell out to the Russians that if they insisted on the inclusion of the Maltese clause, the Treaty would fail and, in those circumstances, Britain would fight on alone.[67]

The Cabinet remained extremely anxious to conclude an alliance with the Russians – it was, after all, the best hope of mounting a realistic challenge to Napoleon on the Continent – so were reluctant to lose the treaty, even for something as fundamental as Malta. Accordingly, Leveson Gower was given a fall-back position. He was instructed to agree that Malta could be placed in the hands of a Russian garrison but only once improved arrangements were made for the future security of Holland and Italy. In addition, Britain would be compensated for the loss of Malta with Minorca.[68]

By the middle of June the Anglo-Russian negotiations had reached an impasse; Leveson Gower's earlier optimism was clearly misplaced. The question of Malta was threatening to kill the nascent alliance stone dead. The Tsar would not ratify the Provisional Treaty and continued to prevaricate. The Ambassador himself now had more time on his hands – official business was less pressing and summer had arrived – and sought fresh amusements to while away the days. With this in mind he took a small house on a lake in the countryside a couple of miles outside St Petersburg. Even this proved unsatisfactory: "the gnats or Mosquitos are so extremely troublesome among the Trees near the water that I am not much inclined to repeat these expeditions".[69]

If his earlier hopes of forming an alliance with the Russians now seemed to be fading, Pitt had no more reason to be confident that the Austrians would join a coalition against the French. Indeed, all the recent evidence pointed in the opposite direction; Vienna seemed bent on appeasement. Outwardly the situation did not improve during the latter half of 1804. Warren and Paget sent home a stream of negative reports: Austria, they emphasized, was not in a state to commit herself to war, nothing should be expected from her.

Britain's already faint hopes that the Austrians might join an anti-French alliance received a setback when, on 10 August 1804, in retaliation for Napoleon's adoption of an Imperial title, Francis II announced that he, too, was adopting an Imperial title. From now on he would be known as the Hereditary Emperor of Germany. The Cabinet feared that the Russians would take umbrage at this piece of Austrian presumption and make the already fraught process of forging an alliance yet more difficult. Leveson Gower was sent on his way to St Petersburg with exhortations ringing in his ears to mollify Russian sensibilites on the subject.

In fact relations between the Austrians and the Russians were good – good enough that on 6 November 1804 the two countries signed a secret convention by which the two Powers agreed to take steps to guard against further French encroachments in Europe. Although purely defensive in character, it was a step in the right direction.

This, however, was kept well hidden from Pitt and his ambassadors; to them the picture looked as gloomy as ever. Sir John Warren reported in November 1804 that the Austrians has demanded £2m up front and £4m a year as their price for coming into a war on the British side. Sir John described this as "exorbitant".[70] Nor had matters improved by the following spring; Leveson Gower reported from St Petersburg that the Austrians were still dragging their feet over joining the Anglo-Russian alliance. And, to make matters worse, their ambassador had by this time seen the terms of the Provisional Treaty of 11 April, promising them an unrefundable "primer" of £1m. Then on 10 June the news arrived in St Petersburg that Leveson Gower had been dreading: the Austrians' formal refusal to join the Anglo-Russian coalition. The blow was softened by the inclusion of a counter-proposal, that Britain join the Austro-Russian defensive compact of November 1804.[71] But this was no good to Pitt; he wanted offensive action against the French and he wanted it now; somehow the somnolent Austrians had to be stirred into life.

To the British Cabinet in the late spring of 1805 the outlook was not promising. Despite a year and more of diplomatic activity and six months of hard negotiation the Anglo-Russian treaty, so keenly desired, seemed to have foundered on the rock of Malta. The Austrians, a key component of any anti-French combination, continued to drag their feet, despite a generous and improved offer of subsidy. Then, suddenly, when all seemed lost, Napoleon, as he had done a year earlier, revitalized the faltering coalition.

In 1804 *l'affaire d'Enghien* and Napoleon's self-proclamation as Emperor of the French had breathed life into the moribund alliance ranged against him. On 26 May 1805 he crowned himself King of Italy in a splendid ceremony in Milan cathedral. It was the second time in six months that he had crowned himself: first, in December 1804, Emperor of the French and now "*Rex totius Italiae*". He used the iron crown that had supposedly been Charlemagne's, the first Holy Roman Emperor. The threat, strategically and symbolically, to the Hapsburg monarchy could hardly have been more explicit. It was an unambiguous statement of intent: Austria's interest in Italy was all but over. To ram the message home Napoleon said, as he crowned himself, "God gives it me; woe to him who touches it".[72] The formalities of the coronation over, the Emperor was due to leave Milan on 10 June and three days before his departure summoned the Legislative Assembly and announced that he had appointed his step-son, the twenty-three-year-old Eugène de Beauharnais, as the viceroy of Italy to rule the country in his absence.

The assumption by Napoleon of the kingship of Italy was a sign that the vaulting ambition of previous years had in no way diminished. The

51

menace to European stability and to the territorial integrity of the Continent's states was as potent as ever. It was a threat that no country could afford to ignore.

The reality of the threat became apparent within days. On 4 June Napoleon annexed Genoa and the Ligurian Republic to France. This was a direct breach of the Treaty of Luneville and confirmed the darkest suspicions about French ambitions in Italy and the contempt in which they held the obligations of international conventions. It was proof, if proof were needed, of the hopelessness of re-establishing peace in Europe by relying on any degree of moderation from Bonaparte.

The effect on the governments of Europe was immediate and startling. On 17 June Francis II agreed to join the Anglo-Russian alliance; only a week previously Leveson Gower, in St Petersburg, had received notice of the refusal of the Austrians to accede to the treaty. What a difference a few days made. The news of the annexation arrived in St Petersburg on 22 June and was greeted with outrage by the Russian court.

The annexation of the Ligurian Republic was regarded by the Russians as "so gross an insult" that their special emissary, Count Novosiltsov, who was in Berlin waiting to travel to Paris to open negotiations with the French government, was ordered not begin his journey.[73] The general opinion in British diplomatic circles, where Francis II's announcement of 17 June was at this point still unknown, was that the annexation had stiffened the resolve of the Austrians to stand up to French aggression. "It is," Sir Arthur Paget wrote from Vienna on 22 June, "felt here that the annexation of Genoa and Placentia are Acts which nothing but an Appeal to Arms can afford a proper Satisfaction for."

The aborting of Novosiltsov's mission to Paris and the Austrian determination to resist this latest act of French aggression constitute the point of no return in the formation of the Third Coalition. What had proved beyond the wit of Europe's finest diplomats for more than a year Napoleon had achieved in a fortnight. Henceforward there was no realistic prospect that a peaceful settlement could be cobbled together; the slide into war was unstoppable.

But, despite the new-found political resolve, some old difficulties continued to dog the negotiations. The British ratification of the treaty of 11 April arrived in St Petersburg on 24 June; the Russians did not ratify it until 28 July. The question of Malta continued to provide them with an excuse for delay, even if by now they appeared to have accepted the British stance.

The Austrians managed to drag proceedings out too. They were understandably anxious to negotiate the best possible subsidy from the British and Count Stadion, the Austrian ambassador in St Petersburg, drove a hard bargain. He was helped by the fact that the summer was drawing on and the British were anxious not to delay the start of hostilities until the following year; nor would the Russians begin their advance until the Austrians had formally joined the alliance.

Leveson Gower, negotiating for the British government, was in a quandary. Stadion was asking more than the Cabinet had authorized, but failure to accede to the Austrian demands on subsidy risked forfeiting the entire coalition. Leveson Gower, over a barrel, gave in to Stadion and on 9 August the Austrians joined the Anglo-Russian alliance. At the cost of conceding an advance of five months' worth of subsidy, and some amendments to the territorial settlement in Italy, the British ambassador in St Petersburg had achieved what had for so long seemed so unlikely, the accession of the Hapsburgs to the alliance. The Third Coalition had come alive.

Once the diplomatic foundations had been laid the military men could begin to formulate their plans; indeed the process had started before the formalities were complete. On 16 July a group of Austrian top brass, the Archduke Charles along with Generals Mack and Schwarzenberg, met Count Wintzingerode, the Russian adjutant-general, in Vienna to discuss plans for the forthcoming campaign. They agreed on a grandiose plan of attack from the Baltic to Italy which presupposed, amongst other things, the participation of Prussia. One historian of the period has described their deliberations as building "castles in the air".[74]

By the middle of September the Third Coalition was preparing to move into action along a front which stretched from the North Sea to the Mediterranean. "The Grand Scheme" was as ambitious a strategy as could be imagined. In the north the Russians would combine with the Swedes, the British and the Hanoverians to liberate Hanover and push into the Low Countries. In the central theatre of operations, expected to be the decisive one, the Austrians and Russian armies would combine along the Danube and in southern Germany. In northern Italy the Austrians would seize the initiative, while the British would protect Sicily, help the Russians liberate southern Italy and prevent any further encroachments by the French in the Adriatic.

In practice the plan was compromised, particularly in the northern and central theatres, by the failure to recruit Prussia to the coalition. Her presence would have greatly strengthened the allies in the field and enlarged their scope of operations in northern and central Europe. Every effort had been made to cajole or coerce the Prussians into joining the coalition. Pitt, as a last throw of the dice, dispatched Lord Harrowby, his former Foreign Secretary, to Berlin in the autumn of 1805 to make a final attempt to bring the Prussians into the fold. It failed. Even Napoleon himself, by violating the Prussian territory of Anspach during his march to the Danube, did his best to persuade the Prussians to throw their lot in with the coalition, but to no avail.

The nearest that the allies came to securing the help of the Prussians in the struggle against France was the signing, on 3 November 1805, of the Treaty of Potsdam between Prussia and Russia. Being no more than an offer by Prussia to provide armed mediation in the disputes between the warring parties, it fell far short of what the allies had hoped for. But worse, and fatally, it included a secret clause that specified that Prussia's price for fighting with the coalition was Hanover. This could never be acceptable to the British; indeed the Foreign Secretary, describing the proposal as "in any shape, utterly inadmissible", refused even to mention it to George III.[75]

The remaining member of the coalition in northern Europe was Sweden. Thus far we have heard nothing of the role of Sweden in the Third Coalition since she had only a minor part to play. Her usefulness as an ally was limited by the insistence of King Gustavus that the proper and legitimate aim of the war was to reinstate the Bourbons on the throne of France. By the end of 1804 he had granted asylum to the Comte de Provence, who was later to become Louis XVIII. The Swedish King was an eccentric figure, even by the standards of the time: according to a British diplomat the King, while on a tour of Germany, walked around Dresden with the Duc d'Enghien's dog.[76] Such eccentricities nothwithstanding, however, after a lengthy courtship, Britain and Sweden signed a secret convention in December 1804. By this agreement Sweden, in return for a handsome subsidy, was to provide Britain with a base at Stralsund on the Baltic and access to northern Germany. However, it quickly became evident that the Swedes had no intention of exerting themselves beyond the defence of Pomerania against the Prussians.

If the "Grand Scheme" was likely to be less than effective in the north, it appeared to have every chance of success in the more southerly theatres of operations. The Austrians were mobilizing their armies to face the anticipated French attack in southern Germany, while the Russians were massing in force in Poland and were shortly expected to join General Mack's Austrian army. In Italy the Archduke Charles had 90,000 men under his command and, with the bulk of the French armies far away on the Channel coast, every prospect of making sweeping gains. Further south still the Russians were a formidable presence in Corfu (by August 1804 they had 11,000 men on the island) and Craig's little army had reached the safe haven of Malta on 18 July after a perilous voyage from England, during which it had been forced by the threat of Villeneuve's squadron to take refuge in the Tagus at Lisbon.

Pitt had now achieved what he had been striving for since he returned to office in May 1804. A European coalition, albeit one without Prussia, was ready to take the field against Napoleon, to challenge the greed and ambition of the French Emperor and restore stability and peace to the Continent. Just as important, he had forced the Emperor to abandon, for the time being at any rate, his long-cherished plan to invade Britain. On 24 August Napoleon dictated to Marshal Berthier, his chief of staff, the order for the Grande Armée to abandon its positions in the Pas de Calais and three days later his troops broke camp and began their epic march south-east to the Danube. Pitt had succeeded in setting "Europe at Napoleon's back".

Any optimism that the leaders of the Third Coalition might have had in September 1805 as their armies took the field across Europe was short-lived: Napoleon, in a campaign that was as swift and devastating as it was daring, smashed the forces of his enemies in little more than eight weeks. The story of that campaign, of the Grande Armée's rapid descent into central Europe from the Channel ports, of Mack's dithering at Ulm, of Napoleon's bold advance to Vienna herself and of his ultimate, brilliant and overwhelming victory at the battle of

Austerlitz, is so well known that I do not propose to recount it here. It was an alarmingly brief episode, which shattered the diplomatic work of years, brought the Third Coalition to its knees and hastened the death of its principal creator, William Pitt. As Macaulay wrote "The peculiar look which [Pitt] wore during the last months of his life was often pathetically described . . . [as] 'the Austerlitz look'".[77]

Everything, it seemed, that could have gone wrong for the allies did so. The Austrian army was understrength, poorly deployed – too many formations were committed to the Italian front – and slow to mobilize. Worse, it was commanded by generals who were on such bad terms that, according to one report, by the time of Ulm they were communicating with each other only in writing.[78] Mack had calculated that the Russians would be able to join his forces in southern Germany before Napoleon was able to sweep down the Rhine to attack him. In fact, as it turned out, the reverse was the case: the Russians made slow progress and Napoleon, reaching the Austrians before they could, was able to tackle his enemies one by one. Mack, once he realized Napoleon was upon him, hesitated and allowed the trap to be sprung. Once caught, he surrendered at Ulm on 20 October 1805, virtually without a fight.

The Austrians, defeated and demoralized, were unable to prevent the French advancing up the Danube towards Vienna and made, seemingly, no effort at all to prevent the French taking their capital and continuing into Moravia to attack the Tsar and his armies. Austerlitz, fought on 2 December 1805, sealed the Coalition's fate; the Battle of the Three Emperors, as it is sometimes known, was a resounding triumph for Napoleon and the death-knell of the Third Coalition.

It was the speed of the collapse of the coalition's armies as well as the completeness of it that startled observers. Lord Grenville, soon to be British Prime Minister, wrote of Ulm that "contrary to what is usually the case, the calamity very much exceeds the first reports of it". The spinelessness of the capitulation, too, furrowed brows in London. "An army of 100,000 men, reckoned the best troops in Europe, totally destroyed in three weeks, without even sustaining any one considerable action, and 36,000 of them capitulating on a bare statement of the position occupied by their Enemy."[79] What he thought of Austerlitz is not recorded.

56

Outnumbered, outgeneralled, outmanoeuvred, the armies of the Third Coalition in the Danube campaign of the autumn of 1805 did not put up much of a fight. Napoleon was able to brush them aside with one sweep of his hand. By Christmas, with Austria humbled, Russia in retreat and Prussia cowed, he was the undisputed master of Europe. The only shadow on his glory was cast by Nelson's defeat of the combined French and Spanish fleet at Trafalgar on 21 October, the day after Mack's craven surrender at Ulm. In fact, there could have been no better, more emphatic reminder of the order of affairs in Europe. The French dominated the land and the British ruled the waves; neither power, it seemed, could strike effectively at the other. An *impasse* prevailed: Napoleon was unable to break the British but the British, in turn, were, it seemed, unable to land a blow against the French where it mattered, on the continent of Europe.

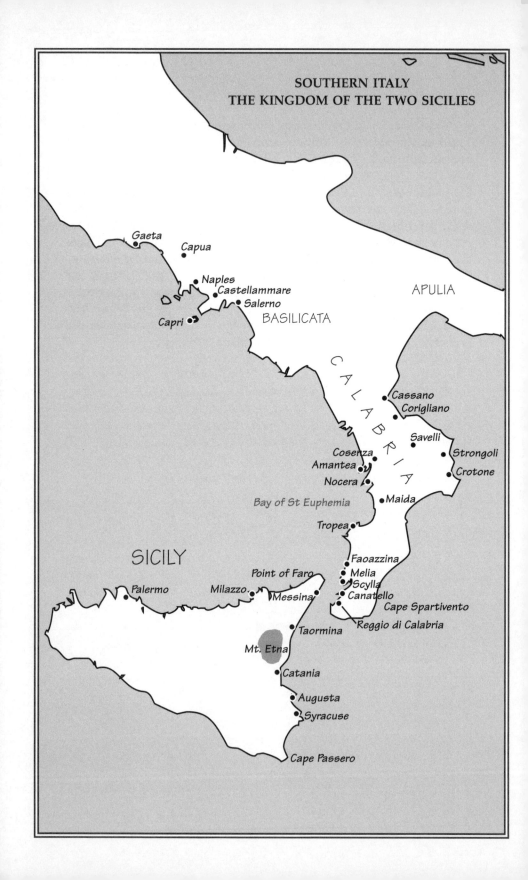

SOUTHERN ITALY
THE KINGDOM OF THE TWO SICILIES

APULIA

Gaeta
Capua
Naples
Castellammare
Salerno
Capri
BASILICATA

CALABRIA

Cassano
Corigliano
Savelli
Cosenza
Strongoli
Amantea
Crotone
Nocera
Maida
Bay of St Euphemia
Tropea

SICILY

Faoazzina
Melia
Point of Faro
Scylla
Palermo
Milazzo
Canatello
Messina
Cape Spartivento
Reggio di Calabria
Taormina
Mt. Etna
Catania
Augusta
Syracuse

Cape Passero

Chapter Four

NAPLES & SICILY: THE THIRD
COALITION IN THE SOUTH

On 30 November 1805 Ferdinand, King of the Two Sicilies, reviewed the newly-landed British troops at Castellamare near Naples. Craig's little army paraded against a dramatic backdrop: Vesuvius towered above the magnificent sweep of the Bay of Naples, the nearby lava fields providing a potent reminder of the volcano's untameable, destructive power. The British ranks stood smartly to attention as the King drove past in "a shabby old carriage drawn by six miserable horses" which, in the eyes of one British officer, compared most unflatteringly with the "eight proud cream-coloured Hanoverians and the gilded trappings of our own Sovereign". The same officer was fascinated to see the Queen, whom he described as "that elegant ruin", although he did add that her "figure was erect and her mein princely and graceful".[80] The parade was watched by, among others, Samuel Taylor Coleridge who was in Naples at the start of his long journey home from Malta, where he had served as secretary to the Governor, Sir Alexander Ball. The poet had become friendly with some of the British officers, in particular the Engineers Pasley and Boothby, during their sojourn in Malta that summer and, later that day, dined with them before continuing on his way northwards.

Ferdinand was reviewing the British troops commanded by General Craig that had landed at Castellamare on 21 November after a seventeen-day voyage from Malta. This British army, some 7,500 strong, along with their Russian allies, represented the southernmost arm of the Third Coalition: their role in the "Grand Scheme" was to assist Ferdinand in the defence of his kingdom, above all Sicily, and to contain the spread of French influence in the Adriatic region.

Despite the impoverished eccentricities of the Royal Family, the

British expedition to Naples had begun promisingly with expressions of good will on all sides. Craig says that his force was greeted with "every Attention & Civility", although one senior officer records that the populace greeted the British with complete indifference. All the British generals were presented to the Royal Family and dined with Ferdinand.[81]

Once Craig had arrived in Malta in July he started planning the military operation with the Russians for the protection of the Kingdom of the Two Sicilies. The aged Russian General Lacy – he used to fall asleep at councils of war – commanded the 14,000 Russian troops stationed on Corfu. Lacy and his staff presented the first Russian plan on 3 August but it was rejected by Craig as ill-conceived. According to Sir Henry Bunbury, who served with the expedition as head of the Quartermaster-General's department and later became its principal chronicler, the plan's genesis lay in the desire of the Russian commanders to allow their troops to occupy the prosperous areas around Naples. The plan did not impress the British who wrote it off as motivated by "treachery, as well as professional ignorance".[82]

While these discussions continued between the British and the Russians the Neapolitan court was charting its own course. In doing so it amply demonstrated why the British government had doubted the trustworthiness of the Neapolitans as allies and why it had granted Craig his wide discretion to secure Sicily without the prior consent of Ferdinand. On 10 September the Queen of the Two Sicilies, terrified that a French invasion was imminent, signed a secret treaty with the Russian ambassador at Naples, Tatischev. By its terms the Russians agreed, in the event of war with France, to provide an army large enough to preserve the integrity of the kingdom and guaranteed, furthermore, that this force would be supplemented by 6,000 British soldiers.[83]

Meanwhile, on 22 September Count Gallo, the Neapolitan ambassador in Paris, signed a treaty of neutrality with France; it was ratified by Ferdinand on 8 October, characteristically, in a vineyard. This treaty was a flagrant breach of the earlier agreement with Russia whereby the Anglo-Russian army was preparing to come to the defence of the Kingdom of the Two Sicilies. Worse was to come. As soon as the Neapolitan court had ratified the treaty with the French they secretly delivered a repudiation of it to the Russians, assuring them that as the treaty had been extracted by force they had no intention of abiding by it. Craig, told of the duplicity of the Neapolitan court by Elliott, the British Minister in Naples, was appalled and not surprisingly described it as "An Act of Perfidy".[84]

Despite this episode, which could hardly have enhanced the trust that the British or the Russians had in the Neapolitan court, the planning for the expedition to Naples continued. Diplomatic relations between the parties might have been strained by the manoeuvring of the Neapolitan court but the military position in southern Italy was changing too. Napoleon feared that Saint-Cyr's men in Apulia might be cut off from the main French armies in northern Italy under Massena. Accordingly, Saint-Cyr, who had commanded the French troops in Apulia since the resumption of war in 1803, was ordered to prepare for a withdrawal to the north. He was to remain in the south until the Neapolitan court had ratified the treaty of neutrality with France concluded by Gallo on 22 September, but, if ratification was not forthcoming, Saint-Cyr was ordered to march on Naples. Ferdinand duly ratified the treaty and the following day, 9 October, Saint-Cyr began to withdraw his forces from Apulia.

Although Saint-Cyr had led his forces off to the north to rejoin the main body of the French army, thus removing the immediate threat to the Kingdom of the Two Sicilies, the British and the Russians carried through their plan to land near Naples. The British transports arrived in the Bay of Naples on 20 November escorted by HMS *Lively* and three other frigates and the following day Craig's army disembarked. It numbered 241 officers, 52 paymasters, surgeons and the like, 369 sergeants and 6,991 rank and file, a total of 7,653 officers and men.[85] The Russians landed at the same time.

The commander of the British expeditionary force, Lieutenant-General Sir James Craig, who by the time he was appointed to his Mediterranean command was in his late fifties, had served in America, in the Cape, in India and in the Netherlands. Bunbury, who came to know Craig well, described him as "a pocket Hercules", adding that Craig was "not popular, for he was hot, peremptory, and pompous".[86] Neither was he in the best of health, a state of affairs that would in the end force him to resign his command.

Once the welcoming formalities were over the troops marched off to take up their positions on the northern border of the kingdom, but

61

in the field the deficiencies of the two armies swiftly became apparent. Lack of cavalry was a serious problem: the British had only 300 light dragoons, the Russians none at all. Craig regarded this as a major impediment to military operations in Naples, particularly as the terrain was suitable for mounted action. Lack of cavalry meant that, should the allies defeat the French, they would be unable to follow up their victory; our "Success would have been nugatory, from our Inability of pursuing it", as Craig put it.[87] Nor could he "foresee when it may arrive, and when arrived, how it is to be mounted".[88] Equally serious, however, was the shortage of transport horses which restricted severely both the mobility of the army and its capacity to supply itself. The Neapolitan court had agreed to provide the allies with draught horses but had in fact provided about 600 fewer horses than promised.[89]

While the Anglo-Russian army was taking up its position on the borders of the Kingdom of the Two Sicilies, to the north events had started to move very rapidly. By the end of November 1805 the Austrians were in full retreat, devastated by the disaster of Ulm; Napoleon had already entered Vienna and was now preparing to attack the combined armies of Russia and Austria at Olmütz in Moravia. The Anglo-Russian expedition to Naples had, at least in part, been planned as a diversion in favour of the Austrians to the north but Ulm and Austerlitz removed any diversionary purpose that the expedition to Naples might ever have had. But Craig and Lacy in Naples did not, at this juncture, know the turn that events in the north had taken. "There is no Disadvantage under which we labour, that affects us so materially just now, as that of the want of Communication."[90] In the absence of reliable military intelligence Craig was forced to rely on rumour and reports put out by the French.

Following the defeat of the Austrians and Russians at Austerlitz, Napoleon imposed terms on them by a treaty signed at Pressburg on 26 December. In it Napoleon made his famous denunciation of the Bourbons of Naples as being "without faith, without honour, without reason". "The royal house of Naples has ceased to reign," he thundered, "its existence is incompatible with the peace of Europe and the honour of my crown. Soldiers, march, hurl into the waves, if they wait for you, the feeble battalions of the tyrants of the seas."[91] The first unofficial news of Austerlitz reached Naples on 22 December, causing, not surprisingly, great consternation. The future looked bleak indeed for Ferdinand.

Craig himself was less than sanguine about the prospects of the Anglo-Russian force in Naples. The expedition's diversionary purpose having disappeared with the defeat of the Austrians in the north, the allied commanders were now confined, at best, to a wholly defensive role, but Craig doubted the capacity of the combined army to achieve even that limited goal. Writing to Castlereagh on 9 December, before the news of Austerlitz had reached Naples, he said: "I have little Hesitation in giving as my Opinion that if France chuses [sic] to take the present opportunity of becoming Mistress of the Kingdom of Naples, it will not be in our Power to prevent it".[92]

It was in this state of mind that Craig received the news on 2 January 1806 that a large French force, estimated at above 30,000 men, was on the march towards Naples. It was expected to reach the frontier within ten days and he reports that the general opinion among the allied commanders was that withdrawal was the only prudent course. Certainly they did not hold out any realistic prospect that the long border could be defended against a large attacking army. Craig also had his orders from the government to bear in mind: the security of Sicily was paramount. He realised that his army ran the risk of being destroyed if committed to the defence of Naples against the French. "If we failed in Naples, nothing could save Sicily; whereas by giving up the former, & transporting the Army to that Island we at least secured . . . the most important object of the two [sic]".[93]

Craig, despite these reservations, obeyed his orders and remained loyal to his superior officer, Lacy. He made it clear that if the Russians decided to defend Naples the British force would remain under his command, expressing at the same time his opinion that if the troops were to re-embark then they should do so at once as a forced re-embarkation in the face of the enemy would be fraught with risk.

Lacy, however, was unwilling to act without direct orders from the Tsar. This lack of independent spirit was the result, so Craig thought, of Lacy's years in the service of a government which "admits of little discretionary Exercise of Judgement in its Servants".[94] Eventually, on 7 January, one of the Tsar's ADCs arrived, hotfoot from Moravia, with orders for Lacy to withdraw to Corfu. These orders, which were dated 7 December, reflect the anxiety of the Tsar in the wake of Austerlitz to preserve intact his remaining forces. Once the Russians had received their orders to withdraw Craig could, no doubt with great relief, follow suit. Even at this ignominious parting of the ways, the Russians had to draw on their ally. They were so poorly supplied as to be compelled to ask for 194,000 pounds of biscuit and a line of credit to the tune of £25,000. The request was met. The British began to leave their positions on 10 January and the first troops arrived on the coast at Castellamare three days later. The army started to embark on 14 January and the transports sailed for Messina on 19 January.

General Lacy had called a council of war once the news of Austerlitz had reached Naples at which it was agreed that since the diversionary purpose of the expedition had been removed, the allies should restrict themselves to the defence of Calabria alone. This ignored the terms of the treaty between the Neapolitan Court and the Russians of 10 September, which committed the Russians to the defence of the whole kingdom. This decision, not surprisingly, caused howls of outrage from the Court and the Queen in particular. "The smell of gunpowder," she wrote, "sickens the feeble organs of General Craig . . . I hope he will go and become a monk, after having dishonoured his country and made it lose all influence in the commerce of the Mediterranean, the Levant and Egypt."[95]

The evacuation of the British force from the mainland portion of Ferdinand's dominions was, in the circumstances, undoubtedly prudent, especially when one considers the goals laid down by the government in Craig's orders. But it has attracted criticism from contemporaries and from later commentators. One historian commented that "This scampering off a month before the kingdom was attacked was joke in questionable taste".[96]

Others, however, have been more charitable to the Anglo-Russian commanders. The allies, it seemed, had scuttled away from Naples without firing a shot weeks before the enemy even crossed into the Kingdom of the Two Sicilies. They had, on the face of things, achieved nothing. It was an expedition which was defeated by its own deficiencies and by the events beyond the control of its commanders. Yet, while the expedition to Naples did not provide any stirring tales of derring-do, it did yield some positive results. As one historian of the war in the Mediterranean put it: "[Craig's army had] without striking a blow, deprived Napoleon of a considerable force in garrison in the north, and the whole of Saint-Cyr's corps of nearly twenty thousand in Apulia: a total considerably greater than their own strength."[97] If the expedition secured a reprieve for Naples, it was to be only a temporary stay of execution.

The decision to withdraw without a fight may have been tactically prudent and in accordance with Craig's orders but the shame of it was keenly felt by the army. John Colborne, who later rose to the rank of Field Marshal, served in Craig's expedition as a junior officer. Colborne describes the withdrawal from Naples as "a most inglorious, ridiculous retreat". In his view "[o]ur precipitate retreat has given the Neapolitans a very unfavourable impression of the spirit of English soldiers".[98] An officer in the 20th Foot also describes the Naples campaign. "[W]e disembarked at Nocera, and after marching and countermarching for a few weeks and never having seen the enemy, or even smelt powder, we left the country".[99]

These sentiments were echoed by Charles Pasley, serving in the Royal Engineers, who blamed "this shabby retreat" on the Russians. He had much enjoyed what he had seen of Italy, a land "whose beauty, variety & fertility exceed every idea that could be formed from description" but deplored the spinelessness of the withdrawal. The "warriors marched to the Frontiers, full of Ardour, fury & revenge," he wrote, seething with derision and indignation, and "in the full height of our glory . . . we retired & from what, from vacancy and airy nothing".[100] It was hardly the stuff of heroes. Indeed, the shame that the retreat from Naples brought on British arms lingered until gloriously expunged by the victory at Maida.

The British expeditionary force arrived in Messina on 22 January 1806. The security of Sicily was now the first priority with the French threat looming larger by the day; Craig was "unwilling to run any possible hazard as to its safety".[101] With the British transports anchored in Messina harbour there now began a period of ludicrously protracted, almost farcical, negotiation between the British and the Neapolitan court. The Neapolitan court was in a quandary, albeit one of its own making: the thrust of Napoleon's declaration at Pressburg had become known in Naples on 25 January, by which time the court also knew that a large French army was marching south, implacably intent on wreaking revenge. The Neapolitan armies, understrength, poorly-led and badly-equipped, were in no condition to resist the advance of the French. Yet the King and Queen were desperate to retain their mainland dominions, to avoid an ignominious exile to Sicily. Negotiation was the only way out; the French would have to be placated in some way.

The British, on the other hand, were rapidly losing confidence in the *bona fides* of the Neapolitan court. Craig was very anxious to secure Sicily and its ports for the Royal Navy; the consequences of failing to do so were unthinkable and he was aware of the need to act solely in the British interest in securing Sicily. It was, as he put it, "necessary to guard against the want of good Faith in our Friends, as against the open projects of our Enemies".[102] Craig did not want the British presence in Sicily to be used as a bargaining counter in the negotiations between Ferdinand and the French. Any treaty between the Kingdom of the Two Sicilies and France would, almost of necessity, be inimical to the British interest. On the other hand, of course, Ferdinand knew that the British presence on the island would be regarded by the French as highly provocative. Indeed, Ferdinand had originally wanted the British to withdraw to Malta once they had abandoned Naples.

The *impasse* continued and, as the French armies marched ever closer to the borders of Ferdinand's kingdom, the Neapolitans grew more desperate. Differences too began to appear within the British ranks. Craig was becoming increasingly irritated with Elliott, the British Minister in Naples, whom he suspected of having gone "native". Craig wrote tartly to him during these negotiations: "the Difference of Opinion that exists between us Appears to me to be, that you seem to regard solely the Benefit of the King of Naples and the means of extricating him from his present Difficulties, while I, willing to contribute to that object also, am nevertheless anxious that in doing it, no detriment shall arise to the Interests of our own Country".[103] Meanwhile, the British force of 7,500 men was cooped up on the transport ships in Messina harbour.

On 9 February news reached Naples that the French were insistent that they would only accept an unconditional surrender of Naples. On the same day the vanguard of the French army crossed into the Kingdom of the Two Sicilies. On 11 February Craig reported to Castlereagh that Sir John Stuart had been sent to Palermo to seek permission from the government for the British troops to land in

Messina.[104] Stuart had orders to return to Messina by 13 February. Although the French were closing the net on Naples the court still held out hope of some compromise with them. Still, on 11 February, Stuart, in Palermo, was unable to obtain permission to land despite bombarding Sir John Acton, Ferdinand's English Prime Minister, with a plethora of reasons why the landing should be allowed. The Neapolitans, desperate to avoid provoking the French, even at this late stage, stuck to their refusal.

Eventually it became obvious even to the most blinkered of Ferdinand's courtiers that there was no hope of reaching an accommodation with the French. On 13 February the King capitulated and granted permission for the British troops to land and occupy the citadel at Messina. Stuart sent the King's order to Craig in Messina, where it arrived on 15 February and the British troops, who had spent nearly a month shut up on board ship in the harbour, immediately began to disembark. "This Order has been tardily wrung from them," Craig said and at that only once the prospect of accommodation with the French had disappeared; it was hardly an auspicious start to an alliance that was to last for the rest of the Napoleonic Wars.[105] But the British had acquired the highly-prized foothold in Sicily. With Sicily and her ports defended against the French the Royal Navy could consolidate the gains made at Trafalgar and maintain its dominance of the Mediterranean. For his part, Ferdinand had acquired an ally capable of defending what remained of his dominions from the vengeful French. It would also in the future be possible, as Stuart reminded Acton, to use Sicily as a base from which "his Majesty's Enemies may be most effectively disturbed in their insolent and unjust Aggressions".[106] The seeds of Maida had been sown.

*   *   *

The French invasion of the mainland part of the Kingdom of the Two Sicilies was quickly accomplished. Having crossed into Neapolitan territory on 9 February, the French advanced so rapidly that Joseph Bonaparte, the king designate, was able to make his triumphal entry into Naples within a week, on 15 February. The Neapolitan resistance was so feeble that the French suffered only two officially-reported casualties in the advance on Naples. One of them was a general whose head was blown off while making a reconnaissance and the other was

67

one of Regnier's ADCs who was mistakenly shot when sent to parley with the enemy at Gaeta under a flag of truce. Capua, an important fortress to the north of Naples, surrendered without a shot being fired and now only the fortress of Gaeta held out against the French. Even Napoleon at his most optimistic could scarcely have believed that his threats against the Kingdom of the Two Sicilies, issued at Pressburg in late December, would become reality in less than two months.

The Neapolitan royal family did little to encourage their subjects to resist the invaders. Ferdinand disappeared to Palermo as soon as he could and the Queen and her daughters joined him there on 16 February, escorted to safety once more by two Royal Navy warships. The Hereditary Prince (Ferdinand's heir) stayed on the mainland with the remains of the Neapolitan army, which, in the face of the French advance, had retreated south into Calabria. Elliott, the British Minister, fled to Palermo with the Queen. Although the evacuation of its capital had been swift, the government, anxious not to leave anything of military value for the enemy, had removed all military and naval stores, men of war and other vessels from Naples.

Once the French had established themselves in Naples, they turned their attention to the conquest of the rest of Ferdinand's kingdom, in particular Calabria. General Regnier was appointed by Massena, the commander of the invading army, to lead the conquest of Calabria and he set out from Naples on 1 March. Nominally the nineteen battalions of Regnier's force, the Third Corps of the Army of Naples, were more than 15,000 strong, in fact they mustered 11,706 infantry and 1,010 cavalry. The shortfall in numbers was due to the fact that some formations were understrength, while, in other cases, troops had been detached to take part in the siege of Gaeta or were incapacitated by illness or wounds.[107]

The Third Corps comprised two divisions the first of which, commanded by General Verdier, was made up of the 1ère Légère, the 42nd Ligne, the 23rd Légère and the 6th Ligne. Serving under Verdier as his "generaux de brigade" were Compère and Digonnet. The Corps's second division, commanded by Peyri and Francheschi-Delonne, consisted of the 1st Regiment of Polish Infantry, the 10th Ligne, a battalion of the 1st Regiment of Swiss Infantry and the cavalry, the 6th and 9th Chasseurs. So far as quality was concerned the army that Regnier commanded was a mixed bag: the 23rd Légère, for example, were steady troops but the Polish troops, who had been recruited to the French colours from among Austrian prisoners of war in Northern Italy, were poor and very unreliable.

To support his infantry and cavalry, Regnier had been allocated only one company of foot artillery and one of horse artillery. This small detachment was largely equipped with mountain guns which, it was felt, being more manoeuvrable, would be more practical in the difficult terrain that the army would encounter. The mountain artillery had been formed for the invasion of Calabria and its men had received special training in the tasks that lay ahead of them.

The French encountered some resistance during their conquest of Calabria, certainly more than they had faced in the advance on Naples. The Neapolitan army, numbering 14,000 and commanded by Roger de Damas, took up a strong defensive position at Campo Tenese, where on 9 March Regnier, his troops drawn up in columns, attacked. This was the preferred formation among French commanders when they wished to achieve the maximum physical impact on the enemy; it was a particularly effective tactic against inexperienced or unsteady troops. Despite the defensive strength of their position, the Neapolitans were unable to resist the frontal assault by the French columns and were routed. A French artillery officer who fought at the battle estimated that the enemy had suffered between 1200 and 1500 casualties.[108] Campo Tenese was the end of the formal military resistance to the French; Roger de Damas and the remainder of his defeated army crossed to Sicily on 22 March. The same French artillery officer wondered aloud at the ease with which the Kingdom of the Two Sicilies had fallen to the French. "I admire especially those who have been so obliging as to give it up to us". The kingdom could, he thought, have been defended very easily, particularly had the fortress at Capua resisted with any vigour.[109]

Having disposed of the Neapolitan army Regnier was free to advance to the Straits of Messina. The surrender of Reggio and the important fortress of Scylla to the French on the same day, 21 March, virtually completed the conquest of Calabria. On 25 March Craig reported to the Secretary of War that the French were in possession of the coast on the other side of the Straits of Messina, with part of their army in cantonments in Reggio. With the enemy now established on the opposite shore, Craig hastened to reinforce his army by sending for the 81st Foot from Malta. He was under no illusions as to the task that lay ahead; he told the government at home that "we may be consider'd as left to ourselves" in the defence of Sicily.[110] Indeed, with the French army now camped just across the Straits of Messina, it appeared to be only a matter of time before the British garrison in Sicily would face an attack.

Although the Straits of Messina are at their narrowest – the Point of Faro – considerably less than two miles wide they nevertheless represented a formidable barrier to the French. The difficulties for shipping posed by the extremely strong currents in the waters of the Straits had been notorious among sailors since ancient times. The forces of nature at work in the narrows between Sicily and the mainland left an indelible impression on one eighteenth-century British traveller:

> "Whilst we were still some miles distant from the entry of the straits, we heard the roaring of the current . . . This increased in proportion as we advanced, till we saw the water in many places raised to a considerable height, and forming large eddies or whirlpools. The sea in every other place was as smooth as glass."[111]

Navigating the Straits was a difficult proposition for all vessels; for the type of flat-bottomed landing craft that would be needed to transport infantry across to Sicily it would be fraught with danger. For Craig's small army the Straits were the first and perhaps the most effective line of defence against any attack that the French might make.

The capture of Sicily was now the key objective of French military strategy in southern Italy and the Emperor was keen that an attack be pressed as soon as possible. To this end he bombarded Joseph with letters of encouragement and advice; on 20 March Napoleon wrote, urging action, "Your movements are much too slow. You should already be the master of Sicily." Joseph was not as optimistic as his brother about the prospects of taking Sicily and on 7 March he sounded a cautionary note. "Your Majesty knows that it is now impossible to take the island without extensive preparations, and without having command of the seas for several days. Not less than 25,000 men would be needed to take and hold that island."[112]

Urged on by the stream of letters from Paris Joseph and his generals set about planning the capture of the island with a will. French soldiers were dispatched to the various ports between Pizzo and Reggio to report on the number of craft – fishing vessels, feluccas, coasters – that could be commandeered to transport Regnier's men across the Straits of Messina. Joseph was told that the searches had revealed 198 vessels of various descriptions capable of carrying 4,460 men.[113] By 19 April he was able to report to Napoleon that he had given all the orders for the preparation of the expedition to Sicily. At the end of May Joseph wrote to the Emperor setting out the tactics he intended to adopt in the attack on Sicily. "I am counting on leaving Massena on the mainland with a minimum of available troops and to entrust the initial crossing to General Regnier. Once he is master of Faro, when he will have established a battery opposite the one we have put up at Pezzo, I will myself cross over with the rest of the army in the same boats that carried the advance party. I suppose that the Straits will be closed to English vessels by the cross-fire established between the nearest points on the two shores." This looks straightforward enough but ignores completely the difficulty of getting the first wave of troops across the water, with the Royal Navy still commanding the Straits. To take Sicily by an assault from across the Straits of Messina without naval support was a tall order and the French, whose fleet had been largely destroyed by Nelson at Trafalgar, had no ready means of challenging the Navy's mastery of the Mediterranean.

As the weeks went by without an attack being launched Napoleon became frustrated by the lack of progress. His frustrations were reflected in the increasingly aggressive, hectoring tone of the letters he wrote to Joseph at the time. "It is very important that you do now, at last, start your operations against Sicily," Napoleon wrote on 6 June. This letter discusses in detail the conduct of the operation and which general should be appointed to lead it. It reveals an arrogance mixed with ignorance of local conditions and an utter contempt for the British that is surprising for a military commander at the height of his powers. "My experience," he wrote, "of war would mean that with those 9,000 men I would be able to beat 30,000 English". "The expedition to Sicily is easy," he opined. "I repeat: thirty-six hours after the nine thousand men have landed, the English will have been toppled; if they are beaten, they will re-embark."[114] It seems as if his recent triumphs over the Austrians and Russians had gone to his head, perhaps the Emperor now really did consider himself invincible.

Napoleon was as keen to conquer the island as the British were to keep it from him: it was the first, vital stepping-stone in the renewed pursuit of a successful French foreign policy in the Levant and further east. Possession of Sicily was an important step in establishing French hegemony, for so long as the Royal Navy continued to have the use of the island's ports the French would never achieve supremacy in the Mediterranean. Furthermore, until his armies took Sicily the French conquest of Italy would remain incomplete and the hated Bourbons of Naples would continue to rule; to fulfil the Pressburg denunciation the Bourbons had to be ejected. An unconquered Sicily was also a threat to the stability of Italy and a bolt-hole for deserters and smugglers. While no doubt many of the Emperor's troops shared his reasons for crossing the Straits of Messina, there were some who had other, more elevated reasons for wishing to do so. Paul-Louis Courier, the artillery officer quoted earlier, was a keen antiquarian and found it frustrating to be so close to the famous sites of Sicily, yet not be able to visit them.

★   ★   ★

Messina, which sits in a bowl beneath the spectacular peaks of the Pelorus Mountains, has one of the deepest and safest natural harbours in the Mediterranean. The anchorage is protected from the rushing currents of the Straits by a long curving spit of land and from other dangers by the fort of San Salvatore, built at the entrance to the harbour by the Spanish in the sixteenth century. When the British arrived in 1806 there was a castle in Messina – it no longer exists, destroyed no doubt by one of the many natural or man-made disasters that have devastated the city over the centuries – which dated back to the Middle Ages and formed the defensive hub of the city. The previous year one Lt.-Colonel Smith, ordered to report to the British government on the state of Sicily's defences, concluded that for the most part they were in poor condition. The sole exception was the citadel at Messina which he found to be in a reasonable condition; Smith reported that 3,000 troops should be able to hold the city indefinitely. Messina was, for the next nine years, to be the headquarters of the British presence, naval and military, on the island and the centre of the defensive line against an invasion from the mainland.

Once the British forces had received permission to land and occupy the citadel, Craig and Stuart could start to make arrangements for the defence of Sicily against the expected French attack. But by the time the troops landed in Messina there was another even more pressing concern: Craig was in poor health and the fact was evident to everyone in the army. Boothby, a junior officer in the Royal Engineers, commented on it: "The necessity of this resignation had long been painfully obvious to the army . . . by the ghastly and suffering appearance of our revered commander".[115] Craig wrote to Castlereagh from Messina on 16 February requesting to be relieved of his command. He was ill enough to feel justified in asking that he be allowed to resign before a replacement was nominated but did not leave the island until the end of March, arriving back in England on 7 May.[116]

After Craig's resignation Stuart assumed command of the British forces; he was also appointed by Ferdinand to command the defence of the east coast of the island from Milazzo to Cape Passero. In this capacity he would have command of the Sicilian and Neapolitan troops as well as the British troops engaged in the defence of Sicily. With the arrival of reinforcements – Craig had sent for the 81st Foot from Malta and the 78th Foot, a Highland regiment, arrived in Messina on 25 May – the British had about 8,000 men with which to defend the island. This is a startlingly lower figure than the 25,000 men that Joseph Bonaparte considered necessary for the capture and defence of Sicily.

Stuart also had under his command some local troops, although these were of very poor quality. The official returns of the Sicilians showed a strength of 9,566 but an inspection carried out soon after his appointment to the overall command showed this figure to be a gross exaggeration. The inspection revealed that there were in fact fewer than 3,500 Sicilian regulars and many of those, especially in the cavalry, were in a poor state. The appearance and the substance were greatly at odds; as Craig had noted a few weeks before, there is "Nothing being less to be relied on than a Neapolitan return." If the regular Sicilian army gave Stuart no realistic expectation of worthwhile support in the defence of the island, the militia was completely useless. Having inspected the militia he reported that it was "at present altogether an Illusion – without Arms, without System, without

Organization, and without Pay, it is a mere List of Names."[117]

Stuart considered in February 1806, when he had about 7,000 men at his disposal, that sufficient British troops were in Sicily to make a good defence of the island, although he admitted that if the enemy were able to force a landing he would be at a great disadvantage in any battle which might then have to be fought.[118] Two years later the government canvassed the views of the three generals who were best informed on matters Sicilian. Stuart expressed the view that 10,000 effective soldiers was an absolute minimum for its defence. Sir John Moore stated that 26,000 troops were required to defend Sicily. General Fox agreed with Moore, saying that 25–27,000 troops would be needed to defend the island, particularly if the population was not in sympathy with the British.[119]

Clearly, then, the 8,000 or so troops that Stuart had in May 1806 for the defence of Sicily was a bare minimum. However, it did not make the British position untenable since the main burden fell on the Royal Navy. The Navy had two ships of the line, the *Excellent*, of 74 guns, and the *Intrepid*, of 64 guns, and three frigates deployed for the defence of the island. Captain Sotheron commanded the naval defences of Messina, where the *Excellent* took up station, having deposited the Neapolitan royal family in Palermo. The naval squadron was reinforced on 7 March when Collingwood, at Craig's request, sent two more ships of the line to join the defence of Sicily. Further reinforcements, in the shape of the *Pompée* (80 guns), with Admiral Sir Sidney Smith on board, arrived at Palermo on 21 April.[120]

The Navy's task was to intercept any force that might try to cross the Straits of Messina or attempt a landing elsewhere on the island. It also had an important role to play in disrupting the enemy's preparations for invasion. The appalling state of the roads in Calabria meant that the French were compelled to bring up by sea any heavy artillery and supplies needed for the assault on Sicily. This coastal traffic was vulnerable to attack and the Navy took full advantage of the opportunity to harrass and intercept the transports as they made their way down the peninsula.

The army was needed to secure the ports from which the Royal Navy operated and to guard against raids from across the Straits of Messina. The very strong currents in the Straits meant that it was not always possible for the Navy's ships to keep their station, so there would be times when the island could be vulnerable to an attack from across the Straits. The army was also necessary to protect the ports from attack by the Sicilians themselves, possibly in support of a French invasion. This was a possibility that could never be wholly discounted and one that both Stuart and Fox considered important when asked in 1808 for their views on the defence of the island.

The presence of the army in Sicily and gradual improvements to the port and coastal defences mean that the French, in order to take the island, needed a much larger expedition with greater numbers of troops and heavier artillery. This in turn meant that the Navy would be more likely to intercept the invading force before it could secure a foothold on the island. Surprise was increasingly difficult for the French to achieve, particularly as the British could keep them under close observation across the narrow stretch of water.

The western end of the British position was at Milazzo, round the Point of Faro from Messina, an ancient settlement sitting astride a narrow peninsula and dominated by its castle, which dates back as far as the Arab invaders of the tenth century and was magnificently embellished by the Emperor Charles V. The old Spanish fortifications, adapted and improved, secured both the harbour and the peninsula in British hands and made Milazzo into a formidable base from which to defend the island from attack from across the water. On the eastern flank the coast was guarded as far as the beautiful, clifftop town of Taormina by outposts of troops and as time passed so the British presence crept down the east coast of Sicily past Etna to Catania and beyond.[121] Craig may have resigned his command in 1806 but he had not lost interest in the defence of Sicily, and, once back in London, pressed the government to send more heavy artillery to beef up the defences of Syracuse, Augusta and Milazzo.[122]

By the early summer of 1806 the British had succeeded in establishing a reasonably secure system of defence for Sicily. Although it depended to a large degree on the ability of the Navy to dominate both the Straits and the surrounding waters, it seemed unlikely that the French would be able to transport sufficient men across the Straits quickly enough to seize the ports from which the Navy operated. While it was always possible that a violent storm might force the Navy's frigates and ships of the line from their stations, the land defences were now strong enough to be able to resist attack until reinforcements could be brought to bear on the French.

★   ★   ★

While Craig's expeditionary force was cooped up on board its transport ships in Messina harbour in January and February 1806, great political changes were taking place in London. William Pitt, the Prime Minister, weakened by illness and broken by the failure of the Third Coalition, died in January and the administration that he had led collapsed soon afterwards. The new government, known to history as the Ministry of All The Talents, led by Lord Grenville, took office at the beginning of February.

The new Prime Minister appointed William Windham as Secretary of War in the new Cabinet. Windham was a renowned parliamentary orator who was vehemently opposed to the Jacobinism that flourished in the aftermath of the French Revolution. He had been a member of the Cabinet in Pitt's first administration, also at the War Office, so brought a considerable amount of experience to the job, although Lord Rosebery, himself a Prime Minister, writing about Windham in 1913, was less than flattering about his talents:

> "As a minister there is less to be said. He was always connected with the War Office, a territory which is perilous for a civilian even in narrative to tread. It must be admitted that the few pebbles he left on the shore of military history scarcely constitute a memorial cairn."[123]

Scathing as Rosebery was about Windham's achievements as Secretary of War, he was ultimately responsible for the victory of the British forces at Maida and, in proposing the motion of thanks to the victorious army in the House of Commons, led the country in celebrating the deeds of that momentous day.

The advent of a new administration in London did not lead to a change of policy towards Sicily. The new ministry attached the same importance to it as its predecessor had done. Windham, in his first dispatch to Craig, dated 3 March 1806, wrote: "nothing is left . . . but to impress strongly on your mind the consequence We attach to the securing possession of Sicily". This is, incidentally, a fine example of the vagaries of correspondence between the government in London and its commanders in the Mediterranean. When writing this dispatch on 3 March Windham had before him only those reports from Craig dated before 14 December 1805, since which time, of course, the situation in southern Italy had radically altered.[124] Yet Windham's dispatch reached Messina within three weeks.[125]

Indeed, the new ministry was anxious that the army in the Mediterranean should be put to better use. On 5 May Windham, by now knowing of the withdrawal from Naples and the intention of landing in Sicily, gave Craig his blessing, indicating that a large consignment of arms and ammunition would be sent to the Mediterranean. Five days later Windham (by which time he still did not apparently know that the General had arrived back in England) wrote urging action. Craig was ordered to consider any operation which would not jeopardize the main object of the expedition, the security of Sicily: "The nature of your Command will I presume authorize you without special Instructions from here, to detach any part of your Force which you think can be safely spared." Windham reiterated the position of the previous administration, promising that "a most liberal construction" would be placed on any attempt that he might make to attack the French, thereby checking their progress and disrupting their plans for the invasion of Sicily. Indeed, as Windham hinted, the army in the Mediterranean was likely to be reinforced. This call to arms had very likely arrived in Messina by the time that Sir John Stuart started to plan the expedition to the Italian mainland that would result in the Battle of Maida.[126]

★   ★   ★

On the other side of the Straits of Messina the French occupation of Naples and Calabria was running into difficulties. Conquering Ferdinand's mainland possessions had proved remarkably easy, controlling them was to prove rather more troublesome. The first and more serious difficulty was the insurrection that had begun to flare up almost from the very beginning of the French occupation of Calabria. The other problem that faced Joseph and Massena was the fortress of Gaeta, which continued to resist all attempts to reduce it.

Gaeta was a powerful fortress on the coast about fifty miles to the north of Naples. It occupied a narrow neck of rocky land sticking out into the sea, which surrounded it on three sides. On 13 February a small French detachment summoned the fortress to surrender; it was answered by a cannon shot and the main body of Joseph's army bypassed Gaeta and continued the advance towards Naples. The siege of the castle began in earnest in March with General Lacour in charge of operations and on 21 March the fortress was again summoned to surrender. Once more, the summons was refused. By this time the defenders had mustered some eighty guns in the batteries to the landward side of the fortress, which were able to return the fire of the French artillery.

The garrison, which numbered about 6,000 men, was commanded by the eccentric and bibulous Prince of Hesse-Philipstadt, a leader who inspired the greatest loyalty in his men. Brave as the Prince undoubtedly was, his military *savoir-faire* was perhaps questionable. Charles Pasley was sent to Gaeta by Sir John Stuart in April 1806 to report on the progress of the siege. Pasley, although young, was no fool – he had established something of a reputation while in Malta as an expert on the geopolitics of the Mediterranean – and he had no doubt where the blame lay for the fall of Gaeta. The Prince was "a Man who without the smallest Military Knowledge or talents, believed that he was a greater general than Caesar, who obstinately refused the assistance of the English Army, of whom he was jealous & hateful, and without the smallest foresight expended his Powder Shot & shells in an incessant fire, with little adequate effect".[127]

It was by now becoming apparent to the French that taking Gaeta would be no easy matter; more extensive siegeworks were needed if the fortress was to be reduced in reasonable time. By early June, with General Campredon replacing Lacour in command, the siegeworks had reached approximately half-way across the rocky neck of land in front of the walls: the French front line was now about 200 yards from the glacis. They had some 200 guns in position and reinforcements were starting to arrive, so that by 28 June the French army before Gaeta numbered 8,000 men. On that day Massena himself arrived from Naples to take charge of the siege.

The defenders had not sat idly by while the French closed in on the fortress: on 13 and 15 May they made sorties against the besiegers which achieved some success. By the time of Massena's arrival in front of Gaeta, the Neapolitan defenders had fired 120,000 rounds of shot and 22,000 shells at their attackers. Their commander kept his men's spirits up by shouting at the French through a loud-hailer from the ramparts "Gaeta is not Ulm! Hesse is not Mack!"[128] The intrepid Sir Sidney Smith had also played his part by delivering provisions, four ship's guns and some gunners to the beleaguered fortress.[129]

The arrival of Massena before Gaeta signalled the start of the final assault on the fortress; Joseph also joined his army to witness the capitulation of the last bastion of resistance to his rule. The French opened fire on 28 June with fifty large guns and twenty-three mortars. By 1 July considerable damage had been done to Gaeta's defences but the French supplies of ammunition were already running low and on 3 July Gaeta received 1500 reinforcements, landed by sea. On 7 July the French opened fire once more, this time with ninety guns and at shorter range, but again their fire was damagingly returned by the four ship's cannons that Smith had landed in the fortress. Then, on 10 July, disaster struck for the defenders when the heroic Hesse-Philipstadt was wounded and was no longer able to conduct the defence of the fortress. Command now devolved to the Prince's deputy, Colonel Hotz, a man who was, according to Pasley, "a Notorious Coward". Massena, despite a severe shortage of ammunition, kept up a heavy fire, gambling on battering Gaeta into submission while Hesse-Philipstadt was out of action.[130]

By 16 July the critical moment of the siege had been reached. Massena had heard of the defeat of Regnier at Maida and knew that he had only two or three days' worth of ammunition left and could expect no fresh supplies. A quick capitulation was now the only hope so on 17 July the French artillery concentrated on enlarging the existing breaches. The following day Massena ostentatiously assembled storming parties in the trenches in full view of the ramparts, a show of strength that was enough to induce the defenders, lacking the stout leadership of Hesse-Philipstadt, to surrender.[131]

Gaeta had fallen at last but only at considerable cost to the French. The siege had tied up 8,000 troops in dull and dangerous operations: during the siege the French soldiers dug over 9,000 yards of trenches and suffered 1,000 casualties, killed and wounded. On 15 June, a full month before the end of the siege, Joseph had written to the Emperor to warn him that the siege of Gaeta was using up valuable resources, particularly gunpowder, that could otherwise have been used in the invasion of Sicily. The expense to the treasury was far from trifling,

79

too: the operations added an extra 90,000 francs a month to the cost of maintaining the artillery, more than half the normal budget. On the credit side, one should add that the fall at Gaeta contributed an extra 170 cannon to Massena's artillery, albeit about one third of them were damaged.[132] The siege became a major commitment for the French army in the Kingdom of the Two Sicilies in the early summer of 1806 and undoubtedly diverted resources from the longed-for invasion of Sicily at a vital time. It allowed Craig and Stuart a breathing space in which to put the defence of Sicily on to a proper footing and, equally importantly, gave Stuart the opportunity to consider striking a blow in Calabria while the French were heavily committed to the siege.

While the French were bogged down in front of Gaeta to the north of Naples, the forces that had marched south under Regnier were becoming embroiled in a vicious guerrilla war with the local population. The trouble started almost as soon as the French arrived in Calabria, as their troops were forced, by lack of supplies and by bad communications which prevented revictualling, to live off the land. Calabria was a poor province and the depredations of the French troops quickly provoked the population into violence.

The first serious incident of the insurrection was at Soveria on 22 March, the day after Scylla and Reggio had surrendered to the French. A detachment of French soldiers, requisitioning some horses in the town, provoked a brawl in the course of which several Calabrians were bayonetted. The soldiers were driven out of the town and Verdier, the local French commander, sent a column of 200 men to restore order. This column was ambushed in a gorge as it approached Soveria and about forty soldiers were killed. In revenge, Verdier ordered that the town be razed to the ground.[133]

After this the revolt began to spread across the province so that by the end of March all the French garrisons in Calabria were threatened. There was no quarter given or offered and the treatment meted out by both sides was brutal in the extreme. For example on 4 April Verdier discovered at Nicastro the remains of twenty-six French soldiers who had been castrated, tortured with fire and then murdered. Verdier ordered executions of Calabrians in retaliation.[134] Paul-Louis Courier commented on the brutality that the Calabrians showed: "When they capture our men, they burn them as slowly as they possibly can".[135]

Regnier faced a war against an enemy who struck and then as quickly melted away into the hills, in fact classic guerrilla tactics. To counter the threat of the insurgents Regnier spread his troops out to cover the main towns of Calabria. General Compère, with 1,000 men, was ordered to Reggio; Verdier, with 3,000 men established himself at Monteleone and Delonne-Franchesci at Catanzaro with 2,000. The French pursued a policy of reprisals for acts of violence committed against them: villages and houses were burned; executions were frequent. During May and June the villages of Savelli, Cassino, Gerenza and Cachari were all burned in retaliation for attacks on the French. As the foment increased, so Regnier further divided his forces, nor was his cause helped by having to supply reinforcements for the siege of Gaeta. According to Finley, by June Regnier's strength was reduced to 9,240 men, including the sick.[136] By midsummer every town of any size had a French garrison to support supply convoys which ran into trouble. By now the countryside was ablaze and the French could not control it.

The travails of the French in Calabria had not escaped the notice of the British and the Neapolitans in Sicily. For Ferdinand and the Queen, the prolonged resistance of Gaeta and the flaring insurrection in Calabria were encouraging signs that they might one day recover their mainland dominions. In 1799 Ferdinand had been restored at least in part by a popular uprising against the Parthenopean Republic and hope sprung eternal that history would repeat itself.

The British, too, were always pleased to see the French discomfited. In late May Stuart reported to Windham that the French were troubled by "all the Disadvantages of an Advanced Position in a Country destitute of Supplies – while the Animosity of an incensed Population . . . has already begun to display itself."[137] Stuart helped to foment the anti-French feeling by landing in Calabria Michele Pezza, known as Fra Diavolo, one of the leaders of the 1799 insurrection. The British saw that the unrest in Calabria would upset the French plans for the invasion of Sicily and to Stuart, confronting a force of potentially overwhelming size, it was a welcome sign of weakness in the enemy. He also realized that a landing in Calabria by British troops and, even, a military success against the French would inflame the Calabrians still further.

Sir Sidney Smith, who had anchored in the *Pompée* off Palermo on 21 April 1806, was a man who revelled in the type of inshore naval operations that the military and political state of southern Italy now demanded. He had a reputation which he assiduously fostered, as a swashbuckling, daring commander. He had, famously, defied Napoleon for sixty days at the siege of Acre in 1799. Earlier, in 1796, in the course of an inshore operation at Le Havre, he had been captured by the French and spent two years as a prisoner of war in Paris before escaping. In 1793 Smith had commanded the raiding party ordered to burn the French fleet at Toulon to prevent it falling back into French hands after the British withdrawal from the port. Despite Smith's long record as a thorn in the side of the French, Napoleon held a low view of his qualities. "Sidney Smith is a man who is easily deceived," the Emperor wrote to his brother. "I often laid ambushes for him; he always walked into them."[138]

Smith had been ordered by the Admiralty to join the Mediterranean fleet, although he claimed later that, before leaving London, he had been briefed on his mission by Pitt in person. He had been, he alleged, charged by the Prime Minister with arranging diversions in Italy for the benefit of the Austrians, with preventing a French invasion of Sicily and with securing Ferdinand in Sicily. In addition to these duties Smith was ordered to do everything in his power to restore Ferdinand to his mainland possessions. Smith's biographer doubts that such a briefing in fact ever took place as Pitt was very ill by the time that Smith left England and died shortly afterwards.[139] That Smith should have bothered to make such claims at all is testament to his powerful ego and sense of *amour propre*.

Whatever orders Smith claimed to have received from Pitt, his orders from Collingwood, the commander-in-chief of the Mediterranean fleet, dated 26 March 1806, were of much narrower scope. Smith was reminded of "the utmost importance that the island of Sicily should not fall into the hands of the enemy, but be defended against any assault that may be made on it". He was to station his ships in such a way as to prevent any enemy landing on the island, Collingwood stressing that the defence of Sicily was the overriding aim of the British presence in the area.[140] In this respect Collingwood echoed the views of the government, as expressed in Craig's orders of March 1805. Smith was also urged to maintain the closest co-operation with the British army in Sicily: the army commander "must be privy to your most secret movements and I beg strongly to impress

on your mind to maintaining the utmost harmony with the army."
Smith's failure to co-operate closely with Stuart during the expedition
to Calabria was to cause a great deal of friction between the two men.

By May 1806 the British and the French confronted each other
across the Straits of Messina. Each was anxious to possess Sicily: the
British to defend their existing position and the French to cross
the Straits and drive the British into the sea. Napoleon badgered his
brother Joseph from afar with his ever more insistent demands that the
island be swiftly overrun, meanwhile Sir John Stuart contemplated
the necessity of defending Sicily. If the French were to become masters
of Sicily, he wrote, "not only the whole of Italy would be irrecoverably
lost – but I think the forfeiture of Malta and indeed of all our Prospects
of any Preponderance in the Mediterranean would be an inevitable
consequence."[141] The stakes were high.

Chapter Five

"THE DESCENT ON CALABRIA": THE BRITISH TAKE THE INITIATIVE

The main purpose of the little British army stationed along the northern and eastern coast of Sicily was to prevent the French taking the island; it was essentially but not exclusively a defensive role. Lord Camden's original orders for the "Secret Expedition" had made clear – and the new Secretary of War, Windham, confirmed – that the commander was not restricted purely to the defensive in securing Sicily from the French. The government allowed him a wide measure of discretion to act as he thought best in fulfilling the main object of the expedition; this included using Sicily as a base for offensive operations against the French on the Italian mainland.

Stuart himself was acutely aware of the practical possibilities opened up to him by the occupation of Sicily. Just after the British had been granted permission to land at Messina by the Court he wrote to the government at home: "if ever again an attempt is to be made to create a new struggle on the side of Italy – I can conjecture no point from whence our Operations may be combined or our Efforts directed with greater Efficacy than from this Island."[142] By the early summer of 1806 the notion of attacking the French on the mainland was becoming increasingly alluring: the obstinacy of Gaeta and the spread of the insurrection in Calabria were distracting the French and hampering their attempts to launch an attack across the Straits of Messina. A strike against the French in Calabria, while their energies were concentrated elsewhere, would disrupt their invasion plans and, thereby, consolidate the British position in Sicily.

In planning an attack on the French in Calabria, Stuart had one dominating advantage over the enemy, namely the Royal Navy's total mastery of the seas. The French would not be able to attack the troop-

84

ships or, from the sea, threaten the landing itself, nor would they be able to prevent a withdrawal from the mainland, should one become necessary. The British, with complete command of the sea and a good-sized fleet of transport vessels, enjoyed a tactical superiority over the French which Joseph was quick to recognize.[143] He wrote to the Emperor that "eight thousand men in English ships is the equivalent of fifty thousand men here, as in eight days, they can be transported to eight different places".[144] Stuart was in the happy position of being able to pick the most advantageous place to attack the French, thereby ensuring that it would be his army not the enemy's who had the tactical advantage and the choice of battlefield and, should events go badly for the British, he would be able to return, largely unmolested, to the safety of Sicily.

Although the army had not had the opportunity to distinguish itself during the abortive expedition to Naples and the mainland at the end of 1805, the force that Stuart had inherited from his predecessor was well-trained and in good spirits. General Craig had not been idle after his arrival in Malta in July 1805 and had used the opportunity to introduce a reform which was to pay a substantial dividend at Maida. It was the usual practice that a certain proportion of the men of each company, selected for their marskmanship, were trained in light infantry duties. These men, called 'flankers', would fight in front or to one side of their company as it advanced into battle and, in addition to this, each battalion had its own light company, whose men would be trained in light infantry fighting methods and act as skirmishers when the battalion was in battle.

Craig went one step further than this by forming a Light Battalion, to fight alongside the line infantry battalions. It was composed of the light companies of all the regiments in his army topped up with the 'flankers' belonging to the other battalions' companies of the same regiments. Lt.-Colonel James Kempt, of the 81st Regiment, was appointed to command this new battalion. At the same time Craig formed a Grenadier Battalion, with Lt.-Colonel O'Callaghan in command, from the grenadier companies of the regiments. Both battalions were to distinguish themselves in the fighting at Maida.

Craig's new light infantry battalion was an *ad hoc* formation but its officers did a good job in melding the disparate elements together during training in Malta. As Richard Church, appointed adjutant of the new battalion by Kempt, wrote in October 1805: "We are . . . a new regiment, as we form a battalion of light-companies from every British regiment in Malta: facings of every colour: men of every country: yet in my whole life I never saw such harmony as pervades the whole".[145] Church's enthusiasm for the new idea continued unabated as he described the purpose for which Craig intended the Light Battalion.

> "Into our charge is given the first contest with the enemy, and we must endeavour to give a good account of veterans who have for ten years been conquerors. The task is arduous. The Commander-in-chief, when he formed our battalion, made a most impressive speech . . . when in the most solemn manner he told us that he had formed two battalions for the purpose of making all attacks upon the enemy: and who were never intended to think of anything but going forward, without regard to numbers or situation, when ordered to commence an engagement . . . 'To die or conquer', says the General must be the motto of the men he has chosen for that express purpose."

Church tells us that Craig even went so far as to commission a special piece of martial music for the new battalion. "Every soldier pants for action, and pines at the delay: everyone feels the glorious idea of the first tremendous charge of 1,700 men, the flower of England: their impetuosity will be the only thing to endanger their success."[146]

The preparation of the new battalion was not confined simply to generating *esprit de corps* and raising morale; the soldiers were trained hard in the methods of the light infantry, which placed greater reliance on the individual and on initiative than was required in the line battalions. Church gives a positive account of the benefits of the new formations and both the Light and Grenadier battalions proved their mettle at Maida, but the practice of removing the best marksmen from the battalion companies of line regiments had an obvious disadvantage. Sir Charles Oman, writing about the battle before the First World War, described the practice of denuding those formations of their best marksmen as "an execrable device".[147] Maida was the only battle in the Peninsular War period in which Oman found any reference to the British employing 'flankers'. The system was only an experiment and, while it more than proved its worth at Maida, it did not long survive

1. The Scott Memorial, Edinburgh. Sir Walter Scott was so stirred by the British victory at Maida that he named his devoted deerhound after the battle. *(Author)*

. Lt.-Col. Patrick MacLeod by Sir Henry Raeburn. He commanded the 78th Foot at the battle. *(Queen's Own Highlanders Amalgamation Trustees)*

3. This magnificent piece of silverware, worth £100 in 1806, was awarded to Lt.-Col. Patrick McLeod by the Lloyd's Patriotic Fund for his part in the victory. *(Queen's Own Highlanders Amalgamation Trustees)*

4. Sir James Kempt's batman caught this tortoise on the evening of the battle and made his master supper from it; the shell was later mounted on silver and presented to Kempt's regiment, the 81st Foot, as a memento of Maida. *(The Queen's Lancashire Regiment)*

5. Maida Vale, along with Trafalgar Square and Waterloo Station, is the only major London landmark named after a victory of the Napoleonic Wars. *(Author)*

6. Sir James Kempt, who commanded the Light Battalion at Maida, fought throughout the Peninsular War and at Waterloo. He was Governor-General of Canada, 1828-1830. Painting by William Salter. *(NPG)*

Sir Lowry Cole commanded the 1st Brigade at Maida and a division during the Peninsular War. He too later became a colonial Governor, in his case of Mauritius and then the Cape Colony. Painting by William Dyce. *(NPG)*

8. Joseph Bonaparte, Napoleon's brother, was placed on the throne of Naples after the French conquest of 1806 and became King of Spain in 1808; he was succeeded as King of Naples by Murat, the Emperor's brother-in-law. *(NPG)*

9. Sir John Stuart, the victor of Maida
(NAM)

10. A sword, worth £100 in 1806, awarded to Lt.-Col. J. Moore, 23rd Dragoons, by the Lloyd's Patriotic Fund, in recognition of his part in the victory at Maida. *(NAM)*

the battle. Sir John Moore, who, in effect, commanded the army in Sicily after the replacement of Stuart, in July 1806, abolished the system.

Stuart was fortunate in the senior officers who served under him, in particular the officers in command of the 1st and 2nd Brigades, Brigadiers Cole and Acland. Cole, a younger son of the Earl of Enniskillen, had risen rapidly (at the time of Maida he was only 34) by purchase to the rank of Brigadier. His lack of combat experience was not a handicap at Maida, where he displayed enviable sang-froid in battle. He was promoted Major-General in 1808 and commanded the 4th Division with distinction throughout the Peninsular War, combining his military duties with sitting as the, presumably mostly absentee, MP for the Irish constituency of Fermanagh. Acland, who commanded the 2nd Brigade at Maida, also served Wellington throughout the Peninsular War. He was promoted Lieutenant-General in 1814 and appointed KCB at the same time. If Stuart was well served by his senior officers, he was equally fortunate in his more junior officers, many of whom distinguished themselves during the course of the battle; their contributions will emerge as the story of Maida unfolds.

This army was commanded by Sir John Stuart, a general who has not enjoyed the historical reputation that the victory of Maida might be thought to warrant. The general of an army always takes the blame when things go wrong and should (indeed, usually does) take the credit at moments of victory. That this has not happened in Stuart's case is largely due to Bunbury, the Quartermaster-General of the army at Maida. Bunbury wrote an account of the war in the Mediterranean which has become the starting point for historians interested in Maida. He was less than complimentary about Stuart's part in the battle; the General was, he wrote, "rather a spectator than a person much, or the person most, interested in the result of the conflict". According to Bunbury, Stuart "formed no plan; declared no intention and scarcely did he trouble himself to give an order" and he himself had to go from brigade to brigade in the heat of the battle, offering what help he could. This is a harsh, and somewhat self-serving, assessment, but in one respect, however, Bunbury gives Stuart credit: he was "perfectly regardless of personal danger".[148] Overall, however, it is probably fair to conclude that the victory at Maida owed more to the discipline and musketry of the troops than to the inspired generalship of Stuart. As Cole wrote shortly after the battle: "Everything is due to the steadiness and good discipline and gallantry of the troops, without which we must have been defeated."[149]

Stuart had, by the time of Maida, had a long and distinguished military career. Born in the American colony of Georgia in 1759, he was educated in England, at Westminster School, and joined the army. He fought against the colonists in the American War of Independence and was present at the surrender of Yorktown. He took part in the capture of Minorca in 1799 and was again in action in the Mediterranean in 1801 when he commanded a brigade in Sir Ralph Abercromby's expedition to Egypt.

Abercromby defeated the French troops in Egypt at the Battle of Alexandria in March 1801 and Stuart's brigade played a vital role in driving off the enemy's attacks. This battle gave rise to a long-standing jealousy on Stuart's part of Sir John Moore. While Moore had won golden opinions for his part in the battle, Stuart felt that the contribution made towards the victory by the actions of his own brigade had never received the recognition it deserved. Interestingly, the French commander at Maida, General Regnier, was also present at Alexandria and formed an opinion there of the competence and fighting spirit of the British generals that may have cost him dear at Maida.

Stuart, who had succeeded to the command as Craig's deputy, was replaced as the commander of the British forces in the Mediterranean by Generals Fox and Moore immediately after his victory at Maida. He was reappointed to the post in 1808 and enjoyed a second successful tour of duty, during which the British captured Ischia and Procita and, in October 1810, repelled the long-expected French attempt to invade Sicily. Most commentators agree that Stuart was a vain, prickly man (the long-held grudge about Alexandria is a good example) and his failure to cooperate with Sir Sidney Smith was, at least in part, due to this failing. The idea of striking a commemorative medal for the senior officers at the battle was also Stuart's idea (it was common practice in the Navy) and is typical of the man.

The French army was commanded at Maida by General Regnier, as it had been throughout the invasion of Calabria. Although younger than Stuart – he was 35 at the time of Maida – he had also served in

Egypt and, like Stuart, had fought at the Battle of Alexandria and in the campaign that followed it. Regnier was Swiss, having been born into an aristocratic family in Lausanne in 1771; his elder brother, a distinguished botanist, accompanied Regnier to Egypt and to Naples, where he served as Director-General of Forestry. Regnier was a tall, upright man with a prominent nose and chin, blue eyes and blonde hair, more Germanic perhaps than French.[150]

Regnier had originally joined the French army as an engineer, enlisting in the ranks at the outbreak of the Revolutionary Wars in order to see action, but was soon recalled to resume his engineering duties. He was clearly a promising officer who was held in high regard by his superiors as he was offered promotion to general rank at the extraordinarily early age of twenty-three in June 1794. Perhaps wisely – this promotion was offered during the Terror, when the slightest slip or suspicion of a slip could lead to the guillotine – he refused, citing his extreme youth and inexperience. Shortly thereafter, in 1796, he was appointed chief of staff to General Moreau in the Army of the Rhine and, although successful in this post, his reputation was tarnished by his failure (along with Moreau and Desaix) to alert the Directory to the existence of a royalist plot. His friendship with Moreau saved his military career and secured him a posting to Egypt with the Army of the East.

Regnier distinguished himself in the eastern campaigns, particularly at the battles of El-Arish, where he defied 20,000 Turks with four battalions of French troops, and Heliopolis, where he ensured victory by routing the elite janissaries. Once Napoleon had returned to France Regnier supported Kléber's decision to evacuate the army from Egypt but quarrelled with Menou, Kléber's successor, and was ordered to return home. Back in France and with time on his hands, Regnier wrote a book about the Egyptian campaign which was highly critical of Menou and most disparaging about the military capacity of the British. This book and the death of one of Menou's officers in a duel with Regnier resulted in his exile from Paris and ensured that he would not be offered further military employment in the foreseeable future.

It was only after the resumption of war in 1803 when the need for experienced officers became pressing that Regnier was recalled to the colours. He was posted to the Army of Naples, which was considered by regulars to be a backwater; it has even been suggested that the

French military authorities regarded the army in Naples as a safe haven for officers who had in some way blotted their copybooks.[151] Certainly this was true of Regnier at that point in his career. After Maida he continued to serve the Empire, fighting at the Battle of Wagram, in Spain and in Russia. His career came to an end at the Battle of Leipzig in October 1813 when he was captured, along with about 15,000 French soldiers, when the attempt to abandon the town misfired after a bridge was mistakenly blown up. Regnier was released from captivity but, sadly, never lived to see his baby daughter, Louise Marie, as he died of gout before she was born on 25 March 1814.

Regnier had a reputation as a cold, reserved man but also as a fine general and tactical thinker. It was said of him at the time of the Egyptian campaign that "no one could conceive or organize a plan of attack better, nor discuss more cogently the chances of its success".[152] This assessment of Regnier's capacity for dispassionate analysis is not entirely borne out by his book on the Egyptian campaign. He is slating in his criticism of Menou and blames him entirely for the defeat at Alexandria in March 1801, ignoring the fact that the French were considerably outnumbered by Abercromby's men. It also reveals a strong streak of vanity. At one point Regnier referred to those French soldiers who were "too frank to disguise their esteem for General Regnier". In a similar vein, Regnier notes that Menou came to hear of the "expressions of the esteem and confidence with which the troops distinguished General Regnier".[153]

From the point of view of what was to happen at Maida, the opinions Regnier expresses about the British in this book are even more interesting. He had nothing but scorn for the way in which the British conducted their Egyptian campaign. The rank and file of the French army come in for consistent praise; the British rank and file earn it only grudgingly and Regnier reserves his most scathing criticism for the British generals.

"The expedition of the English has succeeded; but they have gathered only the laurels of success; for never did they insure victory either by their military movements, their courage, or their enterprise. Their timid march, notwithstanding their enormous superiority, perfectly points out what would have been their fate if the chief of the army of the East [Menou] had been worthy of his troops."

There is little doubt that Regnier's experience in Egypt imbued him with a contempt for British troops and their leaders which induced fatal overconfidence at Maida. The presence on the other side at Maida of Stuart, who had been one of the British generals in Egypt, no doubt exacerbated his tendency to underestimate the fighting potential of the British and the competence of their generals.[154]

★   ★   ★

The invasion of Sicily remained the highest priority for the French and Joseph, constantly prodded by Napoleon to invade the island, ordered Regnier to make the necessary preparations. The problems which faced the French in attempting to organize an invasion of Sicily were formidable indeed. The siege of Gaeta was becoming increasingly burdensome, while the insurrection in Calabria was starting to threaten the French position in the province. Without reinforcements, Regnier had too few men to be able to maintain control of Calabria and invade Sicily.

The gravest practical difficulty facing Regnier in organizing the invasion was transport. How was he to deliver the huge quantity of artillery, munitions, supplies and all the other equipment on which an army depends to the point at which it was needed, the Straits of Messina? The Royal Navy's mastery of the seas made any attempt to move goods by sea extremely hazardous, yet the roads in Calabria were impassable. When the French invaded the province there was no road south to the Straits of Messina passable to wheeled traffic and such tracks as existed in the mountainous countryside were often steep and, being prey to landslips, dangerous. This was a problem that Regnier needed to address most urgently and it is here that the first tangible signs of progress are to be seen. By May 1806 the French had built a road from Basilicata to Reggio on the Straits of Messina which followed the west coast of the peninsula. As a result heavy artillery could now be brought to the Straits by road – the first pieces, two twenty-four-pounders, arrived on 17 May – thus avoiding the dangers of coastal transport. This meant that both Reggio and Scylla would now be properly defended from attack by the British and henceforth could be used as bases in which to accumulate supplies for the invasion of Sicily.[155]

While the French were mustering their strength for the invasion of Sicily, the British were not sitting idly by. Sir Sidney Smith, who had arrived, it will be recalled, off Palermo on 21 April, soon swung into action with characteristic energy. In his first three weeks on the station Smith succeeded in landing two convoys at Gaeta, one of which included the four lower-deck guns from the *Intrepid* which were to prove such a boon to the defenders of that fortress. He also mounted a diversionary attack on Capri, in an attempt to draw off some of the forces besieging Gaeta. This operation was a complete success and the French commandant, unable to hold the island, surrendered to the British on 12 May.[156] The capture of Capri was an important blow against the French position in southern Italy as it gave the Royal Navy a base very near Naples from which it could attack French coastal shipping. Capri remained in British hands until the French retook the island in October 1808.

At the beginning of June Smith arrived in Messina fresh from his operations along the coast of mainland Italy. He asked Stuart if he would be prepared to contribute troops to take part in further coastal raids, a request the General declined on the grounds that the proposed sorties were "too trivial". Windham's dispatch of 10 May, urging action, would most probably have arrived in Messina by the beginning of June so it is no surprise to find the two men discussing the possibility of an "Enterprize upon as larger a scale which could promise permanent advantage and Credit to the Service and to Ourselves".[157] Stuart suggested an attack on the French in Italy (which he christened the "Descent on Calabria") as a highly effective way of ensuring the future security of Sicily. One of his more senior officers later wrote that Stuart's principal motive for the expedition was "to give eclat to his command before the arrival of General Fox appointed to supercede him".[158] It is characteristic of Stuart that in deciding to launch the operation practical and strategic considerations should be coloured, however lightly, with vanity and the hope of self-aggrandisement.

By the beginning of June 1806 circumstances appeared favourable for a British strike at the French on the mainland. As Bunbury (who would certainly have known) has written, the British considered the French to be overstretched in Calabria; Regnier, they believed, had only 5,000 men in the province, all well-dispersed, and very long, difficult lines of communication to the north. Nor was there any realistic possibility that Regnier would be reinforced since Verdier to the north was fully occupied in containing the *massi*, the Calabrian irregular militia, and defending his headquarters at Cosenza while the main part of Joseph's army was embroiled in the siege of Gaeta. Stuart believed that, if he was able to force a battle, his army would enjoy a numerical advantage over the French. He calculated that if he could land 5,000 men in Calabria while the circumstances remained propitious Regnier would retreat, Massena would raise the siege of Gaeta and the insurrection in Calabria would flare up. Certainly, he had received "constant and reiterated tokens" of the willingness of the Calabrese to revolt should help arrive.[159]

Stuart offers further justification for the "Descent on Calabria" in a letter to Sir John Acton, the Neapolitan Prime Minister now sheltering in Palermo. The circumstances were favourable for the attack, Stuart wrote, because the forced levy raised by the French in Calabria had further inflamed the populace against the invaders. By landing, the British would demonstrate their support for the Calabrese, even if the populace failed to rise in revolt against the French. If, however, they did, the expedition was certain to be successful. It was a good time to strike, too, because the government at home had indicated that reinforcement of the army in the Mediterranean was imminent. The expedition would act as a diversion for Gaeta and would expose Naples should the French elect to reinforce the army facing the British. It would also be able to withdraw, if necessary, at will. It was, Stuart added, very important to destroy the enemy's "Establishments for Maritime Protection" on the mainland side of the Straits of Messina. "Sicily," Stuart wrote to Acton, "could never be in Peace or Security while the French remained, as at present, Masters of the contiguous Shore of Calabria."[160]

This is the overriding rationale of the plan for the "Descent on Calabria". The army had, since it set off from England fourteen months earlier, been charged with ensuring, above all else, the security of Sicily. This entailed doing everything possible to frustrate the French desire to take possession of the island. Here, suddenly, was a golden opportunity to strike at the French while they were weak and overstretched, and disrupt, or destroy entirely, their preparations for the invasion of Sicily. And, because of the Royal Navy's command of the sea, there was little risk attached to the operation; whatever happened in Calabria, the army could escape back to Sicily and resume a purely defensive role. What Stuart had in mind was a pre-emptive strike which, if successful, would secure the British position in Sicily for months, perhaps even years.

Stuart and Smith had formulated their plan by the second week of June, whereupon the Admiral left for Palermo in order to carry the news of the intended operation to the Court. Stuart says that Smith, at this stage, agreed fully with the plan but from the time Smith left Messina relations between the two men began to deteriorate until, by the end of the campaign, they had descended into mutual distrust and accusation. Stuart complained that "I was left [by the end of the expedition] . . . with difficulty to reconcile the personal proceedings of Sir Sidney those attributes of Candour; of disinterested Zeal and of honest Exemption from any Impulse of selfish motives".[161] The first sign of trouble was Smith's failure to keep Stuart abreast of developments in Palermo, an oversight that, after a fortnight without news, the General found most frustrating.[162]

Smith's silence was broken by a letter dated 26 June from Palermo. In it Smith suggested that he command an expedition up the west coast of Calabria, with the relief of Gaeta as its ultimate objective. This, he said, would throw the French under Regnier in the south into disarray thereby enabling Stuart to tackle them alone. This letter shows that Smith, whether or not he had agreed to the original, limited idea of a pre-emptive strike, had developed more grandiose ideas while in Palermo.[163] The concept of a sweeping, inshore operation up the Italian coast was more to Smith's taste than simply escorting soldiers to a landing point.

While Smith was in Palermo he fell under the spell of the Queen's flattery who, in turn, thought of the Admiral as the next Nelson, the saviour of the Kingdom of the Two Sicilies. On 28 June he entertained the Neapolitan royal family on his flagship, the *Pompée*, at Palermo; Ferdinand returned the compliment by issuing a decree giving Smith overall command of all Neapolitan forces, on both land and sea. As this plainly ignored the authority that the King had already granted Stuart over the Neapolitan forces, Smith was forced to explain, rather unconvincingly, that he had not asked for the commission: it had been thrust upon him.[164] The appointment led one British officer to describe him as a "floating viceroy".[165] The episode was to cause a lot of ill-feeling between the two British commanders. Smith's acceptance of Ferdinand's commission also got him into hot water with the government at home. Lord Grenville, the Prime Minister, was convinced of "the absolute necessity, on grounds of public duty, of our expressing a decided, tho' mild, disapprobation" of Smith's conduct in accepting a commission from Ferdinand and usurping Stuart's command.[166]

Meanwhile Stuart, continuing to plan and organize the "Descent on Calabria", chose the Bay of St Euphemia, which is about seventy miles north of Messina on the western side of the Italian peninsula, as the landing point for his army. The British camp had received encouraging intelligence suggesting that the army would not encounter any significant resistance in coming ashore there.[167] The principal attraction of the Bay of St Euphemia was its position, by landing there Stuart would place his army between Regnier and the main body of the French to the north. This would immediately pose a threat to Regnier's lines of communication, already menaced by the Calabrian insurrection, and confer a tactical advantage on the British. As the bay lay at the narrowest part of the Italian peninsula, where it was no more than 20 miles wide, the presence of a British army at this point would force Regnier either to stand and fight or compel him to make a dangerous retreat north under the guns of the enemy. By choosing to land at St Euphemia Stuart was doing his utmost to ensure that his army would draw the French into battle.

All the necessary stores and equipment were loaded on to transport vessels at Messina which were then sent, one by one, past the Point of Faro to Milazzo and other more westerly ports. This was to try to keep the preparations secret from the French and, for the same reason, the troops selected for the expedition were kept on the move, changing quarters and encampments. Stuart says, perhaps rather complacently, that all the preparations were conducted in the greatest possible secrecy. He adds that the French had, to begin with, regarded the troop movements in particular with suspicion, but notes that they came to see them purely as exercises.[168]

The French accounts of the events of the last week of June, however, do not support Stuart's claim. Indeed, given the proximity of the two

95

opposing forces and the view that each enjoyed of the other's activities across the narrow waters of the Straits of Messina – a telescope was the most that was required – it is hard to imagine how Stuart could have prepared the expedition with any degree of secrecy. On 29 June Regnier was able to report to Joseph the details of the fleet that the British had mustered to transport their army; he added that his spies in Sicily had informed him that three English regiments were to embark.[169] It was, as it happened, an inaccurate report but it shows that secrecy was more difficult to achieve than Stuart claimed.

The commander of the French artillery, Griois, says that by the end of June Regnier had known for a long time that the British were planning an expedition to the mainland. He adds that at this juncture fresh intelligence arrived that pinpointed St Euphemia as the most likely landing point, information which helped Regnier to assemble his forces in the right place to confront the British.[170] Even Charles Boothby, who was wholly loyal to Stuart, doubted that the French were in complete ignorance of the expedition. Boothby, describing Stuart's departure from Messina, wrote: "A nice military figure, he jumped gaily into his carriage, laughing with his aide-de-camp, and nodding kindly, drolly, and significantly to the vivaing Messinese, who, nothwithstanding the profoundest secrecy had a pretty good guess what he was after, drove rapidly off".[171] If the Messinese knew what Stuart was up to, it is fair to assume that the French, too, would have known.

The army that Stuart embarked for the expedition to Calabria was essentially the same as the one Craig had led to Naples the previous autumn. It was a mixed bag: seasoned troops rubbed shoulders with new recruits. The 20th Foot had seen action in the campaign in Holland in 1799, where the young John Colborne had distinguished himself. The regiment had joined the British expeditionary force in Egypt and, although they arrived too late to take part in the defeat of the French at the Battle of Alexandria, the 20th nevertheless earned its spurs with a daring and wholly successful night attack on the enemy at Fort des Bains. From Egypt the regiment was posted to Malta, where the commanding officer, Robert Ross, only too aware of the drudgery of garrison duty, kept his men fit and fully occupied with regular route marches and drill. Ross himself was a first-class officer who rose to the rank of general and later, during the brief war with the

United States in 1812, led the expedition to Washington that burned the White House.

The 27th Foot were, in Bunbury's phrase, "hard-biting fellows", who hailed from Northern Ireland and Scotland. The regiment had, like the 20th, campaigned in Holland in 1799 and had been in Egypt in 1801. The second battalion took part in the landing at Aboukir Bay and fought at the Battle of Alexandria, while the first battalion – nominally, at any rate, the battalion that fought at Maida – did not arrive in Egypt until later and saw only minor action. Both battalions were posted to Malta after the end of the Egyptian campaign.

The 35th Foot contributed its Light and Grenadier companies to Stuart's army and 150 hand-picked men commanded by Major Robertson also fought in the Light Battalion. The 35th had also taken part in the dismal expedition to Holland and later participated in the final stages of the siege of Malta.

These regiments had some experience of battle and in each case also contributed their Light and Grenadier companies to the newly-formed Light and Grenadier battalions. In this way these two new, *ad hoc* formations acquired seasoned troops to stiffen the other, less experienced men. Both battalions were composed of men who were anyway probably above the run of the normal soldier and had been subjected to rigorous training while stationed in Malta during the summer of 1805.

On the other hand the 58th, 78th and 81st Foot were considered to be inexperienced, green troops, the 78th in particular being very young soldiers; of the 650 of its men who fought at Maida, 600 were under age.[172] A recently-raised Highland regiment, it had arrived in Messina in May 1806, having been ordered from Malta to reinforce the Sicilian garrison and had caused something of a sensation among the local population. One British officer remembered that the Highlanders' "picturesque national dress made a great impression upon the Sicilians, though the women, indeed, seemed to think it due to modesty to say the dress was very ugly".[173] Stuart was disappointed to have been reinforced with "a corps of boys", although in fact they fought gallantly at the battle and, along with the 81st Foot in Acland's brigade, they sustained the heaviest casualties on the British side.

In the case of the 58th Foot this disparaging assessment of their qualities might, in view of their recent record, be somewhat unfair. The regiment had fought with great distinction under Sir John Moore in the Egyptian campaign, playing a prominent role in the landing at Aboukir Bay and in the Battle of Alexandria. The 58th was also engaged in all the more important later operations of that campaign, such as the capture of Rosetta and the sieges of Cairo and Alexandria. A second battalion was raised in 1803, but it was the first battalion that joined the Secret Expedition; what is less certain is how many of the veterans of Egypt remained on the strength by the time the regiment returned to Mediterranean duty.

The 81st Foot had been raised at the beginning of the Revolutionary Wars and had served in the West Indies where, in common with most regiments on that station, it was devastated by disease. In 1799 the 81st was posted abroad once more, this time to Cape Town, returning to England after the Peace of Amiens. Once back at home the regiment took in a large draft of recruits to make good the losses of years of foreign service. It was this newly-constituted and inexperienced formation that joined Craig's army. The British regiments were joined by a battalion of Swiss infantry from de Watteville's regiment and by detachments of the Royal Corsican Rangers and the Royal Sicilian Volunteers.

The infantry were accompanied by a sizeable detachment of the Royal Artillery. Commanded by Major Lemoine, the artillery consisted of ten four-pounders, four six-pounders and two howitzers. In this department at least, the British enjoyed a significant advantage over the French, who were able to deploy only four light mountain pieces at the battle. So far as cavalry was concerned, however, the reverse was the case. Although there was a squadron of the 20th Light Dragoons attached to the garrison at Messina, they were not present at Maida. Stuart was to complain after the battle that his lack of cavalry had prevented him from turning the defeat of the French into a rout. The French, by contrast, had 300 horse of the 9th Regiment of Chasseurs who played a prominent role at the battle.

Stuart left Brigadier Broderick in Sicily to guard the island in the absence of the expeditionary force, with a skeleton garrison which consisted of the battalion companies of the 61st and 35th Foot (less the 150 'flankers' of the latter who had been detached to Kempt's Light Battalion). He also had at his disposal the Chasseurs

Britanniques, the 20th Light Dragoons, some artillery and some Sicilian troops.[174]

While the troops earmarked for the expedition to the mainland were gathering in Messina, the battalion companies of the 20th Foot were detached from the main body of the army to provide a diversion. Lt.-Colonel Ross was ordered to embark his soldiers into feluccas, a type of small boat with a capacity of about 100 men, and to cruise the coast between Reggio and Cape Spartivento, that is, in the opposite direction to Stuart's intended line of attack. This they did and it may well account for the various sightings of British boats along the coast by the French in the last days of June. It is also possible that some of Ross's men may have landed near Reggio on the 29 June.[175] Their task complete, the 20th returned to Messina on 3 July and embarked on transports to join the main force at St Euphemia.

Meanwhile the troops chosen to participate in the "Descent on Calabria" boarded their transports at Milazzo and Faro on 25 June. According to Bunbury, the embarkation was carried out quickly at

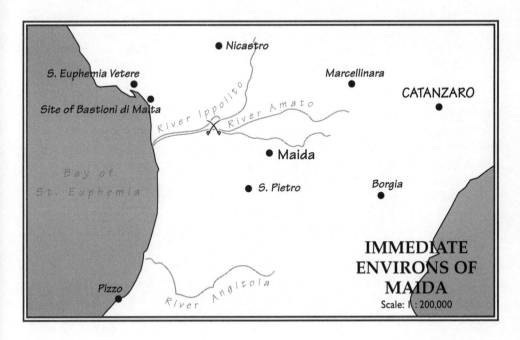

99

daybreak, the regiments in question having been ordered to march down to the harbours by night. There was no means of transporting any significant number of horses, hence the lack of British cavalry at the battle, although space was found for a few horses for the more senior officers and for use as draught animals.[176] The force sailed for St Euphemia the following day, 26 June, escorted by the *Apollo* and two other men-of-war.[177] The adventure had started. As one British officer of the 27th Foot wrote from Malta on hearing news of the expedition: "I need not say how much we all wish to be with them. Something dashing is expected: all the peasantry are in our favour, the troops are the finest in the British service, they were ordered only to bring one shirt per man. All this looks well; if the General was not pretty sure he would not hazard the top of Sicily."[178]

Chapter Six

"SOMETHING DASHING IS EXPECTED": THE BATTLE OF MAIDA

On the night of 30 June 1806, Stuart's small army arrived in the Bay of St Euphemia.[179] The beach which skirts the bay is about twelve miles long and forms a gentle crescent from north to south. The British landed at the northern extremity of the beach which extends to the south past the mouth of the River Amato as far as the River Angitola. The strand itself is flat, wide and composed of coarse sand and pebbles, while along its landward side there is now, as there was in 1806, a thick belt of scrub, mainly broom. The wide expanses of the beach made it an ideal place to land an army and its equipment, and, once the transports had anchored in the bay, the troops began to wade ashore, although their progress was hampered by heavy surf.

At daybreak Lt.-Colonel Oswald led an advance party to secure the beachhead. Regnier had been expecting a landing in the Bay of St Euphemia and there was a small detachment of Polish troops on the beach when the British landed. Stuart, anticipating opposition, had asked Captain Fellowes of the *Apollo* to order his ships to cover the landing.[180] But instead of attacking the British while they were coming ashore the Poles quickly retreated into the hinterland, allowing Stuart's men to land unopposed. Oswald's party consisted of troops from the Light Battalion, the Grenadier Battalion and the 78th Foot. They moved off from the Bastione di Malta, a square, squat fortified tower which stood behind the beach; nowadays it is several hundred yards inland. Away from the sea a "vast plain with much cover of brushwood extended from the beach to the receding mountains".[181]

Oswald and his men advanced into this scrub and soon encountered

101

the enemy, who consisted of two companies of French troops and five companies of Polish troops, amounting to perhaps 400 troops, commanded by Colonel Grabinski.[182] A fierce skirmish followed which resulted in the Poles being forced to retreat further inland and to the south, towards the main rendezvous for Regnier's forces on the River Angitola.[183] It was the first opportunity that the newly-formed Light Battalion had had to prove itself under fire and it acquitted itself with honour. One British officer recalled that no "fox-hunters after a long frost could appear to enjoy their sport more keenly".[184] Sergeant O'Neal, of the Light Company of the 81st Foot, distinguished himself by single-handedly taking several Poles prisoner.[185] The French and Poles lost about twenty men killed and eighty-one were taken prisoner by the British, including two officers of the rank of major.[186] The British suffered only one casualty, a sergeant in the Light Battalion, who was wounded in the skirmish.[187] Oswald's men, having seen off the Poles, advanced inland and began to establish themselves in positions near the village of St Euphemia, about a mile from the beach, where the ground starts to rise towards the hills.

The beachhead was, at least for the time being, secure and the Royal Engineers began to fortify it by digging a defensive position behind the landing beach. This, Stuart hoped, would have a double function: not only would it protect the beachhead in the event of a forced re-embarkation, but would also act as a rallying point for those Calabrians who wished to join the British colours.[188] The remainder of the troops landed on 1 July and were deployed in defensive positions with the sea to their right and the village of St Euphemia to their left, facing to the south, from where it was confidently expected that the French would appear. The following day, 2 July, Stuart ordered an advance guard to take up a position at Nicastro, a village high on the northern scarp, about seven miles from the beach, which commanded a fine view of the whole plain of Maida. While Stuart was establishing and consoli-dating his position artillery and stores continued to be brought ashore from the transports, although the heavy surf ensured that the process was not completed until 3 July.

Regnier knew that something was afoot. If he was to counter the threat to his extended lines of communication there was not a moment to be lost: he must concentrate his forces, which the insurrection had compelled him to spread throughout Calabria. The largest part of his army had been reduced to 1,000 men by the demands of the siege of Gaeta and by the need for troops for service in Apulia; of this 800 were stationed to the north at Cosenza and 200 to the east at Crotone. Other, smaller, outlying detachments from places such as Pizzo, Tropea and Bagnara were ordered to make all possible speed towards the Bay of St Euphemia, the expected landing point. The General himself, with his *etat major*, left Palmi on 1 July for St Euphemia, leaving behind small detachments of troops at Reggio and Scylla to guard the castle and the hospital with orders to resist the enemy until Regnier returned to relieve them. Compère, who commanded the two battalions stationed between Scylla and Reggio, was also ordered, on the afternoon of 30 June, to join the main body of the army.

Regnier advanced quickly northwards and by evening on 1 July he had arrived at Monteleone. As he later explained to Joseph, he wanted "to advance swiftly on the English, to throw them back into the sea". "I thought," he continued, "that this was the wisest and tactically the best course of action."[189] The following morning the French continued their march north; to speed their advance Regnier ordered all baggage and non-essential personnel to be left behind at Monteleone. This affected officers and men alike: Griois was thereafter accompanied by only a single orderly. By the evening of 2 July Regnier had reached the River Angitola, where he pitched camp on the heights above the river. Regnier's men had marched from Palmi to the Angitola, a distance of more than thirty-five miles, an exhausting experience in only two days in the full heat of the *mezzogiorno* summer through difficult, mountainous country. By now the French were converging on the Bay of St Euphemia; on the night of 1 July General Digonnet arrived on the River Amato with a company of Polish grenadiers and a detachment of the 9th Chasseurs, the only French cavalry to take part in the battle.

On 3 July Regnier took up a position above the Amato. The route north from the Angitola, a distance of about ten miles, had taken the French along a large part of the Bay of St Euphemia; inland, woods of myrtle and pomegranate and olive groves spread out over a vast, occasionally marshy and mainly uncultivated plain, where herds of buffalo roamed.[190] At this time of the year the myrtle was in full bloom, its white flowers adding colour to the picturesque mountainous landscape. The French pitched camp on the lower part of a thickly-wooded scarp that rose from the southern edge of the plain, most probably between the modern villages of Maida and S. Pietro di Maida. At least some of Regnier's men were high enough up the ridge for their camp fires to be visible from across the plain; had they been on the plain itself folds in the ground might well have concealed these lights from the British.

His position on the ridge to the south of the plain of Maida offered Regnier several advantages. First, he was no more than three hours' march from the British position and, it might be added, commanded a fine view of the ground in front of his lines, making it unlikely that he would be taken by surprise. Secondly, from there Regnier could attack the enemy's centre on a line between the mountains and the sea, thereby reducing the risk that his troops would come under fire from the ships of the Royal Navy. Thirdly, Regnier believed that this position gave him some measure of protection against the Calabrian brigands.[191] This was a most important consideration as anti-French sentiment among the populace and the brigands, incited by the Court and by the priests, was now at boiling point. It was here on the hills above the plain of Maida that Regnier formed his battle plan and waited, on the evening of 3 July, for General Compère and his troops to arrive from the south.

Meanwhile, less than ten miles away on the north side of the plain the British had established themselves between the sea and the village of St Euphemia. Stuart, once his army had landed, issued a proclamation in the name of George III to the Calabrian people exhorting them to rise up against the French. He stressed that the British had come as friends, not as invaders, to re-establish Ferdinand as the legitimate ruler. The proclamation emphasized the good record and intentions of the British troops; in particular contrast to the French, Stuart assured the Calabrese that "I ask merely quarters from you. I require no contributions; the provisions furnished shall be punctually paid."[192] He was careful to appeal to them as Commander-in-Chief of the British army; he answered only to his king, George III, and had no need of a commission (unlike, by implication, Sir Sidney Smith) from Ferdinand.[193] This was intended to bring the Calabrese flocking to the British colours. Indeed, before the expedition had left Sicily Stuart had hoped that a large body of Calabrese would join the fight against the French. Events did not, however, turn out quite as had been anticipated. Stuart recorded that in general people received the British "with

Acclamation", but that, by 2 July, this was the extent of their practical assistance. Oddly, in view of the opinions expressed before the expedition left Sicily, Stuart claimed that he was not surprised by the reluctance of the Calabrese to volunteer for military service.[194]

For two days following the landing Stuart was in the dark as to Regnier's plans, for as he wrote to the Secretary of War on 2 July: "I am not apprized of the Movement of the Main body of the Enemy". This state of uncertainty was soon dispelled as by the afternoon of the following day Regnier had taken up his position on the other side of the plain which, between the two camps, was about eight miles across. The British position was in the north-western corner, where the sea, the plain and the scarp of the mountains converged. The French were astride the ridge which ran along the south side of the plain, but, unlike the British, who had the sea at their backs, Regnier's men were about seven miles inland. The middle of the plain is completely flat but there are some small ridges as the ground starts to rise up towards the scarps of the surrounding mountains. The plain is at its widest at the coast and, as it recedes inland, so it becomes narrower, the ridges of the mountains funnelling the flat ground away to nothing. There are several rivers cutting across the plain, flowing mainly from east to west; the two principal ones are the Ippolito and the Amato, which is the more southerly of the two. At this time of the year the Amato was easily fordable by infantry, although the ground near the rivers remained marshy even in summer.

Seen from the coast the plain of Maida (or St Euphemia) looks like a great, natural amphitheatre, the plain itself the stage surrounded by a huge semi-circular tier of steeply-banked seats. Some of the land in the middle of the plain was cultivated, but, apart from the marshy areas by the rivers, it was predominantly dry, dusty and covered with scrub. It is easy to see why Stuart chose St Euphemia as the ideal place in which to bring the French to a decisive battle; there was nowhere else for miles around where the British troops and artillery could be brought so easily by sea to the field of battle and where their deployment would not be hampered by steep, hazardous mountain roads.

This, then, was the ground that Stuart, escorted by a detachment of the Grenadier Company of the 61st Foot, set out to reconnoitre in the afternoon of 3 July. As luck would have it, the recently-arrived Regnier also descended at about the same time from his camp among the myrtle and pine to survey the ground that lay between the two armies. As the two generals with their escorts conducted their reconnaissances they came within yards of running into each other. Fortunately they did not and each, having inspected the lie of the land, returned to his camp to make the final preparations for battle and issue orders for the morrow.

★   ★   ★

One of the stranger aspects of the Battle of Maida is the tactics adopted by the British general, Sir John Stuart. The expedition had been planned as a pre-emptive strike against the French in southern Italy; this, it was hoped, would be the most effective way of securing the future of Sicily in British hands. The Bay of St Euphemia had been chosen for the landing precisely because its position on the peninsula meant that it would be difficult for the French to avoid offering battle to any British force landing there. Stuart's army had no longer-term objective in remaining in Calabria – its principal task was to guard Sicily – yet for the expedition to be counted a success the preparations for the invasion of the island would have, at the very least, to be disrupted and, preferably, the enemy defeated in battle. No one was keener than Stuart that the expedition should succeed, yet he seems to have arrived in Italy without any idea of how the French might be drawn into battle. Indeed, it was almost as if Stuart had no concept what strategy to pursue at all once he arrived on the mainland. In his official dispatch to the Secretary of War describing the battle, he says that he decided to attack the French for two reasons: one, that failure to do so would send discouraging signals to the locals and, two, that the proximity of the French gave him little time to think what to do.[195] This is the most extraordinary thing for any general to say, the more so when he has personally planned the entire expedition. It defies belief that Stuart had not planned how to tackle the French once his army had landed or how to force them into the decisive, glorious battle he sought so keenly; yet it seems that he had no firm idea of what course of action to pursue, no plan of campaign to follow.

Stuart gave orders for the British to attack the French on the morning of 4 July. He issued these orders after the reconnaissance of the previous afternoon had revealed that the French appeared to occupy a very powerful position on the hills to the south of the plain.

Bunbury says that the reconnaissance showed that the French position was weakest on its left and that, accordingly, Stuart planned to try to turn the French left.[196] Interestingly, Stuart himself does not state anywhere in his official dispatches that this was his object and, had it been, it is highly likely that in the aftermath of victory Stuart would have mentioned it. Indeed, he says that had Regnier stayed in his position on the heights above the plain the British "could not possibly have made an Impression upon him".[197] Yet Stuart was fully aware of the strength of the French position when he gave his orders to attack on the evening of 3 July. Nor, at that time, could Stuart have anticipated that Regnier would voluntarily give up his impregnable position to descend into the plain to give battle. It is hard to avoid the impression that Stuart, having landed his army on the Italian mainland, had no coherent plan of action, indeed very little idea of what to do at all. The battle was, in the event, a resounding success, but this had little to do with the tactical *savoir-faire* and astuteness of Sir John Stuart.

The decision of Stuart to attack the French appears even more curious in the light of what was known to the British about the relative strengths of the two armies. The official returns show that 4,795 men marched out of the British camp on the morning of 4 July. Stuart had left four companies of de Watteville's Swiss infantry to guard the beachhead.[198] In addition there were about 550 men of the 20th Foot who might be expected to arrive at some time, but it would have been unwise to have counted on them.

The difficulty for Stuart lay in establishing a reliable figure for the size of the forces facing him, since the British headquarters received widely varying estimates of the strength of the French army. On 3 July, according to Bunbury, several "contradictory" reports put French numbers at anything between 3,000 and 6,000.[199] Stuart himself states that on the same afternoon he received intelligence that the French army numbered about 4,000 infantry and 300 cavalry. Moreover, the French, intelligence suggested, expected to be joined by another 3,000 troops "in a day or two", a reference, presumably, to Compère's battalions which were marching north to join the main body of the army.[200] Indeed, writing to his second in command the day *after* the battle, Stuart estimated that the French had fielded at least 7,000 infantry and 300 cavalry.[201] The fact that the British knew of the arrival of reinforcements in the French lines during the night of 3/4 July is an important piece of evidence on which to assess Stuart's actions.[202] It is possible to explain the decision to attack the French on 4 July, despite their strong position, on the grounds that Stuart knew (or suspected) that reinforcements were on their way to Regnier. Better, therefore, to launch an attack before those reinforcements could arrive and while the two armies were believed to be roughly equal in number. But the decision to attack becomes harder to justify when it can be shown that Stuart knew that the expected reinforcements had in fact arrived in the French camp. He was now committing his men to battle against a numerically superior enemy who occupied a powerful defensive position. This gives added impetus to the argument that Stuart lacked a coherent plan or the capacity to react to changes in the circumstances facing him.

The confusion about the number of enemy troops facing them was not confined to the British commanders; rumours too swept through the lower ranks of the army. Charles Pasley, friend of Coleridge who thought him the "embodiment of the young warrior . . . the heroic Spartan", was present at Maida and recorded in his diary that the British received intelligence on the morning of 3 July that the French had 5,000 men, supplemented by an advance guard of a further 1,200 men.[203] Boothby, too, testifies to the widely varying reports of French strength: one put it as low as 2,000–3,000, whereas another as high as 27,000–30,000. He estimates that by the time the battle began on 4 July, the British had 4,000 men and the French 7,000.[204] An officer in the Royal Artillery, writing to a friend a month after the battle, estimated that the French had 7,000–8,000 men and 500 cavalry.[205] While the wilder reports of the strength of the French could be (and no doubt were) safely discounted, it seems certain that, by the time the British marched from their camp on the morning of 4 July, they believed that they were facing an enemy which was not only superior in numbers but of great experience and high reputation.

If Sir John Stuart appears to have lacked a coherent plan of action, Regnier knew from the outset what his aim should be: he must attack. "*Il faut jeter les Anglais à la mer*". Neither was the spirit of aggression confined to Regnier, for when Napoleon, at Saint-Cloud, heard that the British had landed in Calabria he was delighted. "*Rien n'est plus heureux que le débarquement des Anglais*", he wrote to Joseph.[206] On the evening of 3 July, having returned from his reconnaissance, Regnier held a staff conference, at which he announced his intention to attack. There were several voices counselling caution, urging the General to avoid the risk of attacking the British and to await reinforcements. Prominent among these was Colonel Lebrun, who had been sent by Joseph to Regnier's headquarters once it was clear that something was afoot in Calabria. He had orders from Joseph to inform Regnier that the reduction of Gaeta was the most important military objective in the Kingdom of Naples, that Joseph would not reinforce him and that he should keep the enemy under close observation.[207] Lebrun and the other cautionary voices were overruled.

Regnier explained to Joseph, after the battle, why he had decided to attack the British. Waiting for reinforcements was a non-starter, as they might take twelve to fifteen days to arrive from the north. The position that his army occupied on the hills above the Amato was, even in the short term, untenable, as the surrounding woods made the French extremely vulnerable to attack by the Calabrian brigands. (This, incidentally, is a radical revision of his opinion, given only two days earlier, that the Amato position afforded protection against the local insurgents.) The alternatives were to retreat to Crotone or to a position between the Angitola and Monteleone. Both of these had their disadvantages, not least that in both Regnier would still be surrounded by brigands, whether or not he had fought a battle against the British. A Neapolitan force from Sicily had reportedly just landed to the south near Scylla; Regnier could not march against this new threat with an undefeated British army at his back in a region in which he was so isolated. But perhaps the most important reason for attacking the British was that he was confident that he could beat them. Regnier had assembled about 5,000 French troops from regiments which had often distinguished themselves in the past. He hoped that by launching a vigorous attack he could defeat the British, force them to re-embark, restore order in the countryside and then march against the Neapolitans to the south. Regnier knew that he must act swiftly; time was not on his side. "Every day," he wrote to Joseph, "would increase this foment [the insurrection] and my lines of communication would be cut if I delayed forcing the English to take to their ships again."[208]

The reasons Regnier gave for attacking the British are all, in themselves, tactically sound, but Regnier was undoubtedly overconfident of success. We have already seen that his experience of the British in Egypt had left him with a low opinion of the fighting qualities of their troops and an even lower one of the capabilities of their generals, robbing him perhaps of the dispassionate objectivity so vital to any general. Such was his regard for the effectiveness of his own troops that he believed victory was a certainty: had they not overwhelmed the Neapolitan forces during the invasion of the Kingdom of the Two Sicilies? Was the core of his army not composed of veterans of the great, triumphant campaigns in Italy? The British would not have the stuffing to resist a full-blooded assault by these battle-hardened men.

Certainly, the French regiments were experienced troops. The 1ère Légère was a regiment with a long and distinguished history stretching back as far as the mid-sixteenth century. In action from the very start of the Revolutionary Wars, it had fought throughout the 1790s and had been engaged at the Battle of Zurich in 1799; from 1800–01 the regiment had taken part in the triumphant campaigns against the Austrians in northern Italy. The 1ère Légère enjoyed a formidable reputation among friend and foe alike; one British officer referred to them as "the heroes of Marengo".

The 42nd Regiment had likewise fought throughout the Revolutionary Wars; interestingly the regiment had been engaged against the British at Egmont-an-Zee in 1799 during the Dutch campaign. The 23rd Légère, raised in 1792, had probably seen less action during the 1790s than the other two principal French regiments at Maida but had fought against the Austrians at the Battle of Caldiero in northern Italy in October 1805. The detachment of 300 cavalry that Regnier had at his disposal came from the 9th Regiment of Chasseurs à Cheval. Raised in the reign of Louis XV, they had been in action since the start of the Revolutionary Wars and had fought at Valmy, a victory which saved Paris and perhaps the Revolution itself from the advancing Prussians.

Regnier also had some foreign troops under his command. The 1st Regiment of Swiss Infantry had been raised the previous year from other formations that had had experience of battle; it is an interesting reflection of the strength of the divided loyalties generated by these wars that both sides at Maida made use of Swiss troops. The French Swiss, commanded by Clavel de Bresles, a friend and compatriot of

Regnier, were "old soldiers, firm and calm", who had distinguished themselves at Castelfranco.[209] On the other hand the Polish troops, of the 1st Regiment of Polish Infantry, were known from their chequered history to be of dubious quality and had already, in the skirmish with the British on 1 July, shown some worrying signs of weakness.[210]

One of the most serious deficiencies from which Regnier suffered was the lack of artillery. The haste with which his army had been assembled and the forced marches required to bring it to face the British at Maida had resulted in Griois having only four light field pieces at his disposal. Artillery was an important component of Napoleonic battle tactics; it played a vital role in softening up the enemy infantry prior to the final assault. It could inflict casualties on enemy formations while they were still beyond the range of small arms fire, thereby preparing the way for the assault battalions. A lack of it, therefore, was likely to be a severe disadvantage when the French were seeking a rapid and decisive victory. This disadvantage was, furthermore, likely to be compounded by the fact that the British had enough artillery to bring considerable fire to bear on the advancing French.

The British received widely varying reports of the size of the French army that they faced. Contemporaries and historians are equally at odds on the question of the number of men that Regnier had at his command. Sir Charles Oman, the great British military historian, held that the French had 6,400 men in the field at Maida. Berthier, chief of staff of Joseph's Army of Naples, so as well-placed as any to obtain accurate information, said that Regnier put 5,050 men into the field. Regnier himself, on the other hand, in his official report on the battle to Joseph, implies a total infantry strength of 5,150. Jacques Rambaud, the early 20th century French historian, states in his carefully researched book that Regnier had about 5,500 men in the field at Maida.[211] He also says that Regnier gave (presumably elsewhere) a total strength of 5,360 including the sick who had been left at Monteleone. There seems to be no dispute that Regnier had 300 cavalry of the 9th Chasseurs at his disposal. It would appear reasonable to assume, therefore, that when Regnier marched to attack the British he had about 5,100 infantry and 300 cavalry, giving a total of 5,400 men.

Regnier had made one concession to the cautious voices in the

French camp: he delayed the attack until the morning of 4 July in the hope that Compère and his troops would arrive from Reggio during the night. They did.[212] On the eve of the battle Regnier estimated that the British numbered 6,000 and believed that their forces had been joined by about 2,000 Calabrian brigands (which, in fact, was not the case). So, like Stuart, Regnier believed he too was attacking a force larger than his own. But, unlike Stuart, he was absolutely confident of victory. The plan that he announced to his officers at the conference on the evening of 3 July was to attack the British in their camp. The French would turn the British left (which Regnier assumed to be entrenched) by attacking them from the heights above Nicastro, while the rest of the infantry attacked the British right.

Regnier may have been guilty of overconfidence, but was the decision to attack the right one? The answer is that, in all the circumstances, it was. Berthier criticized, after the event, Regnier's tactics, saying that he had been wrong to attack. Better, Berthier thought, either to confine Stuart to the plain, where disease would have decimated his troops, or to draw him into the hinterland by appearing to refuse battle.[213] But Berthier wrote with the advantage of hindsight, knowing of the calamitous defeat that in fact followed the decision to attack. The reasons for attacking that Regnier gave Joseph were, at the time, sound. He was particularly worried about the effect on the local population of failing to defeat the British force. Above all, Regnier was suddenly confronted with the greater part of the force on which Sicily depended for its defence. If he could seize this opportunity to destroy it he would, at a stroke, improve immeasurably the prospects for the conquest of Sicily. This would bring significantly closer a goal for which he had already done much preparation and which the Emperor himself held so dear. It was too good an opportunity to be missed.[214]

The night before the Battle of Maida was beautiful and warm. There was a magnificent view from the French camp of the hills behind the British position and of their ships in the bay. "*La soirée et la nuit furent superbes.*" The French troops were in high spirits, drinking toasts to their success on the following day.[215] But, across the plain, the British too had every reason for confidence in the outcome of the battle. In fact the two armies were evenly matched and there was no cause to think that one side or the other enjoyed an overwhelming advantage. The French had only marginally more men and some of them were veterans of many campaigns, but this was offset by the dubious quality of the Polish regiments. The British troops were less experienced but well trained, keen and fresher than their enemies as they had not been subjected to a series of forced marches in the heat of summer. Regnier had some cavalry at his disposal, whereas Stuart had none; by contrast the British enjoyed a huge advantage in the artillery arm. Defeat was, of course, an unpalatable, even unthinkable, prospect for both generals but would expose the loser to potentially disastrous consequences. For the French it would necessitate a difficult and dangerous retreat which would be constantly harrassed by the Calabrian bandits, with the possibility that Regnier would not be able to force a passage to the north, towards Naples, reinforcements and safety. For the British there was the dreaded prospect of having to defend a beachhead and re-embark an army while under attack, or, at worst, to face total annihilation with all the consequences that that might have for the future of Sicily.

That Stuart's small army was here in a remote part of southern Italy at all was due to the strategy of the Third Coalition. Most of Pitt's grand edifice, so artfully constructed in London, St Petersburg and Vienna had been demolished by Napoleon at Ulm and Austerlitz and Pitt himself was dead. The British army that looked out across the plain of Maida towards the French lines was the last hope that some pride could be salvaged from the ruins, that some limit be put to the enemy's continental ambitions. It was also, perhaps, a chance to show that the British were not merely a nation of sailors and that they had an army that could hold its own with the best. Similarly, for the French it was an opportunity to throw the British into the sea, to punish them for their temerity and add Sir John Stuart to the long list of generals who had tried but failed to challenge the power of France on the Continent of Europe.

*   *   *

At dawn, or about 4 a.m., on 4 July the British began to leave their lines between the beach and St Euphemia and form up in columns of brigades for the march south along the bay. The reserve, commanded by Oswald, marched along the beach; the Light Battalion, commanded by Kempt, marched on the landward side of the army with the two other brigades, Cole's and Acland's, in the middle. The

113

army made slow progress over difficult terrain. Marching along the beach Oswald's men found themselves sinking into the wet, deep, coarse sand and shingle while those regiments not marching on the beach itself had soft, dry sandy dunes to contend with; neither surface made for easy going for heavily laden soldiers. Kempt's Light Battalion, spared the holding sand of the beach and dunes, had to contend instead with marshy ground further inland. Some of the artillery had left the British lines earlier in the night and had found progress equally difficult. One Royal Artillery officer, who had received his marching orders at 10 p.m. the previous evening, had taken all night to bring the two guns at his command to the mustering point at the mouth of the Amato, such was the poor state of the roads.[216]

Before marching off to attack the French Stuart issued orders for the defence of the beachhead in the absence of the main body of the army. He entrusted Captain Fischer of de Watteville's Swiss regiment with this vital task and allotted him four companies of his regiment's infantry; additional defensive fire-power was provided by Captain Lemoine, who commanded the artillery reserve of four six-pounders and two howitzers. The young Engineer Lieutenant, Charles Boothby, was also ordered to remain at the beachhead to put the finishing touches to the defences, including the construction of a water obstacle. Boothby, later that morning, watched the battle from the top of the Bastione di Malta from where he could also, he claimed, continue to supervise his men in their work.[217]

The French were roused at dawn, too, by the sound of regimental bands striking up and soon the camp was alive with activity. Compère had arrived from the south during the night with the 42nd Regiment, so Regnier had the reinforcements he so desperately needed. Once the Calabrian sun had burnt off the mist which had settled over the marshy plain during the night, Regnier and his officers stared out towards the British camp, but, at first, there was no movement to be seen, so he gave the order to attack the British camp, according to the plans issued the previous evening.[218] Then, far over to his left, Regnier noticed the British marching in two columns along the seashore, but it was not immediately clear what they were doing. Could it be that they were re-embarking? As part of the enemy army crossed the Amato it became clear to the French that Stuart was trying to execute a flanking manoeuvre, possibly with the intention of cutting him off from

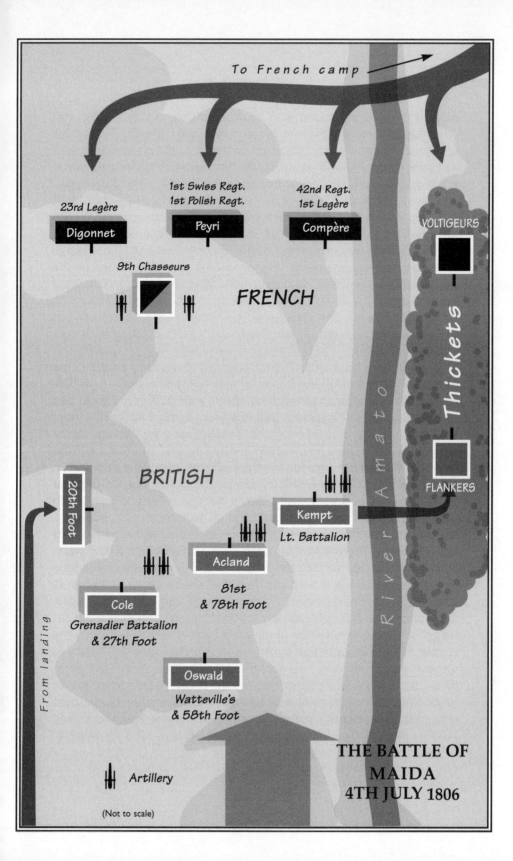

To French camp

1st Swiss Regt.
1st Polish Regt.

42nd Regt.
1st Legère

23rd Legère

Digonnet

Peyri

Compère

VOLTIGEURS

9th Chasseurs

FRENCH

Thickets

River Amato

BRITISH

20th Foot

Kempt

Lt. Battalion

FLANKERS

Acland

81st
& 78th Foot

From landing

Cole

Grenadier Battalion
& 27th Foot

Oswald

Watteville's
& 58th Foot

Artillery

THE BATTLE OF
MAIDA
4TH JULY 1806

(Not to scale)

Monteleone and the south. Regnier decided that, as this was an ideal opportunity to attack the enemy, who had left the protection of his lines and was now out in the open, he would descend into the plain and give battle. Stuart's army would, he reasoned, be at least partly divided by the Amato which would allow the French to attack in detail. The rest of the British, particularly those who had been attempting to turn the French left, would then be cut off from the sea and forced to surrender. Regnier, seeing that there was not a moment to be lost in taking advantage of this opportunity, quickly announced the change of plan to his commanders, recommending that they attack at the charge with the bayonet. The right-hand French column, which had been ordered to attack the British from the heights above St Euphemia, was already under way. Its orders were countermanded and it was now ordered to swing to its left to march towards the sea and the British.[219]

Down by the shore the British stopped when they reached the mouth of the River Amato. It was by now between 6 and 7 a.m. The troops needed a rest, particularly those who had come from the outlying positions at Nicastro, as it was, even so early in the morning, starting to get very hot. The weight of their packs, the sixty rounds of ammunition that each man carried and his musket and bayonet were made all the more burdensome by the difficult underfoot conditions. Stuart could now see the French leaving their powerful positions on the hills to descend on to the plain, a decision which to the British General showed "more Confidence than Judgement".[220] At first it seemed to some who strained their eyes across the plain as the mist cleared that the French were moving so far to their right that they could only be attempting to turn the British left. To others it looked as if Regnier was making a bold bid to avoid giving battle by escaping towards the north and safety. By about 8 a.m. the British had begun to advance inland, keeping the Amato on their right and, taking advantage of the wide open spaces of the plain, deployed into two lines, the standard formation adopted by British infantry in battle. According to one participant, the order to deploy from column into line was given when the British were half-way across the plain.[221] They were drawn up in echelon from the right with Kempt's Light Battalion on the right and Acland's brigade, comprising the 81st Foot and the young Highlanders of the 78th Foot, to their left and slightly behind.

116

Following behind and further to the left was Cole's brigade, consisting of the Grenadier Battalion and the 27th Foot. Behind the front line, between Cole and Acland, was the reserve commanded by Oswald which comprised the remaining companies of de Watteville's and the 58th Foot. At this point, with both sides advancing, the two armies were approximately three miles apart. The mist had cleared; each army now had a clear view of the other, shako plates, buttons and muskets glinting in the bright morning sun. As the two armies bore down on each other the locals, perhaps oblivious to the impending storm, were busy bringing in the harvest.[222]

Regnier, having changed his plan, hurried into action. His troops came down from the steep-sided hills in columns and crossed the Amato. The ground on the north bank of the river was more open and, therefore, more suitable for both a fast-moving infantry assault and cavalry operations than the south bank which was covered with scrub. Once across the river, Regnier ordered Compère to deploy his troops in line; evidently he thought that this was likely to be a more effective formation in which to attack the British.

Much has been written on the question as to whether the French were drawn up in column or line to attack the British at Maida and there is no doubt that Compère's brigade formed into line to attack the British Light Battalion. During the Revolutionary Wars of the 1790s, the column formation was the easiest way for French officers to impose discipline on large bodies of conscripted and poorly trained men. By the time of Maida, however, French infantry tactics had developed great flexibility and were highly responsive to the needs of any situation; by 1806 it was simply not true to say that the French infantry always fought in columns. French infantry did deploy into line, for example, when it was necessary to bring a greater weight of small arms fire to bear on the enemy and, in view of the shortage of artillery at Regnier's disposal here, this consideration might have prompted the deployment into line for the attack. On the other hand the French were short of ammunition (Regnier had ordered his commanders to attack with bayonets alone), so perhaps weight of fire was not the motive for attacking in line. Although, as the most recent historian of French battle tactics put it, "The French rarely deployed in line along the entire battle front", it was by no means uncommon that smaller formations, divisions or especially brigades, would deploy into line.[223] Maida, where the French had only a small force, was one such occasion. The flexibility of French infantry tactics at this time is illustrated by the fact that substantially the same army, commanded by the same general had, four months before, won a resounding victory at Campo Tenese over the Neapolitan army fighting in column.

Regnier had decided that he would concentrate his attack on the British right, so with his army across the Amato, he formed up in line with his best troops, the 1ère Légère and the 42nd Regiment, on the left of the French line. These regiments, deployed in line, would probably have been drawn up with each company in three ranks and the companies dressed in line next to each other: with 2,400 men in the brigade it would have occupied a front of about 530 yards.[224] General Compère, who commanded the brigade, the cream of this French army, was a brave and experienced officer, who in common with Regnier (although for different reasons) had been drafted back into the active list for service in Naples. Born in Péronne in 1768 his parents named him, with splendid resonance, Louis-Fursy-Henri. He joined the army as a gunner and rose rapidly, reaching the rank of Brigadier as early as 1795. He was seriously wounded while serving with the Army of the Danube and, in 1801, was appointed commandant of Les Invalides in Avignon.[225]

The French, like the British, were drawn up in echelon, although in their case echelon from the left. Consequently, slightly behind and to the right of Compère's troops was Peyri's brigade, composed of a Swiss regiment and twelve companies of Polish troops. On the French right General Digonnet commanded the 23rd Légère. The French artillery – such as it was, they had only four small calibre field pieces – was deployed, along with the cavalry, in the centre.[226] As the main body of the Regnier's army forded the Amato, he ordered two companies of *voltigeurs* to keep to the left (or south) bank of the river and to follow the line of the thickets along the Amato towards the British.

The two armies were now closing rapidly; battle was imminent. The two light infantry battalions were, because of the echelon formation adopted by both armies, in the van of their respective armies and would bear the brunt of the first clash between the two sides. As the two armies closed, the opening artillery exchanges disturbed the herds of buffalo on the plain and the beasts, terrified, lumbered away, hooted and jeered by the French soldiers.[227]

The battle began on the south side of the Amato, away from the main bodies of troops. The French *voltigeurs*, ordered to penetrate the thickets on the far side of the river, had done so and were now menacing Kempt's right flank. Major Roverea, Cole's aide-de-camp, was sent to throw some 'flankers' over the river to secure that wing from this threat and the first troops ordered over the river into the thickets to attack the French were a company of Corsican Rangers. As the Corsicans entered the scrub they were greeted by musket fire and then charged by 200 *voltigeurs*, pushing them back in confusion on to the Light Company of the 20th Foot. For some minutes the fighting was very fierce until Kempt ordered Major Robertson across the river with the 'flankers' of the 35th Foot. This settled the issue: the French retreated, pursued by the Corsicans, while the Light Company of the 20th Foot and the 35th's 'flankers' rejoined the Light Battalion on the other side of the river. During this short but fierce fight, a prelude to the main battle, Captain Maclean, the commander of the Light Company of the 20th Foot, was killed, shot in the chest. Remarkably, he was the only British officer to lose his life during the battle. A brother officer and exact contemporary of Maclean's in the 20th Foot wrote of him that "he was a brave fellow, and I believe lost his life by his gallantry".[228]

Meanwhile, as the two armies approached, the artillery exchanges began. The French artillery opened fire at a range of approximately one thousand yards but, at least as far as Acland's brigade was concerned, it was not effective as the shot carried over the front line of British troops but fell short of the second.[229] It is unclear what calibre of gun the French had at Maida but it is unlikely that they were larger than the four-pounders used by the British. If this was so, the French battery opened fire at extreme range.

The British artillery appeared to have made better practice. This may have been due to a greater degree of skill or luck in laying the guns or simply a reflection of the fact that the British had ten guns to the French's four. The first two shots that the British artillery fired hit the 1st Grenadier company of the 42nd Regiment, each round killing three men.[230] The Light Battalion had Dyneley's battery in support, consisting of two four-pounders positioned in front and to the right of its front line. The four-pounder was a light field piece with a limited range; fired at an elevation of two degrees, it had an effective range of perhaps 800 yards. But to be at its most effective against massed formations of infantry it had to be fired at zero elevation, thereby ensuring that the shot was below the height of a man throughout its trajectory; at this elevation its maximum effective range was no more than 500 yards. It is likely therefore that the British artillery would have opened fire on the advancing French infantry with round shot at a range of about 650 yards, gradually lowering the elevation as the enemy came closer.[231]

Once the enemy infantry was within about 250 yards it became possible to employ case shot, which consisted of a number of musket balls contained in an object resembling a large cartridge. This kept the individual musket balls together during firing and ensured that they did not disperse too quickly after leaving the muzzle of the gun. Case shot was a most effective weapon against infantry: one round of four-pounder case contained approximately fifty-five one-and-a-half ounce bullets. Any massed infantry formation exposed to artillery using case shot was likely to suffer severely. Dyneley records using case shot during the battle and there is no reason to suppose that he did not order his men to employ it against Compère's brigade, once it came within range.

The troops of the 1ère Légère and the 42nd Regiment were in high spirits and utterly confident of victory as they marched in line towards the British Light Battalion. As the two armies came within range Colonel Huard, commanding the 42nd Regiment, asked Regnier whether he proposed to order the troops to load, to which Regnier jokingly replied, "Certainly, unless you were going to wait for the English to order it". The troops loaded their muskets and the drums beat the charge along the line.[232] The French cavalry, out in front of their infantry, continued to make feints at the British lines, throwing up great clouds of dust as they did so, obscuring the main body of the French army from the British. Visibility was further impaired by the heat haze which was already, before 9 a.m., thick, and this combination of dust and haze made it difficult for the British commanders to see what the enemy were doing. Until shortly before they attacked Bunbury thought that the French were retreating up the valley.

The advancing French presented a magnificent if intimidating spectacle to the British soldiers. Bunbury wrote that the 1ère Légère were "superb", adding that "never did I see a finer, or more soldier-like body of men". Major Roverea, Cole's A.D.C., wrote: "The *coup d'oeil* was magnificent – our fine troops as steady and in as good order as on the parade ground, *vis-à-vis* the French also in line, their arms glittering in the sun".[233] Several witnesses write of the suspense in the ranks as the two armies closed on each other; to others events seemed to resemble nothing more than summer manoeuvres. "The two armies in parallel lines, in march towards each other, on a smooth and clear plain, and in dead silence, only interrupted by the report of the enemy's guns; it was more like a chosen field fixed upon by a general officer for exercise, or to exhibit a show fight."[234] Sir John Stuart, as the two armies closed, felt, with perhaps a touch melodrama, that "the Prowess of the Rival Nations seemed now fairly to be at Trial before the World".[235]

What happened next was the crucial phase of the battle. It was about 9 a.m. and by now very hot. The various accounts that have reached us offer slightly different versions of events; this is not in the least surprising as battles are, by their very nature, confused and confusing affairs. The 1ère Légère were advancing quickly on the British line, with the 42nd Regiment in support to their right. The British artillery kept up a steady fire into the French ranks while Compère's men got closer; meanwhile Kempt's troops waited. Once the French were within a range of 100 yards, the British Light Battalion fired its first volley. It was devastating. Griois was with Regnier on the right of the 1ère Légère when this first volley smashed into the French ranks. So well-aimed was the volley that gaps appeared throughout the French ranks; those who had survived the impact of the first volley stumbled over the bodies of their comrades, dead or wounded and the 1ère Légère began to lose its forward momentum. Griois also noticed that many men with only slight wounds were going to the rear, further weakening the ranks and adding to the confusion. This irresolution began to spread to the 42nd Regiment. It was particularly unfortunate from the French point of view that as many of the regimental officers of the 1ère Légère were killed or wounded in the first volley – the regiment suffered twenty casualties among its officers in the battle – there were fewer

121

officers to keep discipline in the ranks and maintain momentum.[236]

The Light Battalion fired only one more volley into the advancing French. One version of events has it that before the Light Battalion fired its first volley, Kempt ordered them to discard all unnecessary extras such as blankets and the like.[237] According to another, as the two lines closed Kempt roared to his men, "Now is the time to show that you are British Soldiers". The Light Battalion fired its second volley into the French at very close range, probably no more than fifteen yards, with a deafening crash. As Compère's men were closing on the British at the charge they would, in all likelihood, have covered this final 100 yards in about thirty-five seconds; this would have allowed the British time to fire two battalion volleys at the advancing French but no more. Having fired their second volley, the Light Battalion hurled themselves into the charge through the thick clouds of acrid, choking gunsmoke. The 1ère Légère, who had by now lost all momentum, turned and fled in the face of the British charge. They never reached the British lines.

It was very rare that two lines of infantry charging with bayonets fixed would in fact run into each other; one side or the other tended to break and take flight before the impact. Maida has in the past been offered as an exception to this rule, an example of a battle when the bayonets did cross. Sir John Stuart asserted in his official dispatch home that this did indeed happen, yet no other account of the battle corroborates him and two specifically deny that it did.[238] Rory Muir, in his most recent book, cites these two sources as evidence of the fact that the bayonets did not cross at Maida.[239] Dyneley, positioned as he was with his guns in front of the Light Battalion, was perfectly placed to observe events and confirms the other recollections when he says that the French "turned tail" and fled before they reached the British bayonets.[240]

The Light Battalion charged the French as they turned and fled, panic-stricken; the result was carnage. One veteran, quoted by the editor of Dyneley's letters, wrote that the "French while advancing hesitated, and at last turned and ran away; but they delayed too long in doing so; the British rushed in and laid upwards of 300 of them on their faces with the bayonet." Corroboration of this is offered by a British naval lieutenant who examined the wounded the following day. He noticed that the wounded British were on their backs, having been shot in the front by the advancing French. The wounded French, by contrast, lay on their fronts, having been stabbed in the back while fleeing from the British bayonets.[241] Defeat for the 1ère Légère had become a rout; as one British officer put it, the Light Battalion "ran down the heroes of Marengo like a flock of sheep".[242] Compère was badly wounded leading his men to the charge, one of his arms shattered, and once his horse had been killed under him he was taken prisoner by Captain Roger Tomlin of the 35th Foot. Tomlin's action saved Compère's life, although if some versions of events are to be believed, Compère was hardly grateful for this service as he was led away cursing and swearing. Tomlin himself had lived a charmed life during the battle: a musket ball smashed the hilt of his sword, another grazed his boot and yet another wounded his horse.[243]

The 42nd Regiment, taking their cue from the 1ère Légère, turned in the face of the assault by the Light Battalion and retreated. By now Acland's brigade, in the British centre, was moving forward in support of the Light Battalion, which was fast losing its formation as its soldiers ran off helter-skelter in pursuit of the fleeing enemy. Dyneley, the artillery officer who had been left behind by the rapid advance of the Light Battalion, now fired a few rounds of case shot in support of Acland's men.[244] Regnier, for his part, having seen the failure of his left to break the British, began to switch his attack to his centre and right and could be seen on his charger in the French rear, gesticulating wildly, exhorting his troops to battle.[245] The French centre was composed of Polish and Swiss infantry and, although the Poles melted away in the face of the advance of Acland's men, disheartened by the fate of the 1ère Légère, Regnier did manage to rally the Swiss, who stood firm and perhaps even advanced. Acland's men also came under fire from the French artillery and were attacked by the French cavalry. According to Bunbury they tried to form a square while under fire, a difficult feat for experienced soldiers but for the young Highlanders of the 78th Foot a daunting task indeed. Certainly Acland's brigade suffered the bulk of the casualties on the British side, 52% of both the killed and the wounded. The appearance of the French de Watteville's regiment in the line prompted a momentary doubt in the young Highlanders. The Swiss wore claret uniforms that resembled in the smoke and confusion of battle those worn by the Swiss regiments in the British service; this caused the Highlanders to slacken their fire under a mistake of identity and emboldened the enemy to advance on Acland's troops, whose mounted officer could see better what was happening and ordered them to start firing again. Thus when the 78th and the 58th did reopen fire the Swiss were close and suffered so heavily that it took only ten minutes to clear the line.[246]

Meanwhile Regnier galloped over towards the French right to launch the 23rd Légère against the British line. The advance of Acland's brigade had opened up a gap in the British centre, thus exposing its left flank. However, Regnier found the 23rd already warmly engaged with Cole's brigade on the British left and realized that it was now too far to the right to be redeployed against the British centre. The French cavalry were also involved in the attack on Cole's brigade. Some accounts of the battle refer to the fact that the French cavalrymen could not make their horses, terrified by the noise of battle, charge the enemy and had therefore to fight on foot. Although not entirely clear, it seems that this was during the fighting with Acland's brigade in the centre.

The 23rd Légère and a detachment of the 9th Chausseurs were threatening Cole's brigade. The battle was not going as well for the British on their left as it had done in the centre and on the right. Some *voltigeurs* had advanced, using the scrub as cover, on the left flank of Cole's brigade and were now pouring accurate fire into the British ranks. The French artillery commander, Griois, had brought his guns across to support the 23rd, who were fighting "fiercely".[247] It also seemed that the French cavalry might be about to charge. Major Roverea takes up the story:

"While my General was thinking that he ought not to allow some 'Flankers' to dislodge them, a shell exploded quite close to us and set fire to the dried grass of the field in which we were, and very soon the whole was in flames, and this accident caused some confusion in the centre of the 27th Regiment. But the smoke prevented the enemy from perceiving this. At the same time a body of their Cavalry advanced and threatened our left flank and appeared to be about to charge. So much so that our mounted officers drew sword or pistol and prepared to defend themselves in the mêlée."[248]

Events on the British left were entering a decisive phase. Cole took two companies of Grenadiers from the brigade's right to reinforce the left, but these men suffered heavy casualties. Roverea knew that "the moment [had] become critical for us".[249] The two sides were evenly matched on this part of the battlefield; Regnier thought that the French had contained the British left but would have been broken had he redeployed troops from there for another attack elsewhere.[250] The fire from the *voltigeurs* in the scrub to the left of Cole's brigade was becoming heavier and enemy infantry began to mass behind the cavalry in front of the British line. The flames and smoke of the burning grass in their midst ignited by a shell was an additional hazard for the 27th. Cole, a cool head in the crisis, ordered three companies of the 27th Foot and two companies of the Grenadiers to turn on his left flank to form an angle with the main front so that they faced the French *voltigeurs* and the cavalry who were now also trying to turn the British left.

The outcome seemed to hang in the balance because, although the French had been utterly routed elsewhere on the battlefield, here they were better positioned. Both their cavalry and *voltigeurs* were able to take advantage of the scrub to move further and further round the British flank. It was by now (mid-morning) very hot and the French troops were fresher than the British, who had started marching in the early hours of the morning. Furthermore, most alarmingly, the British were having difficulties in keeping Cole's men supplied with ammunition.

At this moment the 20th Foot, under their colonel, Robert Ross, arrived quite unexpectedly on the battlefield. This sudden reinforcement, in a vital position, settled the issue. The 20th, their diversionary task along the south coast complete, had returned to Messina on 3 July and transferred to the transports *Symmetry* and *Britannia* and sailed for St Euphemia. They arrived there on the morning of 4 July and disembarked, without waiting for orders. By the time the 20th landed the battle was in progress; this much was obvious as "we could hear the firing & see the smoke". Heavy surf on the beach was still making landing difficult and spoiled much of the soldiers' ammunition.[251] Once the troops had been issued with fresh ammunition Ross marched his men off towards the battle.

Bunbury was to the rear of Cole's brigade when news was brought to him of the imminent arrival of the 20th Foot and galloped off to meet the newcomers and brief their Colonel. Ross brought his men up on the left rear of Cole's brigade; forming up quickly, they took up a position in the scrub and began to push back the *voltigeurs*. The 20th were also under attack from the French cavalry; Ross steadied his men to face this new threat, shouting out "You have the advantage, soldiers; the sun is in their eyes! Steady!"[252] Having repulsed the French cavalry with a single, fierce volley, Ross then ordered his men to swing their line to the right, so that they could enfilade the enemy's front. It was the turning-point of the battle; the French, surprised by the unexpected intervention of 550 fresh men in such an important position on their flank, began to retreat and by midday the battle was over. It was, as Stuart put it, "the last feeble struggle of the Enemy".[253] The British had, in the course of a single morning, won a famous victory.

The 23rd Légère was able to disengage itself and, under covering fire from the French artillery, retire in good order, falling back onto what remained of the 42nd Regiment. Regnier, after the intervention of the 20th Foot, felt obliged to retreat as he had no reserves and his broken regiments had fled the battlefield. He needed to conserve those troops he had, to rally those who had fled and await help. There were also the wounded to consider. Regnier was anxious to regroup so that, in due course, he could avenge the defeat, eject the British from the mainland and go to the rescue of the garrisons he had left in Reggio and Scylla.[254] He could not retreat towards Monteleone partly because some British advance parties had reached the town but also (and more importantly) because by doing so he would cut himself off from Naples. Obliged to retreat eastwards, although that necessitated abandoning Monteleone and all their supplies to the British, the French marched off up the valley towards Crotone.[255]

As the defeated French retreated across the plain the British troops followed in pursuit. But their pursuit was not effective: they were exhausted by the battle and the heat and were short of both ammunition and drinking water. But the most serious handicap was their complete lack of cavalry, which allowed the French to escape from the battle with much lighter losses than would have been the case had Stuart had even a squadron at his disposal. As Stuart himself wrote to his second in command: "had I had the few mounted 20th Roy[al]

D[ragoons] from Messina with me not an individual would have escaped."[256]

The main body of the victorious British army remained on the plain while the French retreated to the east. The Light Battalion pursued the defeated 1ère Légère into the hills and some of them had reached Monteleone but the battalion had inevitably become dispersed in the process. Kempt watched his men and, for a while, followed the line of the French retreat, but was anxious to rejoin the rest of the army.[257] Kempt did send the Light Company of the 20th Foot (commanded by Colborne following the death of Maclean in the battle) in pursuit of the French. The day after the battle Colborne and his tiny force (eight-seven men, two dragoons and two officers) had reached the town of Borgia in the hinterland, only to discover that the French had left it a few hours before.[258] The remainder of the British army rested on the battlefield before returning to the shore.

Once the main body of the army had returned to the beach the regiments were detailed off by brigades to bathe in the sea, a most welcome and refreshing respite on such a hot morning, giving the soldiers the chance to wash off the sweat and grime of battle. The men of the 27th and the Grenadier Battalion were in the water at the same time as the alarm was raised: the enemy were approaching across the plain. The entire brigade rushed from the water, threw on their accoutrements but not their uniforms, grabbed their muskets and formed up, stark naked, to face the enemy. Happily for all concerned, it proved to be a false alarm; a panicky staff officer had mistaken a herd of buffalo on the plain for enemy cavalry.[259]

★　　★　　★

Maida was a great British victory, a fine example of the steadfastness and courage of British infantry and of the inestimable worth on the battlefield of disciplined musketry. It is remarkable in that it was won at a cost in casualties that Stuart described as "but comparatively small".[260] The battle was also notable for the difference in the casualties that the two sides suffered, for while the British won their victory at a small cost the French suffered many times greater losses. Forty-five British were killed in the battle and, astonishingly, this included only one officer, Captain Maclean of the 20th Foot, who was shot in the exchanges between the skirmishers on the south bank of the Amato in the early stages of the battle. In addition to Maclean three sergeants and a total of forty-one rank and file were killed. The list of those wounded is, unsurprisingly, longer: twelve officers were wounded at the battle and a total of 270 other ranks, made up of eight sergeants, two drummers and 260 rank and file. This gives a total of all casualties, killed and wounded for all ranks, of 327.

The casualties suffered by the British at Maida were, by the standards of the time, very low. Rory Muir, in his recent book, quotes a nineteenth century statistical study which showed that the British, over the whole Napoleonic period, suffered a mortality rate in battle of 3.3 per cent, or one man in thirty.[261] The comparable figures for the losses at Maida are a mortality rate of 0.8 per cent, which equates to one man in every 117 being killed. At Salamanca in 1812 Wellington's British and German troops lost one man in seventy-nine killed. At the notoriously bloody battle of Albuera, by contrast, one man in twelve of the British and German troops present was killed. The overall number of British casualties at Maida is low, too. The total of 327 of all ranks equates to a casualty rate of six per cent, or one man in sixteen. In other words, fifteen of every sixteen British soldiers present at Maida survived the battle unscathed. At Salamanca the British and Germans lost just over one man in every ten and at Albuera four men in every ten.[262] These figures support the notion that the success at Maida was bought at a human cost that was, by the standards of the day, very low.

It is also rare that casualties in a battle fall evenly across the troops present and an examination of the casualty returns confirm that Maida was no exception. They tell an interesting story: the heaviest casualties in Stuart's army fell on Acland's brigade, composed of the 78th and 81st Foot. Between them they suffered over half the casualties of the entire army – fifty-two per cent of both those killed and those wounded. Even more remarkable are the figures relating to the casualties among officers. It was commonly the case that officers suffered a higher proportion of casualties than their men: the single fatality among the British officers represents an exceptionally low proportion for the period. Of the twelve officers who were wounded all but three of them were in Acland's brigade, two in the 81st Foot and seven in the 78th Foot. The apparent oddities thrown up by the figures for the officers may be attributable to the very small size of the statistical population (or even to luck) but that cannot account for the overall casualties figures for Acland's brigade. Does the fact that it sustained more than half the total loss suggest that Acland's men were in the fiercest fighting? Certainly, if the anecdotal evidence is to be believed, the fighting in the centre was no fiercer than elsewhere on the plain. After all, the Poles opposite Acland fled without a shot being fired, although the Swiss did put up a fight and there is some evidence that the French artillery was brought to bear on the brigade. But it is hard to believe that the fighting was fiercer there than it was between the Light Battalion and the crack French troops on the right or, particularly, between Cole's brigade and the French on the left. It may perhaps reflect the inexperience and youth of the 78th Foot; one remembers the account of their trying to form a square under artillery fire.

The Light Battalion was pitched in against the 1ère Légère and performed heroically against the cream of Regnier's army. It was here that Regnier expected to smash the British line and roll the enemy back to the sea. In the event it was the French who turned tail; Kempt's men proved more than the equals of the French veterans. They also sustained the lowest proportion of the casualties suffered by the three brigades which took an active part in the battle. One officer and ten rank and file were killed, which equates to twenty-four per cent of the total number killed in the entire army, while the Light Battalion's wounded amount to seventeen per cent of the total. These are significantly lower, for example, than the corresponding figures for Acland's brigade. They seem to confirm the impression that the French veterans were shattered by accurate musketry and artillery fire before they themselves could get in a blow at the British.

Similarly, Cole's brigade on the British right was involved in what witnesses say was the most desperate fighting of the battle, yet they too suffered significantly lower casualties than Acland's men and (roughly) the same as those suffered by the Light Battalion. Those killed in Cole's brigade represent twenty-two per cent of the army total and the wounded account for twenty-six per cent.

The casualty returns also show that Oswald's reserve took little part in the fighting. Only five of its men were wounded (about two per cent of the total) and none killed. It was moved up to plug the gap left on Cole's right by the advance of Acland's brigade. Similarly, the returns show that the 20th Foot's contribution, although decisive, was not costly. The 20th had one man killed and six wounded (again about two per cent of the total for the army) during their intervention.

The British casualties at the battle were low, both absolutely and proportionately, and are well-documented in the official returns. The French casualties, it has always been supposed, were significantly higher, but quantifying them with any degree of accuracy is an elusive task. Regnier himself, in his report on the battle to Joseph, admitted that he did not know the exact number of casualties that his army had suffered, although he was able to enumerate the losses among his most senior officers. Compère was wounded – his shattered arm was subsequently amputated – and captured by the British; the commanding officer of one of the battalions of the 1ère Légère, Gastelouis, was killed in the rout of his regiment. Colonel Clavel, commanding the Swiss battalion, was badly wounded and later died of his wounds and Neucha, the commander of the Polish troops, was killed. Both Colonel Rey of the 23rd Regiment and Marchand-Duchaume, the corps adjutant, were wounded; few of Regnier's senior officers, it would seem, escaped the carnage. The day after the battle Regnier's army numbered about 4,000 men and some 300 wounded.[263] This would imply, on the basis that he had 5,400 men before the battle, that the French had suffered about 1,400 casualties, killed, wounded and captured.

The British estimates of French casualties are rather higher: Stuart reckoned on the day after the battle that the French had lost 3,000 men in total and by the following day, 6 July, this had risen to a total loss of not less than 4,000.[264] Of that 700 French dead had been buried on the field of battle and the British had captured more than 1,000 French soldiers, many of them wounded. *The Times* printed Stuart's report of 6 July, so it was these figures that were the publicly acknowledged casualty figures by which the scale of the British victory was measured.[265] The figure of 700 for the number of bodies buried on the battlefield is (one would assume) reasonably accurate, as is the figure for the number of prisoners in British hands. The doubt concerns the balance of Stuart's estimate, that is the 2,300 who, not being dead or in British hands, must be assumed to be wounded but still with Regnier. It is grossly at odds with Regnier's own estimate of the number of wounded with his army after the battle, that is 300.

130

Bunbury said that at least 500 French dead were buried on the battlefield, three-quarters of which were soldiers of the 1ère Légère.[266] As he also estimated that between 2,000 and 3,000 French soldiers were captured, this adds up to a smaller total French loss than that given by Stuart. Other British participants have given their own figures for the French casualties at the battle: the ever-observant Charles Boothby said that 700 French soldiers were buried on the plain and put the total number of French casualties at 3,000 while John Colborne put the total French loss at 2,000, killed, wounded and captured.[267] There is a map of the battle which was engraved and published in early 1807, which in its description of the action put the French casualties at 1,300 killed and 2,770 wounded and captured.[268]

There is no obvious or convincing way in which the various estimates of French casualties can be reconciled. The figure of 1,700 casualties (i.e. 700 bodies and 1,000 prisoners) seems to be a reasonably reliable starting point for computing the French loss and there is no particular reason to doubt Regnier's statement that he had 300 wounded with his army after the battle. This gives around 2,000 as being the total French loss. It might be thought that, in view of Regnier's post-battle estimate of his strength as being 4,000, this figure is out of kilter with the French pre-battle strength of 5,400. But I do not think so, as the figures are all, on the French side at least, uncertain and difficult to verify and wide margins of error should be allowed. The margin of error allowed should be wider for an estimate of 4,000 than for one of 300.

The official returns for the Army of Naples, while appearing to confirm the fact that the French suffered severe losses during the campaign in Calabria, are less specific about the casualties sustained at the battle itself. The earliest return after Maida is dated 18 August and gives the strengths of the various regiments under Regnier's command at levels that are not greatly below those recorded in the return of 30 June. There is a note on the bottom of the return which suggests that it was compiled, perhaps by staff officers in Naples, in the absence of proper, accurate and up-to-date information and certainly it appears not to reflect the casualties that Regnier's army suffered at Maida. The next return, of 18 September, gives a markedly different picture, one which appears to confirm the inaccuracy of the August figures. It shows that the regiments which fought at Maida had, between late June and mid-September, suffered losses of more than 4,200 killed, wounded and captured. It does not apportion the losses between Maida, the sieges of Scylla and Reggio, and the subsequent operations in Calabria, but the figures give a picture of losses that is more credible than those of the August return. In the light of the September return French casualties at Maida of 2,000 does not look unreasonable.[269]

Neither do these French losses, both absolutely and relative to those suffered by the British, seem outlandishly extravagant if one looks at the fire-power to which their infantry was exposed during the battle. In the case of the clash between Compère's brigade and the British Light Battalion – and this is the only phase of the battle for which it is possible to derive any worthwhile statistics – Kempt's men and Dyneley's artillery would have been able, at least in theory, to inflict very heavy casualties on the French.

Since the longest range available to the British belonged to Dyneley's little battery of two four-pounders, it is reasonable to suppose that, at the very latest, Compère's men did not start to come under fire until they were within 650 yards of the British line. From that moment on they would have been exposed to fire from the artillery, firing round shot then case, and ultimately from the muskets of Kempt's soldiers. We know that the 1ère Légère and the 42nd Regiment were ordered to charge when they were about 100 yards from the British line ('half-musket shot') and taking the 'charge' to be the equivalent of six miles per hour, certainly quick enough in full kit, they would have covered the distance in thirty-five seconds or so. I have assumed that the next 100 yards, between 100 and 200 yards of the British position, was covered in forty seconds (i.e. at five miles per hour) and that the first 450 yards took three minutes and fifty seconds (i.e. at four miles per hour). In other words, at these speeds it would have taken Compère's men just over five minutes to cross the 650 yards to the British lines.

Five minutes is not a long time but it would seem an eternity to infantry exposed to enemy fire on flat, open ground and it seems likely that the British took full toll of their enemy. A well-trained gun crew could fire as many as eight rounds a minute, but in practice, for safety reasons, two rounds a minute was the limit; so, in the time that it took for the French to advance to within 200 yards of their lines, the two

132

British guns would have been comfortably able between them to fire sixteen rounds at the enemy. Competent artillerymen would expect to score perhaps ten hits with this number of rounds and, given that a round shot ploughing into massed infantry would be likely to cause about three casualties, could therefore anticipate inflicting perhaps thirty casualties.

Once the enemy had advanced to within 200 yards, the artillery, it is reasonable to suppose, would have started to engage them with case shot; indeed Dyneley specifically states that he fired case in support of Acland's brigade. Shooting at three rounds a minute – case was a less dangerous form of ammunition to load and therefore a more rapid rate of fire was permitted than for round shot – the two four-pounders could have fired at least three rounds each at the enemy in the last 200 yards (taking perhaps a minute and a quarter) of his advance. Each round of case was armed with approximately fifty-five bullets of which two-thirds, say thirty-six, might be expected to hit the type of target that at this range the French infantry presented. So, firing case at the enemy over the last 200 yards of his advance, Dyneley's two guns might anticipate making between 200 and 220 hits.

For the majority of their attack Compère's men had been engaged only by the British artillery; in the final 100 yards they came within range of the Light Battalion's muskets. The India Pattern musket, or 'Brown Bess', the standard British issue of the period, was a notoriously inefficient weapon; it was prone to frequent misfiring and was inaccurate, even in skilled hands. One British officer who fought at Vittoria estimated that at that battle the British and Allied troops scored one hit for every 459 shots fired.[270] Its inherent inaccuracy, the result of loose-fitting bullets or 'windage' and the vagaries of mass manufacture, compounded by any number of factors, including an alarming flash and a heavy recoil, meant that at any range beyond 200 yards it was, for all practical purposes, useless. But, nevertheless, fired in volleys at close range, preferably less than 100 yards, it could be a potent weapon. Well-drilled troops would be able to fire two or perhaps three controlled volleys a minute, at least at the beginning of a fire-fight before the barrels of the muskets became clogged with half-burnt gunpowder.

Kempt faced the French with a total of 730 well-trained men, the

Corsican contingent having gone off in pursuit of the *voltigeurs*, who held their fire, waiting for the moment. The first volley was fired at about 100 yards and the second at very close range indeed; there was no time for a third volley. Both volleys that the Light Battalion fired were lethally effective, the result perhaps of the discipline and marksmanship that had been instilled into the battalion during the previous summer's training in Malta. The impact of the second volley, fired into the French ranks at no more than fifteen yards, must have been devastating. To a body of men that had already suffered considerable casualties to artillery and small arms fire it was the last straw; they broke and fled.

Kempt's 730 men fired two volleys at the enemy and, making some allowance for misfires, we can assume that perhaps 1400 shots were actually fired. The statistics suggest that about 50% of the bullets fired in the first volley, at 90 or 100 yards, and that 75% of those from the second, at fifteen yards, may have hit the target. If this was indeed the case, and it would have represented by contemporary standards exemplary shooting, then it is possible to surmise that the Light Battalion may have scored more than 800 hits in two volleys. Although this would have been musketry of the highest order, eye-witnesses on both sides did comment on the deadly effect of the British shooting.

Taking these figures together it is not over-optimistic to suggest that the 1ère Légère and the 42nd Regiment might have suffered more than 1,000 casualties as a result of British artillery and musket fire during their attack on the Light Battalion. This ignores any further casualties that might have resulted from long-range artillery bombardment of the French before they began their advance; neither does it take account of those killed and wounded by British bayonets as they fled. If the principal strike force of Regnier's army could have lost 1,000 men, nearly half its strength, in five minutes, then a figure of 2,000 for the total French loss does not seem too fanciful.

If we accept a figure of 2,000 as the total French casualties at Maida (and it is perhaps a conservative one) there is a striking difference between the casualties suffered by the two sides. In defeating the French the British inflicted six times as many casualties as they themselves sustained. The French lost more than one man in every three who took part in the battle, which equates to a casualty rate of thirty-seven per cent. The French suffered a mortality rate of thirteen per cent, or about one man in eight. This compares to a mortality rate of 0.8 per cent and a casualty rate of six per cent (one man in sixteen) for the British. In a battle where the numbers engaged on each side were nearly equal the disparity in the losses is remarkable. It emphasizes what a crushing victory Maida was for the British.

Chapter Seven

THE AFTERMATH: "MOPPING UP" AND THE SIEGE OF SCYLLA

"The events of the battle were in some sort told by the mute and motionless, but sad and appalling forms with which the ground was covered; all indeed were still and silent, but all bore the attitude of struggle, of fearful flight or eager chase . . . The route of the flying enemy was thickly tracked through the straggling course of the shallow Amato and up the heights beyond by slaughtered bodies of the 1st Regiment of French Light Infantry, which had ventured to charge ours with the bayonet. All lay in one direction, in the attitude of headlong, desperate flight."[271]

Thus Charles Boothby described the scene on the battlefield immediately after the battle had been won. He had been allowed to leave his post at the beach and had hurried across the plain to see for himself what had happened. Boothby, clearly moved by the human debris of a battlefield, describes finding letters on corpses, many of them in French and written in a female hand.

While his army recovered from its exertions, Sir John Stuart spent the evening as a guest of Sir Sidney Smith (who had belatedly arrived in the Bay of St Euphemia on 3 July) on his flagship the *Pompée*. Smith, as was his wont, regaled his guests with tales of his exploits at Acre and elsewhere, the high point of the evening being his demonstration to Stuart of how to wear a shawl and a turban in the Egyptian style.[272] There was also some discussion between Smith and Stuart of how best to capitalize on the victory. Stuart says that Smith asked him how he (Smith) could be of greatest use, to which he replied that as everything to the south was in the army's power, the best advantage would lie in

Smith "going to the Northward". The following morning Stuart left the *Pompée* with fresh assurances from Smith that he would head north ringing in his ears.[273]

While Stuart and Smith were discussing the finer points of Middle Eastern fashion on the *Pompée* the army was camped on the plain and for one officer at least this was an unpleasant and sleepless night. "The first night we were in bivouac a large snake crawled over me, we were lying down amongst high grass. I felt most uncomfortable afterwards, and hardly closed my eyes again."[274] For two days after the battle the army remained on the plain, idle. Meanwhile Stuart, accompanied by some of his men, went to the village of Maida where he spent the time writing and polishing his dispatches home. For the rest of his army, remaining in the unhealthy climate of the low-lying, marshy plain had more serious consequences: malaria started to set in. As one officer observed: "Great numbers had fever owing to the carelessness of the Quartermaster-General's department, who took up our quarters close to a marsh; although you are sure to get malaria if you sleep anywhere where there is stagnant water and the thermometer between 80 and 90". About sixteen men in the Light Company of the 20th Foot commanded by Colborne died of malaria and Colborne himself was bled for the disease and had his head shaved.[275] By the end of the month the commanding officer of the 78th Foot had reported eight deaths from the disease.[276] Malaria contracted on the plain at Maida was to kill a large number of men in Stuart's army before it was eradicated.

The army remained exposed to malaria on the plain for two days after the battle because Stuart was uncertain what his next move should be. On 6 July he wrote to Smith: "I am going Myself across the mountains with the Chief body of the Army"; in other words he intended to pursue the defeated French.[277] But by then it was already too late; Stuart's failure to mount an effective pursuit immediately after the battle had allowed the enemy to escape his clutches. Colborne's company of the 20th Foot had reached Borgia from where they sent back the news that the French had retreated from Catanzaro. They were now too far away and Stuart, accepting the inevitable, decided against pursuit. According to one source Stuart had been "strongly minded" to pursue the French but wiser counsels prevailed, among them Bunbury and Lefebure of the Engineers.[278] Stuart wrote to Windham, also on 6 July, that he was prevented from pursuing the French by the need to keep the army supplied and, equally importantly, by considerations of the defence of Sicily, the "particular object with which I am charged". He informed Windham that the army would march south before returning to Sicily and cross the Straits as soon as Ferdinand had arranged sufficient of his forces to secure the gains made so far.[279] Stuart also later complained that he had been prevented from pursuing the French by the bifurcation in the expedition's command structure (and the consequent uncertainty) caused by the powers vested in Sir Sidney Smith by Ferdinand in his decree of 28 June.[280] This claim seems rather disingenuous in light of the military considerations that constrained Stuart from giving chase to Regnier. It has more in common with Stuart's wounded vanity and the animus between him and Smith than with any genuine difficulty in commanding the army.

On 7 July Stuart issued orders for the return to Sicily and Oswald's brigade set off towards Monteleone that day, the rest of the troops following later.[281] Stuart may have abandoned the idea of pursuing the beaten French, but he had not forgotten the original aim of the expedition. The army would march south and complete "The Destruction of the Enemy's Establishments on the Shores contiguous to Sicily".[282] Capturing the French strongholds in southern Calabria in order to retard or postpone indefinitely plans for the invasion of Sicily had been one of the objects of the expedition from the outset and now, with Regnier retreating to the north-east, the French strongholds were at the mercy of Stuart's army. The victors of Maida could now reap their reward, the lasting security of Sicily.

The first town to surrender to the British was Monteleone, which, at the approach of Oswald's brigade on 7 July, raised the Sicilian royal standard over its castle. The French garrison of 370 men gave itself up without a shot being fired and on the same day Tropea surrendered to Captain Fellowes of the frigate *Apollo*; here about 100 prisoners were taken. More importantly, the French, intending Tropea to be a secure base for naval operations against Sicily, had stiffened its defences and, as a result, fourteen heavy guns together with a quantity of stores and ammunition fell into British hands. Part of the arsenal that the French had assembled for the invasion of Sicily had been captured.[283]

The next town to fall to the British was Reggio, which surrendered on 10 July. Broderick, who had been left in command in Sicily during the Calabrian expedition, was anxious to prevent the garrison of Reggio joining up with the main French force. Taking the initiative on hearing of the victory at Maida, he gathered together 1200 troops, British and Sicilian (commanded by their brigadier, the Duc de Floresta), and, enlisting the help of Captain Hoste of the *Amphion*, set sail from Messina. After a siege lasting only two days Reggio surrendered and by the terms of the capitulation the garrison was allowed to march out with the honours of war before being taken to Messina. The garrison of the town numbered 632 men, of whom eighty-seven were from the 1ère Légère; 358 of the captured men came from the 42nd Regiment, including their commanding officer and sixteen other officers.

Once Reggio had fallen Scylla remained the only stronghold in French hands between Palmi and Crotone. The commander of the garrison, Colonel Michel, had already, by the 14 July, refused a summons to surrender and preparations for the siege were under way.[284] The British artillery left Maida for Scylla on 6 July, Thomas Dyneley and Captain Pym taking two six-pounders and one howitzer overland and the remainder going by sea. Dyneley and Pym arrived with their guns in front of the castle on 13 July after an arduous journey across the rugged, mountainous country of southern Calabria. The other strongholds along the coast had fallen to the British without any difficulty but Scylla was a different proposition. Boothby, who was present at the siege, described the town as being "in a good state of defence, impregnable to assault, fully garrisoned, and commanded by the chief engineer of Regnier's army". Reggio might have capitulated after two days but Scylla would be a tougher nut to crack.

Colonel Michel, a spirited and experienced officer, was the commander of the engineers attached to the Third Corps. On 1 July, at Regnier's orders, he established himself in the castle with around 250 men, some sappers, about forty gunners and two companies of the 23rd Légère, and at once set about securing supplies and improving the fortifications. When Michel arrived at Scylla the only defences were a pair of batteries guarding the roadsteads and the entrance to the castle was barely defensible; even more alarming was the fact that the water cistern was full of rubble. He had a few days in hand and his men busied themselves to such good effect that by the time the British arrived on the heights above the castle Scylla presented a formidable obstacle. The French had managed to lay in 40,000 rations of biscuit, five oxen and fifty-eight sheep, as well as a quantity of wine. The most serious deficiencies were a shortage of water and a complete lack of medical supplies.

The first skirmishes were with local irregular troops and on 8 July Michel and his men retreated into the castle; two days later some British gunboats opened fire on Scylla. From 11 July the garrison watched Oswald's brigade invest the castle and begin its preparations for the siege. When summoned to surrender once more, he replied that he must see the means whereby the castle could be reduced, i.e. heavy artillery [285] As at present there was none, he would not contemplate surrender.

Scylla occupies a spectacular position on a rocky promontory above the Straits of Messina. The site has been famous since mythological times as the home of Scylla the sea monster who terrorized those mariners who steered too wide a course to avoid Charybdis, the whirlpool. Later it was visited by Odysseus during his long voyage home from the Trojan War. In historical times there has been a castle on the promontory since at least the eighth century and it has always, because of its position, been an important stronghold. The castle that confronted Oswald's men dated largely from after 1783, the year in which a massive earthquake virtually destroyed the previous, seventeenth-century structure.

When the British arrived the tricolour was flying above the castle. The besieging troops would have enjoyed a fine view of the bay below Scylla, of the Straits of Messina and of the Lipari Islands out in the Mediterranean. Many have commented on the beauties of Scylla's position, although one French visitor was less than impressed with the town itself, which to him was "for the most part inhabited by sailors and fishermen and has a pretty miserable look to it".[286] To the left of the castle is the beach and the town and to the right the shore sweeps away round a bay. On the far side of this bay, opposite the castle, Sidney Smith had established a battery and raised the British colours. To the landward side there is a cliff overlooking the castle at a distance of 500–600 yards, in front of which several houses had been built and it was behind one of them that the breaching battery was established.[287] From the top of the cliff the ground rose steadily towards the mountains. It was here that the army was camped, safely out of range of the French artillery. On 15 July, as the British were gathering on the slopes above the town, to the seaward side the soldiers of the 20th Foot, returning to Reggio in transports and feluccas, came under fire from the castle, having foolishly strayed within range of the French guns.

The British began to construct the earthworks from which the heavy artillery would attack the walls. The position of the castle high on a rocky promontory was both a defensive strength in that it was more difficult to take by storm and a defensive weakness in that it meant that no glacis could be erected to protect the walls themselves from artillery fire. Captain Lefebure, who commanded the siege operations, detailed Boothby to construct a breastwork from which the lighter artillery, two twelve-pounders, could fire. Being so close to the enemy – the breast-work was within half-musket shot of the castle – the work had to be carried out under cover of darkness. Boothby and his men succeeded to the extent that by dawn they were adequately protected and could complete the work in relative safety despite being under fire for an hour and a half.[288]

The siege proper of Scylla could now begin and the British batteries kept up a constant fire. Dyneley, who commanded a battery armed with a twelve-pounder and a howitzer, remembered the deafening noise that his guns made.[289] Meanwhile Lefebure continued to bring more and heavier artillery to bear on the castle and by 23 July a battery of three twenty-four pounders had been established within range of the castle. As the firing continued and became heavier the British began to display scaling ladders within 100 yards of the castle, so as to leave the garrison in no doubt as to what was intended.

This demonstration had the desired effect and Scylla surrendered to the British on 23 July. Oswald, anxious to spare the fortifications the effects of a prolonged bombardment, offered Colonel Michel generous terms. Michel, short of drinking water and perhaps aware that there was no likelihood of relief, accepted the terms offered and on 24 July the garrison marched out of Scylla with the full honours of war.[290]

At the fall of Scylla 281 French prisoners surrendered to the British, comprising fifteen officers, thirty-nine NCOs, 199 rank and file and twenty-eight civilians. Scylla also yielded a large amount of booty for its British captors: among the serviceable guns taken were a sixteen-pounder and three twenty-four-pounders. The British also captured a great deal of ammunition, including seventy barrels of gunpowder, 114 filled cartridges for sixteen-pounders, 5,000 ball cartridges and a large amount of roundshot, among many other things. All this was achieved at a very low cost: three soldiers were killed and only eight were wounded.[291] The capture of Scylla was an important achievement; it set the seal on the success of the expedition to Calabria and secured the western end of the Straits of Messina for the British, thereby ensuring that Sicily would be safer still from invasion by the French.

★   ★   ★

The remnants of Regnier's army had retired from the battlefield under artillery cover and protected by their cavalry. The failure of the British to pursue the beaten French army allowed it to escape without further casualties and Regnier hoped that by withdrawing from the battle in reasonably good order he would be able to rekindle his troops' morale. The French army retreated eastwards from Maida towards the Adriatic coast and by the evening of the battle they had reached the village of Marcellina.

The retreat after the defeat at Maida was an unpleasant experience for the defeated French. The hostility of the local population, who frequently attacked the French, and the perennial problem of scarcity of food made it an agonizing trial for Regnier's men.[292] Their progress was further impeded by the presence in the column of some 300 wounded men and, to make matters worse, ammunition was so short after the battle that they could not defend themselves properly against the attacks of the *massi*. Indeed, so acute was the lack of ammunition that Regnier ordered his men to fight with the bayonet alone and to fire their muskets only in the most extreme circumstances. Nor were the officers exempt from the hardships of the retreat: one complained that, for them, conditions were even worse as they had left all their baggage at Monteleone, where it had by now fallen into the hands of the enemy. The officers were denied even the comfort of a clean shirt.[293]

On 6 July the French reached Catanzaro but not before they had been ambushed *en route* and on 8 July entered Crotone, which is on the Adriatic coast to the east of Catanzaro. However, as Crotone proved to be incapable of providing sufficient quantities of food the army returned to Catanzaro, where food was more plentiful, to await reinforcements. Dispatches captured by the British indicate that Regnier had been ordered to retire to Cosenza, on the western side of the peninsula to the north of Maida, to join forces with Verdier, who was himself in an awkward position. Between 1 and 9 July Verdier was attacked by the insurgents and at this point, having suffered 200 casualties, run out of ammunition and received the baleful news of Maida ("*cette fâcheuse nouvelle*") he decided to retreat to Cassano. His objective was as much to avoid fighting the insurgents as to cover Regnier's retreat at that point.[294]

By 25 July Regnier realized that his position at Catanzaro was untenable. He was surrounded by a hostile population and his communications with Verdier to the north had been severed, nor were reinforcements likely to reach him at Catanzaro. He decided to retreat to the north, up the Adriatic coast and so on 26 July Regnier set out once more towards Crotone.

Regnier had been constantly harassed by the insurgents during his retreat from Maida but had, so far, escaped being attacked by the British. This was about to change. On 25 July the 78th Foot, commanded by Lt.-Colonel MacLeod and escorted by the frigate *Amphion* under Captain Hoste, departed to cruise up the Adriatic coast of Calabria. Their object was to assist the Calabrian insurgents in their struggle against the French. On the morning of the 26 July MacLeod spotted a French column on the coastal road, apparently heading for Crotone and, as the French were marching within range of the *Amphion*, she opened fire. The rear of the French column broke, the men fleeing from the frigate's guns to the safety of the mountains.[295] The Polish troops in Regnier's army, we are told, reacted poorly to the attack by a British frigate, so it may be that they were the troops who fled into the mountains in the face of the *Amphion*'s attack.[296]

The *Amphion* and the transports arrived at Crotone on the evening of 27 July to find that the French had not yet reached the town. The British vessels positioned themselves to await the enemy; when the French troops arrived they were fired upon and forced to retire out of range. Deserters brought to the British camp reports of low morale and

143

poor conditions in Regnier's army, but Lt.-Colonel MacLeod was not convinced by these tales of woe: the French had large supplies of food and intended either to mount a stout defence of Crotone or to provide a secure line of retreat for the remaining troops of Regnier's army. Whichever course of action they chose, MacLeod intended to frustrate them.[297]

In the event the French evacuated Crotone on the afternoon of 28 July, leaving their wounded behind, whereupon MacLeod and Hoste summoned the town to surrender. The capitulation allowed for the departure of all the remaining French troops at 10 a.m. on 30 July.[298] The French, having abandoned Crotone to its fate, continued their retreat northwards up the Adriatic coast and on 30 July reached Strongoli. Regnier had done well up to now to maintain discipline among his troops in difficult circumstances but at Strongoli he lost control and they ran amok. Having overcome resistance from the Calabrese, drunken French soldiers looted the town and slaughtered its inhabitants, starting fires which burned much of it to the ground.[299] The town of Corigliano, further up the coast, suffered the same fate. Eventually, sometime after 4 August, Regnier, with fewer than 4,000 men arrived at Cassano, knowing that he would be able to wait there in safety for reinforcements.[300] The hazardous retreat from Maida was over.

The French troops may have reached a safe haven but the war of attrition against the insurgents, the defeat at Maida and the long retreat northwards had inflicted terrible damage on Regnier's army, quite apart from the battle casualties themselves. Uniforms, weapons and kit failed to stand up to the demands of a long campaign in the harsh conditions of Calabria. The men of the 1ère Légère had been reduced to "*une nudité presque entière*"; uniforms that had been end-lessly patched simply fell apart and no replacements were available. Most of the men were barefoot as their boots had disintegrated, worn out by months of marching and counter-marching; their webbing, slings and pouches were in equally poor condition. Worse was the state of the regiment's weapons: a large proportion of the muskets were in urgent need of repair and many of the sabres were damaged. Repairs were difficult to carry out in the field, particularly as the regiment's Master Armourer had been captured at Reggio.[301] The martial splen-dour of the 1ère Légère had evoked the awed wonder of the British as they advanced across the plain at Maida; now, bootless and in rags, they presented a sorry sight.

This picture is repeated in all the regiments of Regnier's army. The 23rd Légère had no boots to replace those worn out by a year's continuous campaigning and its officers, who had lost all their baggage at Maida, were embarrassingly unkempt. The 42nd Regiment were even worse off: their uniforms had entirely disintegrated and the men, with neither tunics nor breeches, were reduced to wrapping themselves in sheets of canvas. Since the beginning of July the regiment had lost 690 muskets, none of which could be replaced in the wilds of Calabria. The Polish and Swiss infantry were likewise suffering from threadbare uniforms, delapidated kit and damaged weapons. The only cavalry attached to the little army, 9th Chasseurs, were in a sorry state: saddles and tack were in urgent need of repair and almost all the troopers needed new boots. The remains of Regnier's corps, cowering in Cassano, looked more like scarecrows than soldiers; half-naked, barefoot and poorly armed, they were a mere shadow of the confident columns that had marched out of Naples to conquer Calabria a few months earlier.

Nor was it just the uniforms, boots and equipment of the French regiments that were in bad condition; their finances were in an equally parlous state. All the regiments reported that pay was in arrears and in some cases the amount owing was substantial. Indeed, overall, by the end of 1806 it was estimated that Regnier's corps was owed about 2,600,000 francs in back-pay and other arrears. Several regiments had lost their cash-boxes and accounts when the British took Monteleone after Maida; the 23rd Légère lost 11,500 francs in this way. The men of the 42nd Regiment had not been paid since 1 May 1806 and the 1ère Légère was owed 13,000 francs of back-pay. The officers were all too often forced, in the absence of regimental funds, to help out their men from their own resources and ruin stared many of them in the face. Several officers of the 1ère Légère, in a few short weeks of subsidizing their men, lost the fruits of fifteen years of saving.[302]

While his men were enduring these privations, Regnier himself, always an independently-minded officer, was in hot water with his superiors. Neither Joseph nor Napoleon was pleased with his failure to defeat the British forces at *"l'affaire de Sainte Euphemie"* but he had also managed to incur the displeasure of his commanding officer in

Naples, Massena. The Marshal had ordered Regnier, after Maida, to join forces with Verdier at Amantea in order to mount an assault on the town. Regnier, retreating northwards along the eastern, Adriatic coast of Italy, knew his regiments were in no condition to cross the mountainous terrain that lay between him and Amantea, on the western shore of the peninsula. This failure to obey orders enraged Massena: he blamed Regnier's disobedience for the failure of his plan to subdue the Calabrian insurrection and he assured Joseph that he had made his displeasure abundantly clear.

The capture of Scylla and the pursuit of the French along the Adriatic coast were the final acts of the expedition to Calabria and by the end of July the British troops had returned to Sicily. Before leaving Calabria Stuart made a tour of the province, escorted by a small detachment of the 20th Dragoons, his purpose being to urge the Calabrese to keep up their resistance to the French. He was also anxious to reassure them that the British withdrawal did not mean that they had been abandoned "totally to the rapacity of the French". Indeed, once the British army was back in Sicily it would have the advantage of secrecy in any future offensive operations against the French which did not exist so long as the army remained in Italy.[303] How reassuring the Calabrese found this argument is, one might think, open to question, but Stuart was genuinely concerned about the treatment that the French had been meting out to the Calabrese. The British regarded the *massi* as, at best, unreliable allies, but, having encouraged (and armed) them in their struggle against the French, felt some degree of moral responsibility for their safety. On 18 July Stuart issued a proclamation in which he drew attention to the attacks by the French on the civilian population of Calabria. In it he made the contrast between the barbarous conduct of the French soldiery and his own humane attitude: had he not, in the aftermath of Maida, offered a reward for each unharmed French soldier brought in to the British lines? The proclamation threatened the French with reprisals should they continue in their attacks on the civilian population and referred pointedly to the 300 or so French prisoners in British hands.[304] Nor was Stuart alone in his concern for the well-being of the Calabrese, for within a week of the news of Maida arriving in London *The Times* was expressing its own sense of foreboding: "While the brilliant success of our army in Calabria is universally felt as a subject of national triumph and exaltation, there are many who shudder for the fate with which the brave Calabrian peasantry are threatened."[305]

Stuart returned to Sicily to find his replacement, General Henry Fox, the younger brother of the Whig politician, Charles James Fox, waiting for him. Fox, who owed his appointment to the change of government earlier in the year, had arrived in Messina on 22 July and assumed command on 29 July. Stuart, having conceived and executed with brilliant success a limited operation which secured the British in Sicily for the foreseeable future, had been relieved of his command. On 30 July Stuart was formally appointed Fox's second in command with responsibility for the conduct of "affairs in the two Calabrias"; that he did not remain to take up the post was, according to Bunbury, due to the news of Moore's imminent arrival.[306] Stuart was prepared to serve under Fox (after all, Stuart had only commanded the army by default at Craig's resignation) but to be junior to Moore as well was more than he could stomach and he resolved to return to England. In fact, although he may not have guessed it, Stuart would in less than two years have the command to himself once more. In the meantime he set off home where he was feted like a hero once the news of Maida arrived.

★　　★　　★

The news of the Battle of Maida caused a popular sensation when it arrived in London. Being a small battle which did not determine the fate of kings, emperors or nations, it lacked the *éclat* of a Waterloo or a Vittoria, but was nevertheless a remarkable victory. The British had inflicted on a proud and battle-hardened enemy a crushing defeat and heavy casualties, yet had themselves suffered very light losses. One of the most notable aspects of the battle was the speed with which the French were defeated, even allowing for the small numbers engaged. Maida, as one French officer put it:

> "was further proof of the uncertainties of military operations: our troops were fired with the spirit which bodes well for victory, they were confident of their strength, every one of them had in previous campaigns given many examples of their courage but nonetheless fifteen minutes was enough to ensure their defeat."[307]

He was referring to the time that it took for the British Light Battalion to break the attack of Compère's troops, the decisive phase, rather than to the course of the whole battle, but nevertheless he makes the point that the issue was decided quickly. The same officer, an eye-witness, expresses the opinion that had Compère's troops kept going forward for only another two minutes they would have reached the British lines and, fired up as they were, would have succeeded in breaking them.[308]

The failure of Compère's troops to smash Kempt's Light Battalion was the decisive phase of the battle. They were the cream of Regnier's army and he relied on them to land the first and crushing blow on the British, thereby opening the way for his other formations to complete the victory. In the event not only did the 1ère Légère and the 42nd Regiment fail to make any impression on the Light Battalion but they were themselves routed. The effect on the morale of the rest of Regnier's army of seeing these revered veterans being slaughtered on the points of the British bayonets cannot be underestimated. Once Compère's men had been defeated the advantage shifted to the British, both in tactics and in morale and Regnier was never able to regain the upper hand.

So what caused the troops of Compère's brigade to be defeated so totally and so quickly? As one might expect, many different explanations have been advanced since the battle was fought. They range from the suggestion that the British attacked the French very quickly, before the latter were formed up or expecting an attack, to the notion that the unfortunately large number of regimental officers killed in the 1ère Légère and the 42nd Regiment resulted in a lack of leadership at a vital time.[309] In the confusion of battle chance plays an important part; the fate of individuals and the turn of a moment can and does have a say in the larger outcome between the conflicting armies. Indeed, the larger outcome is the sum of the individual conflicts. But the experience of the vast majority of those who fought at Maida (or, for that matter, any battle of this era) is lost to us, buried in history.

The received wisdom is that Maida was won by the disciplined and accurate musketry of the British infantry. So far as the decisive phase of the battle is concerned, indeed, this appears to be the case and the statistics relating to British fire-power cited in the previous chapter lend weight to this view of events. Certainly Compère's men were exposed during their advance to withering fire, first from the British artillery, using both round shot and case, and then from the muskets of the infantry. In the five or so minutes that Compère's troops took to advance, they could have suffered as many as 1,000 casualties. Losses on this scale and at this speed, if they occurred, as seems likely, would go a long way towards explaining the defeat of the French.

Kempt's battalion had been recruited from the light infantry companies of the army's regiments precisely with the aim of forming an elite battalion capable of defeating the very best that the French could put into the field. During training in Malta and in Sicily in the earlier part of the year great importance had been attached to musketry and at Maida the results of this hard work spoke for themselves. The Light Battalion fired two volleys into the advancing French in the last 100 yards before the lines met, standing firm while a much larger force (some 2,400 as against the 730-odd British troops) was closing on them in a most warlike and intimidating fashion. It is greatly to the credit of the men of the Light Battalion that they not only held their ground but that they managed to fire two such lethal volleys in such circumstances.

The accurate musketry and discipline of Kempt's troops were major factors in the rout of Compère's brigade, but so too was the superiority that the British enjoyed in artillery, as Stuart himself was quick to acknowledge.[310] The inequality in artillery was a double disadvantage to the French: not only was their infantry exposed to lethal fire while advancing but they were unable effectively to soften up the British Light Battalion in preparation for the assault. The results were disastrous: the British infantry, largely unscathed by artillery fire, were able to mow down the advancing French. Moreover, the fact that Compère's men attacked in line may have increased their losses from British artillery fire. Muir postulates that, at medium to long range, infantry deployed in line presented a better target to artillery than when drawn up in columns.[311]

French generals also protected their massed infantry formations by deploying a swarm of *voltigeurs* out in front of the main body. These troops would snipe at the enemy, causing disruption and loss as well as shielding the main formation from the enemy. Although there were some *voltigeurs* in action at Maida they were confined to the skirmish which was fought out on the far side of the Amato and to the attack on Cole's brigade, but played no part in protecting the main body of

149

Compère's troops. At Maida Regnier sent his best troops into action against the British without either of the elements of protection which they would in normal circumstances have expected. Against troops of lesser quality it might not have been so bad a misjudgment; against Stuart's army and the Light Battalion in particular it was a disastrous miscalculation.

Regnier was overconfident in his conduct of the battle as his decision to attack the British without adequate artillery support or proper provision of skirmishers shows. Regnier simply did not believe that he could fail to win. His overconfidence can be traced to two sources. The first was the contempt, noted earlier, in which Regnier held both the British troops and their commanders. The second source of his overconfidence was the high regard in which he held his own troops, in particular the 1ère Légère and the 42nd Regiment. Their recent victories may have created a false impression of their prowess as the opposition put up by the Neapolitan forces during the conquest of Naples and, latterly, of Calabria could scarcely be described as stiff. Campo Tenese was a victory achieved against a Neapolitan army of doubtful resolution. The British forces they encountered at Maida proved to be a very different proposition. Regnier was defeated but that does not necessarily mean that his decision to attack was wrong; he had to make a decision to act in the way he thought best and was able cogently to justify it to Joseph and should not be judged with hindsight.

Regnier himself blamed the defeat on the irresolution shown by his troops in the battle. He concluded his report to Joseph by saying:

> "I am extremely vexed by these events: I did as I thought best in difficult circumstances and I reckoned that the advantages of a quick and decisive action far outweighed the dangers to which one would have been exposed by delay. But I was not backed up by the . . . heart of my troops."[312]

He did, however, exempt his officers from this criticism. Joseph received an initial report of the opening exchanges of the battle from one of his ADCs who had arrived in Naples from Regnier's head-quarters on 8 July. It described the battle only as far as the defeat of Compère's brigade at the hands of the British Light Battalion. Joseph's views were passed on to Regnier by the chief of staff, Berthier, in a dispatch dated the same day:

"[Joseph] is greatly perturbed and even more astonished by those troops whose conduct has negated your sound plans. The 1ère Légère ought to remember that they have never been afraid of the English and that until now they had known only how to put them to flight. [Joseph] does not know to what to attribute this moment of terrified panic and would like to think that when you receive this letter the troops will be reminded of their shortcomings. [Joseph] wishes the troops to know that he wants the Emperor to overlook their moment of forgetfulness."[313]

Joseph followed Regnier in blaming the irresolution of the troops for the defeat at Maida. He also attributed the defeat to the British superiority in fire power. Others choose to point to different reasons for defeat, for example the exhaustion felt by the French troops as a result of the forced marches required to assemble the army at Maida. There was also in the aftermath of the battle a certain amount of criticism of Regnier's capabilities as a general. Griois, while recognizing Regnier's courage and his military skill and know-how, said that he lacked "the motivating *élan* and inspiring confidence" necessary to rally a body of men and lead them back into battle.[314] This tallies with observations elsewhere that Regnier was a somewhat cold and cerebral general. Napoleon himself, on hearing the news of the defeat, simply pronounced that "General Regnier drew up poor battle plans".[315] Before Maida Regnier was known as a brave and tactically astute general, but the scale and speed of his defeat ruined his reputation. After the battle Regnier was described as "a feeble and irresolute man, narrow-minded and short-sighted".[316]

For the British, there was no doubt that the victory was a magnificent example of the discipline and firmness of their infantry. Stuart, in his official dispatch, praised his troops and ascribed their relatively low casualties to the "happy Effects of that established discipline". He singled out the 58th Foot and de Watteville's for special praise, even though the latter, as part of the reserve, barely took part in the battle.[317] Stuart was as well served by his troops as Regnier was badly served by his. His senior officers performed well in the battle, too: Acland, for example, is singled out by one observer as having "behaved conspicuously well – seizing the colours, and leading his men to the charge".[318]

Whatever the reasons for the French defeat, the suspicion lingers that Maida was a lucky victory for the British. This notion has its origin (as so much in the historiography of the battle) in the account written by Bunbury. In his view, the French should have won: they were numerically superior and well-handled, albeit overconfidently, by Regnier. Nor did the early reverse suffered by Compère's troops herald the end of the French cause; Regnier could still have achieved a 'draw'. In Bunbury's opinion the arrival of the 20th Foot, not the clash between Compère and Kempt, was the decisive moment of the battle.[319]

In some respects Bunbury was right in taking this view. In the first place Sir John Stuart seemed to have little idea of what to do once he had landed on the mainland, and then, having recognized the strength of the French position, he nevertheless decided to attack. Stuart was rescued by Regnier's decision to descend into the plain to give battle: what would have happened to the British attack had Regnier remained in his position on the hills can only be imagined. Once the battle began, it was the courage and resolution of the British infantry that won the day and justified the expedition to Calabria.

There was, however, nothing lucky about the way in which Kempt's men stood firm and fired their devastating volleys into the advancing French. Or about the way in which Cole's brigade withstood the blazing stubble and sniper fire on their flanks. The intervention of the 20th Foot was certainly timely, but to describe it, as Bunbury does, as decisive is to underestimate the importance of the clash between the Light Battalion and Compère's brigade. Not only was it the opening phase of the battle but Compère's brigade were Regnier's best and most experienced troops. The 1ère Légère and the 42nd Regiment were the battering ram with which Regnier intended to smash the British; once the battering ram had itself been smashed Regnier lost the initiative. The effect on the morale of the rest of his army of the all-too-visible defeat of his crack troops was devastating and it knocked the stuffing out of the French army. In this context, the arrival of the 20th Foot was important in that it put the result beyond doubt, but it did not decide the battle. That had already been decided across the plain on the banks of the Amato.

There has also been criticism down the years, again propagated by Bunbury, that Stuart should have made greater efforts to pursue the beaten French forces rather than allow them to retreat in an orderly fashion. The French themselves seem to have been surprised that Stuart did not make a greater effort to follow up the victory, one French historian commenting that Stuart "was so surprised by his victory that he failed to capitalize on it".[320] This criticism is unfair, as it ignores both the resources at Stuart's disposal and the constraints within which he was acting: his troops were exhausted by the heat and by the battle and were very short of ammunition and drinking water. Most importantly of all, the fact that Stuart had no cavalry at his command meant that he was unable to mount any effective pursuit.

Bunbury also suggests that Sidney Smith should have been sent, with 1,000 troops, to relieve the fortress of Gaeta which was, by the time of Maida, in difficulties. He further suggests that Stuart should have sailed towards Salerno and the Bay of Naples in order to force the French to concentrate their resources on the defence of Naples. This would, in turn, he says, have relieved the pressure on Gaeta, although whether these objects would have been attainable must remain a matter of speculation. The siege of Gaeta was by then well advanced, indeed the fortress surrendered on 18 July, having been under siege since April. Stewart in his book on Maida asserts that "it was Sir Sidney Smith's vanity and egoism which limited the exploitation of the victory".[321] It may well be that Smith ploughed his own furrow for much of the time but Stewart's assertion is wide of the mark and ignores the constraints that faced the British commanders after the battle.

The most important point is that these criticisms ignore the reasons for which the expedition in Calabria was launched. Its aim was to make a pre-emptive strike against the French in Calabria to disrupt their preparations for the invasion of Sicily and to dislodge them from the mainland side of the Straits of Messina. With the capture of Reggio, Scylla and large quantities of equipment and munitions, this object was successfully fulfilled. It was the defeat of Regnier's army at Maida that allowed the British to reduce Scylla at their leisure and secure the future of Sicily in British hands. Once the French had been defeated there was no justification for pursuing them (especially bearing in mind Stuart's lack of cavalry) into the hinterland. Indeed, to do so would have put at risk the safety of the British force and jeopardized the remaining object of the expedition, taking the French strongholds.

As for pursuing the wider object of relieving Gaeta, this was far beyond the scope (as well as the capacity) of Stuart's expedition.

It is important, too, to remember that the "Descent on Calabria" was conceived and planned within the discretion granted to General Craig (and to Stuart as his deputy) by the original orders of March 1805. In these it was made perfectly clear that the principal object of the expedition was to secure Sicily from the French. The expedition that resulted in Maida was never intended to be anything more than a pre-emptive strike at a favourable moment to disrupt the French preparations for the invasion of Sicily. In other words it was conceived wholly as a measure to strengthen the British hold on Sicily.

As such it was a brilliant success. The French army in Calabria and French arms in general suffered a humiliating defeat at Maida. All the preparations that had been made for the invasion of Sicily were set at nought. The capture of Reggio and Scylla forcibly removed the French from the Straits of Messina, which was the only possible jumping-off point for the invasion of Sicily. Large quantities of equipment and munitions fell to the British and the insurrection in Calabria was given great impetus. The French themselves suffered severe losses as a result of the campaign: one historian of the campaign suggests that the French losses in Calabria and Naples during 1806 amounted to around 11,500 men, killed and wounded. Of these, he suggests, perhaps 4,000 casualties were attributable to Stuart's operations on the mainland of Italy.[322]

★   ★   ★

'Column and Line'? French tactics at the Battle of Maida

The attack by Compère's troops on the Light Battalion was the most important, the decisive phase of the battle yet how they launched their attack has long been a matter of controversy. It comes down to whether they advanced in line or in column. The most reliable accounts of the battle point to the French infantry attacking drawn up in line; that is to say, each company was ordered to deploy into three lines, rather than continue the attack in the column formation in which they had descended the scarp from their camp.

The received wisdom is that the French infantry of the

154

Revolutionary and Napoleonic eras went into battle in column, a formation that had been developed to make the best use of the large number of relatively poorly-trained and ill-disciplined troops who had been conscripted into the army during the early years of the Revolution. The column maximized the impact of an infantry formation's assault while allowing its officers and NCOs to keep control of the soldiers. Sir Charles Oman, the founding father of modern military history, is responsible for propagating the idea that the French infantry of this time always fought in columns. The British infantry, by contrast, always fought in line and Sir Charles used the Battle of Maida as his example of the inherent superiority of the line over the column and, hence, of British infantry tactics over those employed by the French.

Nor, at Maida, is the question of 'column and line' confined to the realms of theory. It is a key practical issue, as the tactics adopted by Regnier and Compère would have had a decisive influence on how that crucial phase was contested and therefore on how it was decided and so, ultimately, on the result of the battle. It may be, for example, that Regnier ordered his men forward in line because he thought they would suffer fewer casualties advancing in that way rather than in a dense column which would present an inviting target for the British guns. In making this decision he would have been aware of the fact that he lacked the artillery to 'soften up' the enemy infantry and artillery before attacking. It may also be the case that, fighting in line, the French infantry lacked the momentum that a column would have given them and that this was a contributory factor in their failure to reach the British lines.

The controversy over 'column and line' at Maida has intermittently burst into life since Oman first pronounced on the subject before the First World War. Oman's view that the French attacked in a column formation held the ring, more or less, until the 1980s.[323] Since then the weight of opinion, in a number of books which have covered the subject, has moved in favour of the view that Regnier ordered his men to draw up in line.[324] In 1997 John Stewart published the first (and hitherto only) work devoted entirely to Maida.[325] Any, quite reasonable, expectation that this book would provide a definitive answer to the 'column and line' debate was doomed to disappointment as Stewart, curiously, fails even to address the issue. The most recent contribution to the debate is Rory Muir's *Tactics and the Experience of Battle in the Age of Napoleon*, a fascinating study of how armies fought and what it was like to fight in the battles of the time. Muir does not go into any great detail about the tactics employed by the French at Maida but he does assert strongly that the French infantry attacked in line.[326]

Muir states the fact that the French attacked in line at Maida in a way that suggests that he considers it both obvious and plainly correct, but the question is by no means as simple as that. Diligent historians over a period of eighty years have taken, in good faith, the contrary view. In order to arrive at a definitive answer to the question we must turn to the original accounts of the battle, to the evidence of those who were there, who saw and recorded what happened.

The starting point for any consideration of Maida is Bunbury's eyewitness account. In the key passage he writes: "Their 1ère Légère . . . led on by General Compère (and supported by a regiment of Poles), advanced in line upon the brigade of British Light Infantry".[327] The accuracy of Bunbury's history has been impugned on the grounds that it was written some forty years later, but he had, apart possibly from Stuart, been in the best position to observe the course of the battle and it provides strong evidence that the French attacked in line.

Major Roverea in his account of the battle also states clearly that the French advanced in line. "The *coup d'oeil* was magnificent – our fine troops as steady and in as good order as on the parade ground, *vis-à-vis* the French also in line, their arms glittering in the sun . . . At 9 o'clock all the enemy's line advanced on us and the battle began."[328] Roverea, an experienced soldier, had been sent, in his capacity as Cole's ADC, to order the British 'flankers' across the Amato to flush out the French *voltigeurs* positioned there. So he was in an excellent position to observe the French advance. Moreover, elsewhere in his account of the battle he demonstrates that he differentiates clearly between the column and the line. This is not always the case in the sources – sometimes one is left with the suspicion that the terms 'column' and 'line' are used interchangeably without strict regard for their technical, military meaning. Roverea was killed in 1813, so his account of Maida must have been written within a few years of the battle.

Probably the best view of the oncoming French was that enjoyed (if that is the word) by Thomas Dyneley, an officer in the Royal Artillery. Dyneley was positioned with his guns on the right ten yards in front of the Light Battalion. Writing to a brother officer two months later he said: "Their General [Regnier] told them the English were advancing loaded with riches and that they would go down, plunder and drive them into the sea. And sure enough down they did come, in line, in the finest order it is possible to conceive."[329]

Major David Stewart, second in command of the 78th Foot, wrote a detailed account of the battle as part of his history of the Highland Regiments published in 1822. He refers to Regnier leading his army down the hill in three lines and, once on the plain, forming them into two lines of equal numbers. Stewart, once the smoke had cleared, would have had a better view than most as he was riding a horse and his account has a ring of accuracy and authenticity to it.[330]

Captain Charles Pasley of the Royal Engineers was attached to the Light Battalion during the battle. He notes that the French seemed to be moving off to their right in what appeared to be an attempt to turn the British left and then saw the French "forming a formidable line". He refers also to "the two lines" approaching each other. While Pasley is rather vaguer than some of the other witnesses, we should give credit for the fact that his account is contained in a diary and is therefore presumably a near-contemporaneous record.[331] Pasley, elsewhere in his account, makes it clear, like Roverea, that he distinguishes between columns and lines.

Not all of the records of Maida left by British officers or soldiers cast light on the controversy. Richard Church, the adjutant of the Light Battalion, and John Colborne of the 20th Foot, both had active roles in the battle and left some record of the battle without mentioning the question of 'column and line'. Oddly, Sir John Stuart does not, in any of his official despatches after Maida, mention how the French came arrayed.

One of the best-known French commentators on the campaign in Calabria in 1806, the witty and well-informed letter writer Paul-Louis Courier, did not fight at Maida. Many of the French accounts of the battle are very inaccurate, sometimes even misleading. The more extravagantly inaccurate of these often appear to have drawn on the largely fictitious contemporary account of the battle written by a Neapolitan nobleman of rabidly pro-French sympathies. Some of the

French accounts do, however, throw some light on the question of how their men went into battle.

Regnier himself wrote a long report to Joseph about the battle and the events leading up to it which illuminates many aspects of the campaign and of Maida itself, although it is, perhaps understandably, somewhat self-justifying. In a strange parallel to the reports of his opponent, Stuart, Regnier's report does not say in what formation he ordered his troops to attack. Describing the critical phase of the battle he writes: "*Le 1ère et le 42e régiments, forts de deux mille quatre cents hommes, sous les ordres du general Compère, ont passé le Lamato et se sont formés en bataille, ayant leur gauche au Lamato. Le 4e batallion suisse et douze compagnies du régiment polonais . . . ont passé le Lamato au centre, et se sont formés en second ligne par échelons derrière le droit du 42e régiment.*"[332]

Griois, who commanded the French artillery, wrote an account of the battle between 1827 and 1831. Griois is important because he is one of the very few French eyewitnesses who offers a credible account of the battle. He says that Regnier's original plan was to attack the British in their camp until he saw the British marching towards him, apparently to turn his left flank. Prompted into a change of tactics, Regnier ordered an attack on the British army on the plain and the French then advanced towards the enemy at great speed in columns, the *état major* at their head. "The columns then deployed, while still advancing towards the English who were likewise advancing into battle and who seemed to be waiting for us. The general, counting on attacking with his left, had positioned his main forces there, drawn up in two lines." This, on the face of it, seems to be good authority for the proposition that the French attacked in line. There are other references to the line formation in Griois's account of the battle, too.[333]

The eyewitness accounts of participants from both sides are the best but by no means the only source of evidence on the course of the battle. There are also a number of contemporary accounts by those who, while they did not fight in the battle, were able to give a generally accurate version of events without providing the type of specific, operational detail required by the modern historian.

One such is Boothby's account of the battle in which he says: "Just as that thing, which it is said has never happened, viz. the equal shock of opposing lines of troops, seemed inevitable, just as the two regiments seemed in the very act of contact, the French Light Infantry, as a man, turned round and fled."[334] This has been cited in support of the argument that the French attacked in line but, it seems to me, it scarcely amounts to a positive proof, particularly if one considers that Boothby was not at the battle itself. He had been ordered to remain at the beachhead to strengthen its defences and watched events, at a distance of several miles, from the Bastion di Malta. He was later excused duty and arrived on the field of battle after the day was won. So his account, while having a ring of contemporary authority and authenticity about it, is not an eyewitness account such as those offered by Dyneley, Stewart and the others.

The evidence of the eyewitnesses to the battle, particularly those on the British side, points strongly to the fact that the French did indeed attack in line formation. It is striking that, of the British eyewitnesses, none of them say that the French attacked in column. Most of those whose accounts of Maida survive seem to have been advantageously positioned to watch events unfold. Similarly, the most reliable French account, that of Griois, states that they deployed into line to attack. The contemporary sources are, in this case, the best evidence and their conclusion is clear: General Compère's brigade formed into line to attack Kempt's Light Battalion.

*   *   *

News of Maida filtered only slowly back to the governments of the two sides. Joseph, in Naples, received on 8 July a report of events leading up to and including the defeat of Compère's attack. He received no further news until Colonel Lebrun arrived in Naples with Regnier's full report of the battle on 16 July. Lebrun was immediately sent on to Paris and the news had reached the Emperor at Saint-Cloud by 26 July. Predictably, he was furious: "I see that you are conducting all your military operations off the wrong foot," he wrote to the hapless Joseph in Naples.[335]

The news took a great deal longer to reach London. This was partly because it had further to travel but this was not the only reason as Stuart's ADC, charged with taking the official dispatches to London, was still on board the *Endymion* at Faro on 21 July, more than a fortnight after the battle. Rumours began to circulate in London about a battle in Calabria. The first report of the battle in *The Times* appeared on 8 August, when the newspaper quoted a report from Naples carried in one of the less important Parisian papers. *The Times* comments that "It is difficult to give implicit credit to this intelligence. It is not very likely that nine thousand English would quit the island of Sicily, with the defence of which they were specially charged, for the purpose of making a descent upon the Peninsula, an operation which could be productive of no permanent advantage."[336]

By 21 August *The Times* had changed its tune. Having received the latest batch of newspapers from Paris, it now concluded that reports of a battle in Calabria were "well founded".[337] By 30 August the newspaper was becoming exasperated by the lack of proper news: "It is now near two months since a detachment of our army landed in Calabria, and no official accounts have as yet reached this country of its proceedings."[338] But its readers did not have long to wait.

On 2 September the first official report of the battle arrived in Britain. It was the report published from Palermo by Ferdinand and concluded that the victory won by Stuart was "most decisive".[339] This was published in *The Times* the following day, along with Stuart's letter to Broderick, his second in command in Sicily, of 5 July. On 4 September Captain Buckley arrived at the War Office bearing Stuart's official dispatches. They were published in *The Times* the next day.

★   ★   ★

The news of Stuart's victory at Maida was greeted with rapturous enthusiasm in England. The hero of the hour, the General himself, was summoned on his return to these shores to an audience with the King and basked in the warm glow of royal gratitude: created a Knight of the Bath within a week, he was given permission to use the title of "Count of Maida" he had been granted by the grateful Ferdinand and awarded a pension of £1,000 a year for life.[330] George III ordered a medal to be struck to commemorate the battle: the 'Maida' medal was only awarded to seventeen officers who had fought at the battle; all other ranks who had been engaged at Maida had to wait until 1848 for their campaign medal.

The parliamentary tributes to Stuart and his army were generous and marked by some splendid flights of rhetoric. Lord Grenville, the Prime Minister, proposing a vote of thanks in the House of Lords, told the House that the army at Maida was "most distinguishable for its display of heroic valour". William Windham, the Secretary of War, expressed the nation's gratitude to Stuart and his gallant army in the House of Commons. There has, Windham declared, "been so very general, so very lively, and so very proper a feeling" throughout the country about the victory at Maida. There was, he said, "one peculiar characteristic which belonged to this distinguished service, namely, the accession it produced to our stock of national glory, the most valuable possession of a great nation".[341]

The Lloyd's Patriotic Fund had in recent years become more accustomed to decorating the heroes of naval actions: a fine jewelled sword was often the reward for the naval captain who pulled off some daring stroke against the enemy. On receiving news of the triumph at Maida, it acted swiftly both to mark the momentous victory and to provide for those killed or wounded and their dependants. At a specially convened meeting of the Trustees Sir John Stuart was awarded a commemorative vase to the value of £300. All the officers who had been wounded at the battle were recognized by the Fund in some way: Lt.-Col. Moore, for example, received a £100 sword and Ensigns McKenzie and McGregor were awarded £25 each. But it was not just the officers who benefited from the Fund's largesse: gratuities were awarded to all the soldiers wounded at the battle and the Trustees voted to provide relief for the dependants of all those killed.[342]

Thus was the victory at Maida formally commemorated, but the wide public interest in the battle ensured that it was commemorated in many other, less formal, ways. There was a steady flow of aquatints and engravings of the battle, which were printed for sale to the public: one by Wilson, published by Foden in 1807, offered an engraved plan of the battle supplemented with a detailed narrative of the action. Cardon produced an engraving of Stuart in uniform from a portrait by Wood which was published in 1806. These and the many other images of the battle, as prints, enjoyed a wide circulation at the time.

While the engravers and printmakers were busy keeping pace with the demand for memorabilia of Maida, the songwriters, it seems, were equally hard at work. One of them, according to the unabashed sales puff of its frontispiece, was "Sung with the most Unbounded Applause by Mr Braham, at the Bath & London Concerts"[343]. The first verse runs as follows:

"Strike, strike the Harp to Glory lift the strain,
Victory shouts on bright Euphemia's plain,
Sound sound the chords, let peal of rapture rise
With swelling symphonies, swelling symphonies salute the
    skies."

The poets too joined in with the populist songwriters; one amateur versifier who set pen to paper to commemorate Maida was one Lt.-Col. Richard Scott of the East India Company. Scott's epic poem about the battle is both heroic and rigidly patriotic in tone.

"Behold, in awful march and firm array,
Britain's determined columns shape their way!
Death (in approaching terrible) imparts
An anxious horror to the bravest hearts."[344]

Sir Walter Scott, a rather more accomplished poet than his namesake of the East India Company, also noticed and admired the achievements of Stuart's army and, although he does not seem to have written any commemorative verses, he did name his dog, an imposing deerhound, after the battle. Scott was keenly interested in military matters – he was an enthusiastic officer in his local Yeomanry – and in the course of the war against France he wrote about the political situation in Europe in the summer of 1807 after the Treaty of Tilsit had, seemingly, confirmed Napoleon's hegemony over Europe.

"When Europe crouch'd to France's yoke,
And Austria bent, and Prussia broke,
And the firm Russian's purpose brave
Was bartered by a timorous slave."[345]

A similar sense of powerlessness had prevailed the previous summer: the humiliations of Ulm and Austerlitz were fresh in the memory and Napoleon ruled Europe from the toe of Italy to the Pas de Calais. Apart from Trafalgar the news had been unremittingly bad for Britain and her allies since the resumption of war and, for that matter, for long before then.

The reputation of the Royal Navy was second to none. It had

repeatedly taken on and defeated all comers and the 'walls of oak', Britain's best hope of defence in 1806, stood between the nation and invasion. The reputation of the British army was, by contrast, not so good. It had enjoyed some success in far-flung colonies against poorly equipped native forces, for example Sir Arthur Wellesley in India, but in the European theatre the British army was unproven, perhaps even suspect. The expedition to Holland in 1799 could hardly be counted a success, nor did Lord Cathcart's expedition to northern Germany in late 1805 achieve anything at all. The Anglo-Russian expedition to Naples in November 1805 retreated ignominiously in the face of the advancing French without a shot being fired in anger. Sir Ralph Abercomby, it is true, worsted the French at Alexandria in 1801 but it was hardly a resounding victory. Before the outbreak of the Peninsular War in 1808 the record of the British army did not bear comparison with that of the French. This war was to re-establish the reputation of British arms and generalship.

But in 1806 the reputation of the British army was far from fearsome. General Menou, who led the French forces at the battle of Alexandria in 1801, also thought poorly of the prowess of the British military. Sir John Fortescue wrote of Menou that:

> "he despised his enemy [the British] as very reasonably he might; for the English military enterprises since the beginning of the war had almost invariably failed in ignominy . . . Better testimony could not be found to the contempt into which Pitt's Ministry had brought the British Army".[346]

Regnier, who served under Menou in Egypt and shared his opinion of the British army, had seen nothing by the time of Maida to alter his assessment of the British army.

This was why the British victory at Maida was so rapturously received. It showed that the army was capable of taking on and defeating the French in battle; Maida demonstrated that the French armies, however high their reputation, could be defeated by solid, well-disciplined troops. The armies of Britain's allies had proved no match for the French, but Maida showed that the British army was a force to be reckoned with. It offered the first evidence that the British could mount a challenge to the French on the continent of Europe, the first rays of hope that the army could emulate the deeds of the Navy.

Windham summed up the importance of Maida to the House of Commons: "The enemy . . . had persuaded other nations, that they were as superior to us by land, as we were to them by sea; and the delusion seemed to have prevailed on the continent. But the Battle of Maida had broken the charm".[347]

Epilogue:

THE FRENCH RECAPTURE OF SCYLLA
JANUARY & FEBRUARY 1808

The capture by the British of Scylla in July 1806 was one of the most significant trophies of the Battle of Maida, such was its importance to the defence of Sicily. For the French it was equally vital, as control of Scylla was an essential prerequisite of any attempt to invade Sicily across the Straits of Messina. The Peace of Tilsit, signed between the French and Russian Emperors in July 1807, brought peace to central and northern Europe and allowed Napoleon to shift his attention south once more. The invasion of Sicily was still a project dear to Napoleon's heart: not only would it unify his brother Joseph's kingdom, it would drive the hated Bourbons from Italy and deprive the Royal Navy of the use of the ports on the island.

The local situation in Calabria by the end of 1807 was more conducive to a fresh attempt to invade Sicily because the insurrection that had been blazing since the time of Maida had largely been suppressed. The fall of the town of Amantea, on the west coast of the peninsula, was a milestone in the suppression of the revolt as it had been an important base for the brigands. In December 1806 Verdier made an unsuccessful attempt to storm the town, but, after a siege, it fell to the French in February 1807. By the end of the year Calabria was more peaceful than it had been at any time since the French invasion.

Joseph had not pressed an attack on Scylla during 1807, despite Napoleon's urgings that he should do so. It is not clear whether this is because Joseph failed to grasp the importance of controlling the castle or whether he thought that he could take it at a moment's notice. In any event the French made no attempt during 1807 to recapture Scylla and, by 27 November, when Joseph issued Regnier with orders to start operations, it was clear that nothing short of a full-scale siege would

165

retake the castle. The British had used the intervening period to strengthen Scylla's defences; among the improvements was a stairway cut in the rockface between the castle and the beach. Facing seawards, it was protected from the likely direction of enemy fire, which made it easier to supply the castle from Sicily and also allowed the garrison an escape route should things become too difficult.[348]

The French began the preparations for the siege of Scylla at the very end of 1807. On 31 December Colonel Montmajor, the chief engineer of the French army in Calabria, established a base at Seminara incorporating a magazine, a hospital and a barracks, from which the army could be supplied with all the equipment it would need.[349] The campaign to recapture Scylla had now begun in earnest. Up to then the British had used the *massi* to hamper the progress of the French by, for example, blocking the mountain passes and by destroying the paths that led down to Scylla.[350]

Until the end of the year the *massi* had beaten off all French attempts to dislodge them from the heights of Melia above the town by making full use of the cover provided by some dry-stone walls. On 31 December sappers demolished these walls and, now exposed, the *massi* were attacked by three battalions of French infantry and a detachment of cavalry, commanded by General Millet. Driven back, they were forced to seek safety nearer Scylla, leaving the French troops to occupy the positions above the town. On New Year's Day the French brought up two further infantry battalions and advanced their line to Faoazzina and Bagnara, thus completing the investment of Scylla.[351] Regnier had showed his hand.

The key to Scylla was heavy artillery. If the French were to capture the town and castle they would have to be able to bring up artillery pieces capable of breaching the walls. They could not hope to take the castle by surprise from the seaward side, nor was a frontal assault from the landward side practicable. The main difficulty in bringing artillery to Scylla was the appalling state of the roads in Calabria and, although the French had built some military roads in 1806 as part of the preparations for the invasion of Sicily, these did not reach Scylla. Once his army had driven the *massi* back onto Scylla and had surrounded the town, Regnier ordered (2 January) the construction of a road that would allow siege artillery to be brought up from the arsenal at Seminara to Scylla.[352] Regnier's soldiers began to build the road and, despite heavy rain and snow, by 19 January it had reached the French positions at Melia. It was hard, slow work as the continual rain necessitated the laying of many bundles of faggots to ease the passage of the guns. The effort was worthwhile, however, as by that date two twenty-four-pounders, a sixteen-pounder, four twelve-pounders and eight smaller calibre guns had been brought up to the French lines.

To the British garrison of Scylla the build-up of French troops in the area must have appeared menacing. General Sherbrooke, who now commanded the British forces in Sicily, reported in early January that the French had so far been receiving their reinforcements in small parties.[353] Scylla had been put in the best possible state of repair, but he was not optimistic that the castle could hold out for long should the French be able to bring up siege artillery to within breaching range. But, as he assured the Secretary of War, Scylla would be held "until further resistance would become an act of imprudence".[354] The garrison was commanded by Major Robertson of the 35th Foot (who had distinguished himself at Maida) and consisted of 200 British troops, made up from detachments of the 27th, 58th and 62nd Foot and the Royal Artillery, strengthened by the presence in the town of some 4/500 *massi*. The garrison of Scylla continued to do everything in its power to hold up the French by making frequent sorties against the enemy and one of them, a night attack at Bagnara, resulted in a lively skirmish in the course of which the *voltigeurs* of the 23rd Légère suffered heavy casualties.[355] However, not all of these sorties by the garrison were successful; Regnier reports that one made by 600 troops, half British and half Calabrian, at Canatello on the night of the 26/27 January was repulsed with heavy cost by the *voltigeurs* of the 62nd Ligne.[356]

By the end of January Regnier, despite having assembled a small siege train before Scylla, seemed reluctant to attack, preferring to await the arrival of more artillery. Regnier did not have as long to wait as he might have feared for the necessary reinforcements: the weather, events and the chance of war unexpectedly intervened. Despite the recent construction work the appalling state of the roads in Calabria forced the French to attempt to bring artillery and supplies to Regnier by sea from Naples. The Royal Navy was often able to intercept these convoys as they made their way along the coast, but the prevailing bad weather made it difficult for the British vessels to maintain their inshore stations. The sloop *Kingfisher*, normally stationed off Capri, was blown offshore by gales at the beginning of January. In her absence two or three convoys of guns and ordnance stores had managed to pass down the coast from Naples to Pizzo and thence on to Scylla.

Regnier was further reinforced when the town of Reggio surrendered to the French on 2 February, the large Neapolitan garrison having put up no effective resistance at all. General Cavaignac had begun to close on the town on 30 January but lacked the artillery to breach the walls until 2 February; once it arrived the defenders promptly surrendered. The fall of Reggio sparked off a row between the king and his general due to the fact that Regnier had failed to accept the surrender of the town in Joseph's name. The king took terrible umbrage at this slight to his *amour propre*: "He [Regnier] ignores the fact that I have visited both the town of Reggio and the castle, that I have received in person an oath of loyalty from its inhabitants . . . I only lost this as a result of '*l'affaire de Sainte Euphemie*'; it must be restored to the king of Naples."[357] This outburst makes it clear that the defeat at Maida still rankled and that he held Regnier wholly responsible. But for all the ruffling of egos it caused, the fall of Reggio was, militarily, a great success for the French. Fifty officers and 700 NCOs and other ranks of the garrison fell into their hands and, more importantly, they also captured nine pieces of artillery of varying calibres at Reggio; these were welcome additions to Regnier's siege train.[358] The biggest windfall, by which the French secured the use of a further five twenty-four pounders, was the most unexpected and it sealed the fate of Scylla.

On 29 January four Sicilian gunboats, accompanied by two British transports, the *Ellice* and the *William*, were stationed off the Calabrian shore to prevent supplies and reinforcements reaching the French forces besieging Reggio. The gunboats attempted to run to Messina that night, but conditions were too rough and they were forced to return to their original anchorage, where they were joined during the night by a fifth gunboat. The following morning, the 30th, the weather was much worse; reports had reached the gunboats that the French were advancing from the mountains and at about 10 a.m. the French began to appear in numbers. At 11 a.m. half the crew of each gunboat was transferred to the *William*, by which time the French had taken up protected positions on the shore and were firing steadily at the gunboats. The transports, obliged to defend the gunboats which could neither use their guns nor, because of the wind, leave the shore, were returning a brisk fire of round shot and grape at the French troops. Lieutenant Hawke of the *Glattern*, which had recently arrived at the scene, suggested that the guns (of the gunboats) should be thrown overboard and the boats scuttled in order to prevent them from falling into enemy hands. Before this could be done more French troops arrived on the shore and opened fire with artillery.

The crews of the immobile gunboats continued with muskets to return the enemy's fire, but the French infantry and artillery were now well established on the shore and beginning to pepper the *William*. She had been badly damaged, taking eighteen shot, four of which were below the waterline, through her hull from twelve- and eighteen-pounder guns. She had shipped four-and-a-half feet of water in her hold and her foremast was disabled. Hawke now ordered that the cables of both the transports be cut so that they could get out of range of the French for their own safety. The *Ellice* remained close to the *William* and both transports returned safely to Messina.[359]

The gunboats, trapped on a lee shore, were not so fortunate. The French soldiers, grenadiers from the 62nd Regiment and *voltigeurs* from the 1st Regiment continued to pour fire into the gunboats until the grenadiers waded out, boarded them and forced them to surrender.[360] The French managed to land all the guns from the five captured gunboats.[361] As the gunboats were each armed with a twenty-four pounder this constituted a major success for the French. It had negated in a few hours the efforts of the British over a period of months to prevent the French moving their heavy artillery to the Straits of Messina.

The British did not intend to let the French escape with their valuable prizes. At 3.20 p.m. on 30 January Captain Downe of the *Bittern* received signals from the *Glattern* informing him of the capture of the gunboats. Captain Seccombe (the senior British naval officer at Messina), on receiving this news, went aboard the *Delight* and both ships made towards the Calabrian shore, about two miles north of Reggio, intending to prevent the French from landing the captured guns. By the time the two ships reached the Calabrian shore it was dark and at about 6 p.m. the wind began to strengthen. The *Delight*, manoeuvring in the dark against strong winds and currents, ran aground on the Calabrian shore whereupon she was attacked by the French and, after stiff resistance, captured. Downe had received this disastrous news at about 7 p.m. that evening when the boat party he had sent to Seccombe for orders returned to the *Bittern*. Downe was ordered to go to the *Delight*'s assistance, but the bad weather prevented him from doing so that evening. Shortly afterwards the survivors of the *Delight* reached the *Bittern* bringing reports of the death of the captain of the *Delight*, Handfield, and the serious wounding and capture of Seccombe.[362]

At daybreak on 31 January the *Bittern* attacked the *Delight*; by this time there were many French soldiers on board the *Delight*. There was a fierce fight during which the crew of the *Bittern* fired burning oil-soaked missiles on to the *Delight* in an attempt to set her alight. As this was not immediately successful, Downe dispatched a boat party to set fire to the *Delight*, and at about 3 p.m. she blew up.[363] But Downe's action was too late to prevent the French from removing the *Delight*'s guns, two eight-pounders and sixteen twenty-four-pounder cannonades.[364]

The loss of the five gunboats and the large-calibre guns on board to the French was a serious reverse to British hopes of holding Scylla. It was compounded by the bungled attempt to rescue the gunboats in very difficult conditions and the consequent loss of the *Delight* and her guns. The received wisdom, propagated by Bunbury, is that the Sicilian gunboats defected to the French. Bunbury watched with Sherbrooke, from the Sicilian side of the Straits, as events unfolded, but, despite being an eyewitness to the drama, seems to have jumped to the wrong conclusion.

None of the official reports, British or French, mention that treachery was the reason for the gunboats being captured: Sherbrooke himself simply states that the gunboats had fallen into French hands. Had treachery been involved, Sherbrooke had no reason for not mentioning it, particularly as it would have amounted to a further warning about an ally whose reliability was already suspect. Collingwood and the other naval officers who reported on the incident stress that the gunboats were trapped onshore by the weather and only surrendered after a fight. These accounts leave no doubt that the gunboats did not defect to the French. Even Joseph, who had more reason than most to broadcast any act of treachery by the Sicilians, reported that the gunboats were captured by the French as a result of military action.

The historian who first challenged Bunbury's version of events explains the discrepancies in their accounts by saying that Bunbury may not have read the relevant documents.[365] Bunbury was writing many years after the events in question and, although an eyewitness, he watched events unfold from across the Straits of Messina on a January day in poor weather. These factors (or perhaps some deep-seated prejudice) may account for his treachery theory.

The French, their artillery reinforced by the captured guns, began to tighten the noose round Scylla. They came down from the heights of Melia on 6 February and began to establish their batteries. On 7 February Regnier reported to Joseph that the work of bringing the heavy artillery down to within range of the walls was nearly complete and that the first batteries would be armed and ready by 9 February.[366] Nor had the British been idle during the long period of inaction before the siege proper began. "The English and the insurgents," Regnier wrote, "are shut up in the town and the castle. They have cut loop-holes in the outside houses and cut off all the streets." He added that the British had evacuated the entire civilian population of Scylla and their possessions to Sicily; only British troops and the *massi* now remained in Scylla. "The English," Regnier opined, "will defend the castle and town out of national *amour propre* and will drag the siege out for as long as they can."[367]

With the French in position in front of Scylla the skirmishing between the *massi* and the French became fierce. The *massi*, supported by the artillery in the town, displayed great bravery in their attacks on the French. Matters came to a head when, on 9 February, the French infantry launched a powerful attack and the *massi* were forced back into the town. Once the Calabrese had been driven back into Scylla they were evacuated to Messina; not a single one was captured by the French.[368] This was an act of mercy by the British who were only too aware of the appalling treatment meted out by the French to Calabrian insurgents who fell into their hands.

Regnier had assembled an impressive force for the siege of Scylla; indeed, according to Robertson, he had more than 6,000 men in all. In fact the French had assembled a force of nearly 4,900 men for the operations against Reggio and Scylla, the infantry comprising detachments of the 22nd and 23rd Légère, the 1st and 62nd Ligne, supported by 300 men from the 9th Chasseurs. As for the French artillery, Robertson counted five twenty-four pounders, five eighteen-pounders, four mortars and various field guns. Sherbrooke's gloomily realistic prognosis of the likely fate of Scylla once the French could bring their heavy artillery to bear was coming to pass.

On the morning of 11 February the French artillery opened fire. From the outset they concentrated on the 'Upper Works' of the castle and on disabling the British guns. At the same time, using this as covering fire, the French tried to establish two breaching batteries at distances of 300 and 400 yards. The bombardment continued and by 14 February the castle's parapet had been destroyed and its artillery put out of action. Until this point the British artillery had exacted a heavy toll among the French soldiers in the breaching batteries but from now on the defenders were confined to returning fire with muskets, as the bigger guns were buried under the rubble of the parapet. Meanwhile the French kept their eighteen and twenty-four pounders firing incessantly. While the gunners were blasting the walls away the engineers were attempting to mine the castle; they dug for three nights in their efforts to reach the right-hand bastion, but without success.

Prospects were not bright for the garrison of Scylla and on the morning of 15 February Robertson telegraphed to Sherbrooke the news that the parapet had been destroyed and all his guns either dismounted or disabled. The French had retaken the town; now only the castle remained to the British. The previous night, 14/15 February, the French had made an attempt to destroy the staircase leading from the castle down to the sea, which was beaten off with heavy casualties.

On the afternoon of 16 February the French changed tack. Up until that point their fire had not been aimed at any particular part of the castle, but from then on it was directed solely at the left-hand bastion. This was successful to the extent that a breach formed which would probably have been practicable by the following evening. Sherbrooke was concerned for the safety of his troops and, once they were no longer able properly to defend themselves (i.e. from the 14th) he was anxious to bring them away. It was at this point, the afternoon of the 16th, that Robertson received General Sherbrooke's order to abandon Scylla. Bad weather in the Straits prevented any attempt at a rescue

172

operation until a lull in the storm on the morning of 17 February. The evacuation of the garrison of Scylla in the face of the enemy was a very dangerous operation which was carried out with tremendous aplomb by Captain Trollope of the *Electra*, commanding the naval forces.

The flotilla of boats, which was ready, prepared and waiting for a break in the weather, crossed the Straits in full view of the French, giving the enemy ample warning of what was intended. Despite the fact that the British left Scylla under heavy enemy fire, the operation was a complete success; not a single soldier was left behind in the castle. It was, however, a close-run thing, for the moment Robertson's troops left to embark the French entered the castle; indeed, so quick was the 'change-over' that the French were in the castle before the escaping British were out of musket shot. Those in the castle and on the beach (some of them armed with field pieces) kept up a heavy fire on the retreating British.[369]

The French had retaken Scylla but its garrison had eluded them. Joseph reported, seemingly by way of an excuse, to Napoleon that the rescuing boats had crossed the Straits under cover of darkness. The British, having departed in a hurry, left behind all their effects, provisions and equipment. The French captured seventeen guns of various calibres, none of which had been spiked and a good deal of food, including biscuits, meat and eggs.[370] Captain Jordan, who commanded the detachment of the 27th Foot in Scylla, left a note in the castle bequeathing the mess furniture to the officers who were coming to take over.[371] Civility and humour remained alive, even in the most desperate circumstances.

The rescue of the garrison from Scylla was a brilliant success. As it was impossible to achieve any measure of surprise, the operation had to be carried out under enemy fire. In the circumstances it is astonishing that only four soldiers and one seaman were killed in the rescue; a further five soldiers and ten seamen were wounded. Sherbrooke praised Trollope's part in the rescue of the garrison, saying that "More Judgement, Coolness and Intrepidity was never displayed on any occasion". Sherbrooke, in his account of the siege, emphasized that Scylla had been evacuated on his orders and he praised the garrison for their courage and devotion to duty. He reserved his "warmest Praise and Commendation" for Robertson for his "Ability, Zeal and Gallantry . . . in defence of this little Fortress". He reiterated his opinion that the size of the besieging force and the artillery at its disposal meant that the fall of Scylla was inevitable. Moreover, the defence of Scylla was hampered by the fact that the stormy weather prevailing during the siege prevented the Navy from launching attacks on the besieging French. The British canvassed the possibility of mounting a diversionary attack against the French in Calabria but dismissed the idea because of the numerical superiority of the French, the ease with which they could summon reinforcements and the small size of Sherbrooke's army. Indeed, even had such an attack been considered practical, the weather during the siege would have prevented it.[372]

The total British losses in the siege of Scylla were very light, considering that the garrison was defending a castle which had been reduced virtually to a ruin. Of a garrison of 200 men twelve were killed and thirty-one wounded. Robertson estimated that the French losses ran to "several hundreds"; in fact the French returns show that their casualties were much lighter than this.[373] In the course of the operations at Scylla and Reggio the French lost five officers and forty others killed, while a total of 111 men were wounded. Regnier was delighted with his success and was lavish in his praise of his men, singling out a number of officers for special mention.[374]

The defence of Scylla was, in the face of almost overwhelming odds, unsuccessful, but it and the rescue had been conducted with the utmost resolution and panache. As Lord Castlereagh, the Secretary of War, wrote, the defence of Scylla "affords a very striking example of the skill, bravery and good conduct of a small British Garrison against a very superior force of the Enemy."[375] All the praise for Robertson and his gallant men could not disguise the fact that the French, by retaking Scylla, had re-established themselves on the Straits of Messina. With Scylla in their possession again the French could once more contemplate the invasion of Sicily. The security conferred on the British in Sicily by the Battle of Maida had disappeared. One British officer wrote home from Sicily in a mood of understandable but perhaps exaggerated gloom: "All our hopes are at an end. The French have possession of Scylla, England has nothing on the Continent of Europe but Gibraltar."[376]

174

NOTES

In the footnotes below the following abbreviations are used:

PRO – Public Record Office, Kew.
NAM – National Army Museum, Chelsea.
AN – Archives Nationales, Paris.
BL – British Library, St Pancras.

Chapter One

1 Whitworth to Hawkesbury, 14 March 1804, quoted in *England and Napoleon in 1803*, by Oscar Browning, 1907, pp. 115–117.
2 Hansard Parliamentary Debates, 1807–7, Vol. VIII, p. 216.
3 *The Times*, 5 September 1806.
4 *Macaulay's Essay on William Pitt the Younger*, ed. Leash, London, 1918.
5 Quoted in *Napoleon*, by Felix Markham, London 1963, p. 95.
6 Quoted in *The Years of Victory*, by Sir Arthur Bryant, London, 1944, p. 64.
7 From *Life of William Pitt*, by J. Holland Rose, London, 1923, Ch. XXII.
8 Ibid.
9 *The Younger Pitt: The Consuming Struggle*, by John Ehrman, London, 1995, Ch. XVII.
10 Hansard, debate of 23 April 1804, quoted in Ehrman, pp. 635–6.

Chapter Two

11 *Guineas and Gunpowder: British Foreign Aid in the Wars with France, 1793–1815*, by John M. Sherwig, Harvard, 1969, p. 154.
12 *The Memoirs of Prince Adam Czartoryski*, ed. A. Gielgud, London, 1888, Vol. I, p. 314.
13 Ibid., Vol. I, p. 272.
14 Ibid., Vol. I, p. 335.
15 Ibid., Vol. I, p. 335.
16 Ibid., Vol. I, p. 288.

17 *The Letters and Despatches of Vice-Admiral Lord Viscount Nelson*, ed. Sir Harris Nicolas, 1846, Vol. V, pp. 106 et seq.

18 *Russia and the Mediterranean, 1797–1807*, by Norman E. Saul, Chicago, 1970, p. 184.

19 Ibid., p. 174.

20 *The Paget Papers*, ed. Sir A.B. Paget, with notes by Mrs. J.R. Green, London, 1896, Vol. II, dispatch of 23 June 1803.

21 *Britain's role in the Formation of the Third Coalition against France, 1802–1805*, by G.B. Fremont, Oxford DPhil thesis, 1991, p. 84.

22 *Czartoryski*, Vol. I, p. 317.

23 *Despatches relating to the Third Coalition, 1804–1805*, Royal Historical Society, Camden Series III, ed. J. Holland Rose, 1904, p. 6.

24 Ibid., p. 10.

25 *Paget Papers*, dispatch of 9 April 1804.

26 *Napoleon's Great Adversary: Archduke Charles and the Austrian Army 1792–1814*, by Gunter E. Rothenburg, London, 1995, Chapter IV.

27 *The Course of German History*, by A.J.P. Taylor, London, 1961, p. 27.

28 Sir Philip Francis, quoted in *English Literature in the Great War with France: An Anthology and Commentary*, by A.D. Harvey, London, 1981.

29 *Czartoryski*, Vol. I, p. 282.

30 Ibid., p. 318.

31 See *The Diaries and Letters of Sir George Jackson*, ed. Lady Jackson, London, 1872, Vol. I

32 Holland Rose, *Despatches*, p. 29.

33 *The Bourbons of Naples*, by Harold Acton, London, 1957, Ch. XXIV.

34 *Sicily: An insecure base*, by Desmond Gregory, 1988, Ch. 1.

35 Acton, Ch. XXV.

36 *Paget Papers*, letter of 13 May 1800 to Grenville.

37 Acton, p. 428.

38 *Paget Papers*, letter of 13 May 1800 to Grenville.

39 Ibid.

40 *Letters from Portugal, Spain, Sicily and Malta in 1812, 1813 and 1814*, by the Hon. George Bridgeman, London, 1875, p. 216.

41 Charles Parsons, letter of 22 Oct. 1812.

42 *Paget Papers*, letter of 13 May 1800 to Grenville.

43 Quoted from *Bentinck* by J. Rosselli, CUP, 1956, p. 8.

44 Both quoted in Acton, p. 468.

45 Quoted in Rosselli, p. 8.

46 Quoted in Acton, p. 431.

47 Ibid., p. 472.

48 Ibid., p. 465.

Chapter Three

49   Ibid., p. 486.
50   *Paget Papers,* dispatch of 2 April 1804.
51   *Czartoryski,* Vol. II, p. 15.
52   Ibid., p. 16.
53   Holland Rose, *Despatches,* p. 14.
54   *Czartoryski,* Vol. I, p. 319.
55   Sherwig, pp. 149 & 165.
56   Holland Rose, *Despatches,* various, between pp. 41 & 79.
57   Ibid., Vol. II, letter of 4 July 1805.
58   *The Private Correspondence of Lord Granville Leveson Gower, 1781–1821*, ed. Castalla, Countess Granville, London, 1916, Vol. II, letter of 24 December 1804.
59   Ibid., Vol. I, letter of 14 November 1804.
60   Ibid., Vol. I, letter of 14 November 1804.
61   PRO: WO 6/56.
62   Ibid.
63   *The Years of Victory,* by Sir Arthur Bryant, London, 1944, p. 105.
64   Holland Rose, *Despatches,* p. 151.
65   Ehrman, p. 793.
66   Holland Rose, *Despatches,* p. 145.
67   Ibid., p. 165.
68   Ibid., p. 167.
69   *Leveson Gower,* Vol. II, letter of 4 July 1805.
70   Holland Rose, *Despatches,* p. 60.
71   Ibid., p. 174.
72   *Letters of Napoleon,* ed. J.M. Thompson, Oxford, 1934, p. 118; letter to Cambacérès, 27 May 1805.
73   Holland Rose, *Despatches,* p. 182.
74   Rothenberg, Ch. V.
75   Holland Rose, *Despatches,* appendix on Harrowby's mission to Berlin.
76   *Jackson,* diary, 11 August 1804.
77   Macaulay, p. 77.
78   Sir Arthur Paget, quoted in Rothenberg, p. 117.
79   *The Windham Papers,* ed. L.S. Benjamin, London, 1913, letter to W. from Grenville, 5 Nov. 1805.

Chapter Four

80   *Under England's Flag: From 1804 to 1809, Memoirs of Captain Charles Boothby, Royal Engineers,* London, 1900, pp. 35–37.

81 PRO: WO 1/281.

82 *A Narrative of Military Transactions in the Mediterranean, 1805–1810*, by Lt.-Gen. Sir Henry Bunbury, London, 1851, p. 15.

83 Acton, Ch. XXVII.

84 PRO: WO 1/280.

85 Ibid.

86 Bunbury, p. 2.

87 PRO: WO 1/281.

88 PRO: WO 1/280.

89 PRO: WO 1/281.

90 PRO: WO 1/280.

91 *Memoires et Correspondance du Roi Joseph*, ed. du Casse, Paris, 1853, Vol. II, p. 7.

92 PRO: WO 1/280.

93 PRO: WO/1/281.

94 PRO: WO 1/280.

95 Letter of 4 January 1806, quoted in Acton, p. 524.

96 Acton, p. 528.

97 *The War in the Mediterranean*, by Piers Mackesy, Longman, London, 1957, pp. 89–90.

98 *The Life of John Colborne, Field Marshal Lord Seaton*, by G.C.M. Smith, London, 1903, pp. 48–9.

99 *Reminiscences of my Military Life*, 1795–1818, by Lt.-Col. Charles Steevens, NAM, MS., p. 26.

100 Pasley Papers, BL, Add. MS. 41961.

101 PRO: WO 1/281.

102 Ibid.

103 Ibid.

104 Ibid.

105 Ibid.

106 Ibid.

107 Returns of Army of Naples, 1806, AN, AF* IV 1436.

108 *Lettres de Paul Louis Courier*, ed. Anderson, Blackie's Modern French Texts, London, 1894, letter of 9 March 1806.

109 Ibid., letter of 15 April 1806.

110 PRO: WO 1/281.

111 *A Tour through Sicily and Malta in a series of letters to William Beckford Esq.*, by Patrick Brydone FRS, Dublin, 1774.

112 du Casse, p. 91.

113 Letter of Gen. Delauloy to Joseph, April 1806, AN, 381 AP 10.

114 du Casse, p. 283.

115 Boothby, p. 50.

116 PRO: WO 1/281.

117 PRO: WO 1/281.

118 Ibid.

119 PRO: WO 1/306.

120 Mackesy, pp. 110–112.

121 Bunbury.

122 PRO: WO 1/281.

123 *Windham Papers*, p. xii.

124 PRO: WO 6/56.

125 PRO: WO 1/281.

126 This dispatch was written by Windham in London on 10 May 1806. There is no direct evidence that I can find in the PRO that this dispatch was in fact received in Sicily before the expedition to Calabria was launched. However, given the speed with which Windham's dispatch of 3 March travelled to Messina (it had arrived by 23 March), it seems likely that a dispatch from London dated 10 May would have arrived in Messina by the middle of June. Furthermore, there is a reference in a dispatch from Stuart to Windham, dated 26 May, to a dispatch of 5 April from Windham giving orders for the conduct of the army following its departure from Naples. There is no record of Windham having sent a dispatch to Sicily dated on this day. It seems likely therefore that Stuart was in fact referring to Windham's dispatch of 5 May, which did carry instructions for the army following its departure from Naples. So it is likely that Stuart, in Messina, had received the 5 May dispatch by 26 May. This seems to increase the likelihood that the dispatch of 10 May had arrived in Messina by the time that expedition to Calabria was being planned and that therefore Stuart had the specific blessing of the new administration for the expedition to Calabria. PRO: WO 1/281 & 6/56.

127 Pasley Papers, BL, Add. MS., 41961.

128 Quoted in Acton, p. 545.

129 *The Napoleonic Empire in Southern Italy & the Rise of the Secret Societies*, by R.M. Johnston, London, 1904, vol. I, ch. 3.

130 Ibid.

131 Ibid.

132 Ibid.

133 *The Most Monstrous of Wars: The Napoleonic Guerrilla War in Southern Italy, 1806–1811*, by Milton Finley, USCP, 1994, ch. 2.

134 Ibid.

135 Letter of 15 April 1806.

136 Finley, p. 29.

137 PRO: WO 1/281.

138 du Casse, p. 252.

139 *Knight of the Sword: The Life and Letters of Sir Sidney Smith*, by Lord Russell of Liverpool, London, 1964.

140 Ibid, p. 118.

141 PRO: WO 1/281.

Chapter Five

142 PRO: WO 1/281.

143 Bunbury, pp. 49–50.

144 du Casse, letter, Joseph to Napoleon, 10 July 1806.

145 Letter quoted in *The British in Capri*, by Sir Lees Knowles, London, 1918, p. 83.

146 Ibid., p. 84.

147 *Column and Line in the Peninsular War*, by Sir Charles Oman, from The Proceedings of the British Academy, 1910.

148 Bunbury, p. 61.

149 *Memoirs of Lowry Cole*, ed. Cole & Gywnn, London, 1934, p. 50.

150 *Le Général Regnier à Naples*, by J. Rambaud, Revue Historique, 1908, p. 14.

151 Finley, Ch. 2.

152 *Memoirs du Comte Regnier*, Paris, 1827, p. vi.

153 *The State of Egypt*, Regnier (trans.), London, 1802, pp. 300 & 324.

154 Ibid., p. 349.

155 Finley, Ch. 2.

156 Russell, p. 120.

157 The Royal Archives, 40629.

158 *Sketches of the Character, Manners & Present State of the Highlanders of Scotland*, Vol. II, by Col. David Stewart, Edinburgh, 1822, p. 260.

159 The Royal Archives, 40633.

160 Ibid., 40634.

161 Ibid., 40632. The material in the Royal Archives (40629–40657) is a series of letters, some of them copies, between Stuart and Smith at the time of the expedition to Calabria. The first part, 40629–40632, is a preamble which seems to have been written by Stuart, although it is unsigned and undated. Nor is it clear to whom it was addressed. The assertions of fact made in it should perhaps be taken with a pinch of salt.

162 Ibid., 40633.

163 Ibid., 40635–6.

164 Russell, c. p. 130.

165 Boothby, p. 67.

166 *The Windham Papers*, Grenville to Windham, 9 September 1806.

167 The Royal Archives, 40633.

168 Ibid., 40630.

169 du Casse, letter, Regnier to Joseph, 29 June 1806.

170 *Memoires du Général Griois*, Paris, 1909, p. 307.

171 Boothby, p. 68.

172 Stewart, pp. 259 & 263.

173 Boothby, p. 64.

174 PRO: WO 1/281.

175 Griois, p. 307.

176 Bunbury, p. 50.

177 There are discrepancies in the evidence as to when the British force did in fact sail. Stuart, in 'his' preamble to the correspondence with Sidney Smith, says that the troops embarked and sailed from Sicily on the evening of 29 June. In his dispatch to Windham of 2 July, written from St Euphemia (see PRO: WO 1/281), Stuart states that the troops embarked on 25 June and sailed "the next day". I prefer the latter account as it was probably written much closer to the time. There is some support for this version of events in the fact that Regnier went to Reggio on 29 June to observe the expedition. It is possible that the discrepancies reflect nothing more than the fact that the British force assembling at Faro meant that the transports from Messina had to join them. There is no doubt, however, that the army landed at St Euphemia on the night of the 30 June.

178 Charles Parsons, letter of 5 July 1806.

Chapter Six

179 It is unclear from the sources when exactly the British arrived in the Bay but it was definitely at night and probably in the early hours of the morning of 1 July.

180 There is confusion as to whether one of the men of war fired a broadside in order to clear the Poles from the beach. It is not in itself of any great importance save that it later became a bone of contention between Smith and Stuart. Smith wrote, typically, a letter which was published in the *Messina Gazette* shortly after Maida in which he claimed that one of his ships had, by firing a broadside, cleared the beach of the enemy who were preparing to oppose the landing. Stuart denies that this did in fact happen and hints that Smith made this claim in order to clear himself of the charge that the Navy failed to support Stuart's army during the

campaign. One man, who landed with the 78th Foot, recalled that the *Endymion* had cleared the beach with a broadside. See The Royal Archives, 40652 & PRO: WO 1/281.

181 Boothby, p. 68.
182 PRO: WO 1/281.
183 du Casse, Regnier to Joseph, 5 July 1806.
184 Boothby, p. 70.
185 *The Loyal North Lancashire Regiment*, by Col. H.C. Wylly, London, 1933.
186 PRO: WO 1/281.
187 Bunbury, p. 52.
188 PRO: WO 1/281.
189 du Casse, Regnier to Joseph, 5 July 1806.
190 Griois, p. 308.
191 du Casse, Regnier to Joseph, 5 July 1806.
192 *The Times*, 6 September 1806.
193 The Royal Archives, 40640.
194 PRO: WO 1/281.
195 PRO: WO 1/281.
196 Bunbury, p. 53.
197 PRO: WO 1/281.
198 PRO: WO 1/281.
199 Bunbury, p. 53.
200 PRO: WO 1/281.
201 Letter, Stuart to Broderick, 5 July 1806.
202 Boothby, p. 70 & PRO: WO 1/281.
203 *General Sir Charles William Pasley*, by Col. J.C. Tyler, 1923, NAM, MS., Ch. 4, p. 11.
204 Boothby, p. 70.
205 *The Letters of Lt.-Gen. Thomas Dyneley*, C.B., R.A., 1806–1815, in Proceedings of the Royal Artillery Institute, Vol. XXIII, 1896, p. 401.
206 du Casse, Napoleon to Joseph, 21 July 1806.
207 du Casse, Joseph to Napoleon, 17 July 1806.
208 du Casse, Regnier to Joseph, 5 July 1806.
209 *Naples under Joseph Bonaparte 1806–1808*, J. Rambaud, Paris, 1911, p. 68.
210 For the history and service records of French regiments generally under Napoleon, see *Napoleon's Regiments: Battle Histories of the Regiments of the French Army, 1792–1815*, by Digby Smith, London, 2000.
211 Rambaud, p. 68.
212 du Casse, Regnier to Joseph, 5 July 1806.
213 Rambaud, p. 70.

214 Ibid., p. 70.

215 Griois, p. 308.

216 Dyneley, p. 401

217 Boothby, p. 71.

218 Griois, p. 308.

219 du Casse, Regnier to Joseph, 5 July 1806 & Griois, p. 309.

220 PRO: WO 1/281.

221 *Recollections of a Peninsular Veteran: Joseph Anderson, C.B., K.H.*, Edward Arnold, London, 1913, p. 11.

222 Stewart, Vol. II, p. 263.

223 *Battle Tactics of Napoleon and his Enemies*, by Brent Nosworthy, Constable, London 1995, p. 140.

224 *Tactics and the Experience of Battle in the Age of Napoleon*, by Rory Muir, Yale, 1998, pp. 69–70.

225 Griois, p. 311, note.

226 The strength given here for the French artillery – four small calibre field pieces – is the figure used by Regnier in his report on the battle to Joseph of 5 July. Griois, who commanded the French artillery at the battle, states in his memoirs (p. 309) that it consisted of four guns of the 2nd company of the 1st Regiment of Horse Artillery and a detachment of the 2nd Foot Artillery with two mountain guns. Regnier's account was contemporary, whereas Griois wrote his twenty years later. As against that, it is possible that Griois's is the more accurate figure, given that he was the immediate commander of the battery. Stuart said that the French had four six-pounders and two howitzers. As they say, you pays your money and you takes your choice.

227 Griois, p. 309.

228 Steevens, p. 28, note.

229 Stewart, Vol. II, p. 263.

230 Griois, p. 310. Griois is the only one (altho' the most reliable) of the French sources to refer to the fact that their troops came under fire from the guns of Royal Navy ships in the bay. A cursory consideration of the positions occupied by the respective armies on the plain shows that it simply cannot have happened. The British were between the French and the shore and at least a mile inland. It would have been far too dangerous for the Navy to have attempted to fire at the French infantry over the heads of the British, even assuming that they had guns capable of doing so. It can therefore be wholly discounted. Perhaps the weight and accuracy of the British fire from the ground persuaded the French that naval gunnery must have been involved. Regnier, interestingly, does not refer to gunfire from British ships. He confined himself to stating that the

British flank was protected by the warships. No British witness to the battle mentions the matter at all.

231 *Firepower: Weapons effectiveness on the battlefield, 1630–1850*, by Major-Gen. B.P. Hughes, London, 1974.
232 Griois, p. 310.
233 Cole, p. 46.
234 Stewart, Vol. II, p. 263.
235 PRO: WO 1/281.
236 Griois, p. 310.
237 Dyneley, p. 410.
238 PRO: WO 1/281.
239 Muir, op. cit.
240 Dyneley, p. 410.
241 Ibid.
242 Pasley, Ch. 4, p. 16.
243 *History of the Royal Sussex Regiment 1701–1953*, by G.D. Martineau. Where the French failed, disease succeeded; Tomlin later died of fever and was buried in the glacis at Messina.
244 Dyneley, p. 410.
245 Stewart, Vol. II, p. 265.
246 Stewart, Vol. II, p. 266.
247 Griois, p. 311.
248 Cole, p. 46–47.
249 Ibid., p. 47.
250 du Casse, Regnier to Joseph, 5 July 1806.
251 Steevens, from p. 26.
252 *Regiment of the Line*, Cyril Ray, London, 1963, p. 69.
253 PRO: WO 1/281.
254 du Casse, Regnier to Joseph, 5 July 1806.
255 Ibid.
256 Letter, Stuart to Broderick, 5 July 1806, MS, NAM.
257 The Light Battalion, separated from the main body of the army, had no supplies of any description and were forced to scavenge for food. Kempt's batman caught a small tortoise and prepared it for the Colonel's supper. Kempt kept the shell as a memento of the battle. Later, mounted on silver and converted into a snuff box, Kempt presented the shell to the 81st Foot, in whose Mess it remains to this day. I am grateful to Major A.J. Maher of the Queen's Lancashire Regiment for this anecdote.
258 Colborne, from p. 51.
259 See Bunbury. The tale is repeated in a number of other accounts of the battle.

260 Letter, Stuart to Broderick, 5 July 1806, MS, NAM.
261 Muir, p. 8.
262 Ibid., p. 8.
263 du Casse, Regnier to Joseph, 5 July 1806.
264 Letter, Stuart to Broderick, 5 July 1806, MS, NAM.
265 PRO: WO 1/281.
266 Bunbury, p. 65, note.
267 Boothby, p. 77 & Colborne.
268 *Map of Maida*, published by W. Foden, London, April 1807. NAM.
269 See Army of Naples returns, AN, AF* IV 1436–9.
270 Quoted in Philip J. Haythornthwaite *Napoleonic Firepower*, in *Napoleonic Wars* magazine.

Chapter Seven

271 Boothby, pp. 74 & 75.
272 Bunbury, p. 66.
273 The Royal Archives, 40643.
274 Steevens, p. 28, note.
275 Colborne, p. 55.
276 PRO: WO 1/281.
277 The Royal Archives, 40644.
278 Boothby, p. 79.
279 PRO: WO 1/281.
280 The Royal Archives, 40648.
281 Bunbury, p. 66.
282 PRO: WO 1/281.
283 Ibid.
284 Ibid.
285 Boothby, p. 84.
286 Griois, p. 301.
287 Boothby, p. 84 et seq.
288 Boothby, p. 94.
289 Dyneley, p. 401.
290 PRO: WO 1/281.
291 PRO: WO 1/281.
292 Finley, Ch. 3.
293 Griois, p. 314.
294 PRO: WO 1/281.
295 Ibid.
296 Griois, p. 320.

297 PRO: WO 1/281.

298 Ibid.

299 Griois, p. 323.

300 Bunbury, p. 68.

301 Report on the condition of Army of Naples, summer 1806, AN, 381 AP 8.

302 Ibid.

303 *The Times*, 25 November 1806, unsigned letter.

304 *The Times*, 10 September 1806.

305 Ibid.

306 *The Times*, 15 September 1806.

307 Griois, p. 312.

308 Ibid., p. 312.

309 Rambaud and Griois. Rambaud's idea (that the British attacked before the French were formed up) is culled from the report on the battle by Sénéchal, Regnier's chief of staff. This explanation of the French defeat is discredited by the number of witnesses who comment on the order with which the two sides closed for battle & the fact that no British account relates that the French were unformed when attacked. Had they been so, it is inconceivable that British eyewitnesses would not have referred to it. I have not found Sénéchal's report.

310 PRO: WO 1/281.

311 Muir, p. 49.

312 du Casse, Regnier to Joseph, 5 July 1806.

313 PRO: WO 1/281.

314 Griois, pp. 312–313.

315 du Casse, Napoleon to Joseph, 26 July 1806.

316 Courier, letter 12 August 1806.

317 PRO: WO 1/281.

318 Codrington, p. 117.

319 Bunbury, p. 66.

320 *Memoires de Massena*, by General Koch, Paris, 1850.

321 Stewart, p. 20.

322 Mackesy, p. 139.

323 See, for example, *The British Army*, by Brig. Peter Young, London, 1967. There is a further tuck in the story in that Oman, in his *Wellington's Army* (1912) changed his mind. He states there that the French at Maida did in fact fight in line. He refers opaquely, as justification for his change of mind, to "evidence put before me" and cites the relevant parts of Bunbury and Boothby in support. His contemporary, Sir John Fortescue, had followed Oman's original line in the first edition of his

exhaustive *A History of the British Army* (1899) but he, too, later recanted. In the 1921 edition of the book Fortescue wrote that "[b]oth armies were formed in line, the British two deep, the French three deep". Strangely, the change of mind by these two great military historians failed to overcome the influence of their original pronouncements on the subject.

Oman's French contemporary, Jacques Rambaud, states that the French (or at least the 1st Légère and the 42nd Regiment) fought at Maida in "columns of companies". He emphasizes this conclusion a few lines later, noting, by contrast, that the British were deployed in line. See *Naples sous Joseph Bonaparte 1806–1808*, Paris, 1911. More recently Milton Finley has restated the Oman line: see *The Most Monstrous of Wars: The Napoleonic Guerrilla War in Southern Italy, 1806–1811*, USCP, 1994.

324 The first crack in the edifice appeared with James R. Arnold's *A Reappraisal of Column versus Line in the Napoleonic Wars* (JSAHR, Winter 1982). He argues that the French in fact attacked the British in line formation. He cites as evidence for this proposition two quotations from French eyewitnesses at the battle (both of whom we will encounter later). One of them is the artillery commander, Griois, a plain enough authority for Arnold's proposition. The other is a translated quotation from Regnier's report to Joseph of 5 July 1806, which seems to be at odds with the French version, quoted in du Casse. Du Casse gives the text of Regnier's report on Maida to Joseph and it appears to be inconclusive so far as the 'column and line' argument is concerned. In it Regnier merely states that the 1st Légère and the 42nd Regiment were "formes en bataille". This does not lend support to either the 'column' or the 'line' argument. Arnold, it would seem, translates the same phrase as "formed into line". He also prays in aid a British eyewitness to the battle, Joseph Anderson of the 78th Foot, who was 16 at the time of Maida. He began to write his memoirs, wholly, we are told, from memory in about 1864, when he was 74 years old. Arnold quotes Anderson as saying (on pages 12–13 of the 1913 edition): "Taken under fire by the Acland's brigade the French returned our fire without ceasing, then in part commenced to deploy into line". The 1913 edition of Anderson's memoirs that I read varies somewhat from Arnold's edition. What it says at p 13 is: "Nor were the enemy idle; they returned our fire without ceasing, then in part commenced to deploy into line". But the point about the French deploying into line remains. Brent Nosworthy's *Battle Tactics of Napoleon and his Enemies*, London, 1995, also states that the French fought in line at Maida.

325 *Maida: A Forgotten Victory*, John Stewart, Bishop Auckland, 1997.

326 London, 1998.
327 Bunbury, p. 58.
328 Cole, p. 34.
329 Dyneley, p. 401.
330 See p. 263.
331 Pasley, Ch. 4, pp. 13 & 14.
332 du Casse, Regnier to Joseph, 5 July 1806.
333 Griois, p. 309.
334 Boothby, p. 78.
335 du Casse, Napoleon to Joseph, 26 July 1806.
336 *Times*, Friday 8 August 1806.
337 *Times*, Thursday 21 August 1806.
338 *Times*, Saturday 30 August 1806.
339 *Times*, Wednesday 3 September 1806.
340 *Times*, 9 April 1807.
341 *Hansard Parliamentary Debates*, 1806–07, Vol. VIII, pp. 213, 215–218.
342 Minutes of the Lloyd's Patriotic Fund, Guildhall Library.
343 Bodleian Library, Mus. 2 c. 101.
344 NAM.
345 Sir Walter Scott, from *Patriotism*.
346 *History of the British Army*, by Sir John Fortescue, Vol. IV, Part II, p. 816.
347 *Hansard Parliamentary Debates, 1806–07*, Vol. VIII, p. 218.

Chapter Eight

348 Bunbury.
349 du Casse, Joseph to Napoleon, 6 February 1808.
350 PRO: WO 1/306.
351 du Casse, Joseph to Napoleon, 6 February 1808 & PRO: WO 1/306.
352 du Casse, Joseph to Napoleon, 6 February 1808.
353 Sherbrooke was left in command in Sicily by the departure in September 1807 of Moore. Bunbury describes him as: "A short, square, hardy little man, with a countenance that told at once of the determined fortitude of his nature. Without genius, without education, as hot as pepper, and rough in his language, but with a warm heart and generous feelings."
354 PRO: WO 1/306.
355 PRO: WO 1/306.
356 du Casse, Joseph to Napoleon, 7 February 1808.
357 du Casse, Joseph to Napoleon, 8 February 1808.
358 Ibid.
359 PRO: Adm. 1/414.

360 du Casse, Joseph to Napoleon, 7 February 1808.

361 The sources are at odds as to the exact number of gunboats that fell into French hands. Joseph, for the French, and Collingwood and Sherbrooke, for the British, all say that four gunboats were involved. Captain Downe of the *Bittern*, who was the senior surviving British officer at the scene, reports that five gunboats were captured. This is confirmed by the masters of the two transports (who were also at the scene). Bunbury, presumably following the "higher" reports, says that four gunboats were captured. I prefer to side with the eyewitnesses and therefore adopt the figure of five gunboats captured. See: du Casse, Joseph to Napoleon, 7 February 1808 & PRO: WO 1/306 & Adm. 1/414.

362 PRO: Adm. 1/414. Seccombe was returned to Messina on 31 January where he died of his wounds on 3 February.

363 PRO: Adm. 1/414.

364 Mackesy, pp. 241–2, note.

365 Ibid.

366 du Casse, Regnier to Joseph, 7 February 1808.

367 Ibid.

368 PRO: WO 1/306.

369 Ibid.

370 du Casse, Joseph to Napoleon, 23 February 1808.

371 Charles Parsons, letter of 20 February 1808.

372 PRO: WO 1/306.

373 Ibid.

374 Letter Regnier to Joseph, 27 February 1808, AN, 381 AP 7.

375 From the General Orders of the Mediterranean Forces, 9th July 1808.

376 Charles Parsons, letter of 20 February 1808.

INDEX

Britain, 10; campaigns in Italy, 21–3; returns from Egypt, 22

Nelson, Horatio, 3, 8, 10, 15–16, 19, 33, 36, 57, 71, 94

Nicastro, 80, 102, 116

Nile, Battle of the, 8, 33

Novosiltsov, Count, 17, 41, 42, 52

O'Callaghan, Lt.-Col., 85

Oman, Sir Charles, 4, 86, 111, 155

Oswald, Lt.-Col. 4, 101–2, 113, 141

Oswald's Reserve Brigade (58th Foot & de Watteville's), 114, 117, 129, 138, 140

Ottoman Empire, 18–20, 32

d'Oubril, Count, 39, 40

Paget, Sir Arthur, 23, 25, 32, 33, 34, 36, 39, 50, 52

Palermo, 36, 66, 67, 68, 74, 93, 94, 160

Palmi, 103, 139

Parthenopean Republic, 31–2, 34, 81

Pasley, Charles, 59, 65, 78, 79, 108, 157

Paul, Tsar, 15, 16

Peninsular War, 3, 4, 86

Peyri, *General de Brigade*, 68

Piedmont, 7, 15

Pitt, William, 6, 10, 11, 12, 13, 14, 17, 20, 26, 27, 33–4, 37, 40, 42, 46 48, 50, 51, 55–6, 82, 113; death, 76

Pizzo, 70, 103

Pressburg, Peace of, 3, 62, 68

Prussia, 3, 15, 26–31, 53, 54; and Austria, 24, 27, 29; and Britain, 24, 27, 28–9, 54; and France, 26–7, 28–9, 31, 39, 54; and Hanover, 28–9; and

Russia, 29, 54; Treaty of Basle, 21, 27, 28

Reggio di Calabria, 69, 70, 80, 81, 91, 99, 103, 126, 131, 138–9, 141, 144, 153, 154, 171; recapture by French, 168; Joseph slighted, 168

Regnier, General Jean-Louis-Ebenezer, 68, 69, 71, 79, 80, 81, 88, 88–91, 91, 92–3, 95, 96, 102–4, 105, 107, 108, 108–13, 113–27, 129, 130, 131, 145–6, 147, 150–1; at Battle of Maida, 114, 116, 117, 118, 123, 124, 125; countering British landing, 102–4, 105; "Column & Line", 117–18, 154–9; corps after Maida, 144–5; early career, 89–90; in Egypt, 90–1; Joseph slighted, 168; recapture of Reggio, 168; recapture of Scylla, 165–8, 171, 174; retreat from Maida, 126, 142–4; strength at Maida, 109, 111–12; tactics at Maida, 108–13, 116, 123, 124, 149–50

Robertson, Major George, 97, 119, 167, 171, 172, 173, 174

Ross, Lt.-Col. Robert, 96–7, 99, 125–6

Roverea, Major, 119, 121, 124, 125, 156

Royal Navy, 1, 8, 10, 12, 15, 32, 33, 36, 67, 68, 71, 72, 74–6, 81–3, 84–5, 91, 104, 162, 165, 163; right to search neutral shipping, 15, 16; loss of 5 Sicilian gunboats & the

195